Communications in Computer and Information Science 428

Editorial Board

Simone Diniz Junqueira Barbosa
Pontifical Catholic University of Rio de Janeiro (PUC ᴿⁱᵒ)
Rio de Janeiro, Brazil
Phoebe Chen
La Trobe University, Melbourne, Australia
Alfredo Cuzzocrea
ICAR-CNR and University of Calabria, Cosenza, Ital
Xiaoyong Du
Renmin University of China, Beijing, China
Joaquim Filipe
Polytechnic Institute of Setúbal, Setúbal, Portugal
Orhun Kara
TÜBİTAK BİLGEM and Middle East Technical University, Ankara, Turkey
Igor Kotenko
St. Petersburg Institute for Informatics and Automation
of the Russian Academy of Sciences, St. Petersburg, Russia
Krishna M. Sivalingam
Indian Institute of Technology Madras, Chennai, India
Dominik Ślęzak
University of Warsaw and Infobright, Warsaw, Poland
Takashi Washio
Osaka University, Osaka, Japan
Xiaokang Yang
Shanghai Jiao Tong University, Shangai, China

More information about this series at http://www.springer.com/series/7899

Amir Hossein Jahangir · Ali Movaghar
Hossein Asadi (Eds.)

Computer Networks and Distributed Systems

International Symposium, CNDS 2013
Tehran, Iran, December 25–26, 2013
Revised Selected Papers

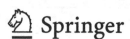
Springer

Editors
Amir Hossein Jahangir
Ali Movaghar
Hossein Asadi
Department of Computer Engineering
Sharif University of Technology
Tehran
Iran

ISSN 1865-0929   ISSN 1865-0937   (electronic)
ISBN 978-3-319-10902-2   ISBN 978-3-319-10903-9   (eBook)
DOI 10.1007/978-3-319-10903-9

Library of Congress Control Number: 2014952776

Springer Cham Heidelberg New York Dordrecht London

© Springer International Publishing Switzerland 2014
This work is subject to copyright. All rights are reserved by the Publisher, whether the whole or part of the material is concerned, specifically the rights of translation, reprinting, reuse of illustrations, recitation, broadcasting, reproduction on microfilms or in any other physical way, and transmission or information storage and retrieval, electronic adaptation, computer software, or by similar or dissimilar methodology now known or hereafter developed. Exempted from this legal reservation are brief excerpts in connection with reviews or scholarly analysis or material supplied specifically for the purpose of being entered and executed on a computer system, for exclusive use by the purchaser of the work. Duplication of this publication or parts thereof is permitted only under the provisions of the Copyright Law of the Publisher's location, in its current version, and permission for use must always be obtained from Springer. Permissions for use may be obtained through RightsLink at the Copyright Clearance Center. Violations are liable to prosecution under the respective Copyright Law.
The use of general descriptive names, registered names, trademarks, service marks, etc. in this publication does not imply, even in the absence of a specific statement, that such names are exempt from the relevant protective laws and regulations and therefore free for general use.
While the advice and information in this book are believed to be true and accurate at the date of publication, neither the authors nor the editors nor the publisher can accept any legal responsibility for any errors or omissions that may be made. The publisher makes no warranty, express or implied, with respect to the material contained herein.

Printed on acid-free paper

Springer is part of Springer Science+Business Media (www.springer.com)

Preface

The 2013 International Symposium on Computer Networks and Distributed Systems (CNDS 2013), the second conference of Computer Society of Iran (CSI) in this series, was held during December 25–26, 2013 in the Department of Computer Engineering, Sharif University of Technology, Tehran, Iran. CNDS 2013 has aimed to be a premier computer science and engineering event that brings together industry professionals and academics to exchange information on recent advances in data communications, wireless networks, and distributed systems, and provide a platform to discuss computer networks, traffic modeling and analysis, grid, cluster, and cloud computing, data communications, multimedia networks and systems, mobile communications and networks, "Next Generation" networks, cognitive networks, distributed- and network-based cyber attacks and defense, wireless, Ad hoc and sensor networks, and modeling and evaluation of communication networks.

The success of the symposium is reflected in the relatively high number of papers and reviews received despite late announcement of the call for papers. The quality and diversity of the accepted papers (with a ratio of ~ 20 %) has allowed a great platform for the exchange of experiences and ideas.

The accepted papers that were presented during the sessions, and are published in this volume, can be classified into five major categories:

- Grid and cloud computing
- Wireless sensor networks
- Network security
- Cognitive radio
- Multimedia communication

A symposium such as CNDS 2013 has become successful using team effort, so herewith we want to thank all contributors, especially the scientific committee and the reviewers for their efforts in the review process as well as their invaluable input and advices. We are hopeful and confident that with the experience accumulated during this and past CSI conferences, beside the growing interest on computer networks and distributed systems, we will have more contribution and participation in the upcoming conferences.

July 2014

Amir Hossein Jahangir
Ali Movaghar
Hossein Asadi

CNDS 2013 Organizers

Honorary Chair

Reza Roosta-Azad   Sharif University of Technology, Iran

General Chair

Ali Movaghar   Sharif University of Technology, Iran

Program Chair

Amir Hossein Jahangir   Sharif University of Technology, Iran

Organizing Committee Chair

Jafar Habibi   Sharif University of Technology, Iran

Registration Chair

Abbas Heydarnoori   Sharif University of Technology, Iran

Workshop and Tutorial Chairs

Mohammad Izadi   Sharif University of Technology, Iran
Maziar Goudarzi   Sharif University of Technology, Iran

Publication Chair

Hossein Asadi   Sharif University of Technology, Iran

Local Arrangement Chair

Mohammad Ali Abam   Sharif University of Technology, Iran

Internet Chair

Hamid Zarrabi-Zadeh   Sharif University of Technology, Iran

Publicity Chair

Hossein Ajorloo   Sharif University of Technology, Iran

Organizing and Technical Committee

Hamid Haghshenas   Sharif University of Technology, Iran
Mohammad Salehe   Sharif University of Technology, Iran
Hamidreza Mahyar   Sharif University of Technology, Iran
Mohammadreza Tahzibi   Sharif University of Technology, Iran
Mostafa Kishani   Sharif University of Technology, Iran

Contents

Clouds and Grids

Cognitive and Multimedia Networks

Random Sensing Strategies in Cognitive Friendly Networks

Atoosa Dalili Shoaei and Siavash Khorsandi(✉)

Computer Engineering Department, Amirkabir University of Technology,
Tehran, Iran
{A.dalili,khorsandi}@aut.ac.ir

Abstract. In this paper, we study the performance of random sensing strategies in Cognitive Friendly Networks (CFN). CFN refers to the scenarios where primary networks conform with some stated conditions in order to assist secondary users in the process of channel detection and utilization. The incentive may come from a unified business model for primary and secondary networks or it may come from regulatory requirements. Random sensing strategies although have low complexity, but they lead to poor performance in the scenarios that are not CFN. However, due to properties of CFN, the situation is different in these scenarios. In this paper, we study the performance of Pure Random Sensing and Cooperative Random Sensing which can be both used in CFN and not CFN scenarios. Moreover, the investigation includes results of Reward based Random Sensing proposed for CFN. The results show that in contrast to not CFN scenarios, these strategies lead to significant performance increase in CFN.

Keywords: Cognitive friendly networks · Opportunistic spectrum access · Random sensing strategies

1 Introduction

With the expansion of wireless services and applications, demand for radio spectrum has increased. Currently the spectrum is allocated in a fixed manner, thus the growing need has led to the scarcity of unallocated spectrum. On the other hand, reports indicate that under fixed allocation of spectrum, most channels remain unused. Therefore a new concept, Cognitive Radio Network (CRN) has introduced in which no licensed channels are allocated to the users. In these networks, the user can transmit over unused channels of primary network [1].

The main concern in CRN is detection of idle channels. In case that the information regarding the state of channels are not provided by primary network, these information are obtained by sensing the channels. However, due to the limited sensing capabilities, obtaining the state of channels need considerable time and energy. Therefore an efficient spectrum sensing strategy should be deployed.

Even an efficient sensing strategy leads to low spectrum utilization, when each secondary user can sense only one channel at each time slot. Therefore in [2], we proposed ordered channel assignment strategy which assists secondary users in the detection of idle channels. This help is done in an indirect way which needs no

© Springer International Publishing Switzerland 2014
A. Movaghar et al. (Eds.): CNDS 2013, CCIS 428, pp. 3–12, 2014.
DOI: 10.1007/978-3-319-10903-9_1

interaction between CRN and primary network. Under ordered channel assignment strategy, detection of one idle channel reveals information regarding the state of some other channels as well. Due to this property, we expect that higher utilization is obtained under this scenario. In [2] we show that the utilization significantly improves when optimal strategies are used. This paper shows that improvement is not limited to optimal strategies even random strategies achieve higher utilization in CFN.

The rest of this paper is organized as follows. After presenting related works in Sect. 2, we introduce system models and assumption in Sect. 3. Then, we propose our random sensing strategies in Sect. 4 and present the results in Sect. 5. Finally, we conclude the paper in Sect. 6.

2   Related Works

Seeking for spectrum opportunities is challenging. Secondary users should exploit efficient MAC protocol to access channels in the best manner. When time is slotted in primary network, it is enough to sense channels at the beginning of time slot because no changes happen until the end of the slot. The problem of choosing sensing action when states of channels evolve as Markov model is first investigated in [3]. In this paper, it is assumed secondary users are aware of the transition probabilities of Markov model and since at each time slot they observe state of some channels, the problem is formulated by POMDP framework and an optimal policy has been proposed. This policy is computationally complex, therefore another policy which is less complicated has been proposed in [4]. This policy is applicable for scenarios which cognitive radio network consists of single user. When there are multiple users in CR network, the interactions of secondary users should be considered to avoid collision happens among them. This issue has been investigated in [5], in which users apply myopic policy for different channels. In [6], multi user CR network is considered, in which secondary users have different QoS requirements. This problem has been modeled by Dec-POMDP. [3–6] assume that secondary users are aware of state transition probabilities, therefore they are not applicable for scenarios that these information are not provided.

In some works it is assumed, each channel is idle at each time slot with unknown probability of p_i. In [7], two sensing protocol has been proposed for this situation. The first one is random sensing and the second one is negotiating sensing. The average throughput and delay for these protocols has been investigated in both saturation and non-saturation network. Applying the proposed strategies leads to low network utilization under low number of secondary users. In [8], performance analysis is done for scenarios that fading may exist. These analyses are done for Different control channel implementation.

When users are unaware of probability of idleness of each channel, they can try to learn these probabilities. Hence, there are works in which each user applies learning method to estimate mean probability of idleness of channels. These problems are known as multi armed bandit problems. In [9], the CR network which is consisted of single user has been investigated. In this paper, user selects each channel according to Gittes index. In [10], this problem for multiple secondary users have been investigated, it is assumed all users have the same observation of channel occupancies. On the other hand, in [11] due to geographic dispersion different secondary users have different observations of primary user activities. All proposed strategies in [9–11] need considerable time to reach to acceptable utilization. Therefore, they are not proper for short transmissions.

In this paper, we propose simple random sensing strategies for situation that fully ordered channel assignment is applied in the primary network. Unlike our previous work [2], secondary users don't need to be aware of state transition probabilities. We show that due to the properties of fully ordered channel assignment, random sensing strategies achieve high utilization regardless of number of secondary users and amount of time that has past.

3 System Model and Assumptions

In this section, we describe system assumptions and parameters. We assume that there is a Cognitive Friendly Networks with fully ordered channel assignment. CFN refers to the scenarios where primary networks conform with some stated conditions in order to assist secondary users in the process of channel detection and utilization. The incentive may come from a unified business model for primary and secondary networks or it may come from regulatory requirements. The definition of fully ordered channel assignment is as below.

Definition: In a fully ordered channel assignment,

a) if $i < j$ and channel j is occupied, then channel i is also occupied,
b) if channel j is idle, then every channel $i > j$ is also idle.

Our CFN strategy is governed by the following principles:

- The network consists of N channels.
- A channel not used by a primary user can be assigned to another primary user.
- The time is slotted in both primary and secondary networks and slots of secondary network are synchronous to the primary network.
- Each transmission from a secondary user on a given channel is allowed only when that channel is not in use by the primary network. That is, the cognitive network should not cause interference for primary network.
- To facilitate the process of channel sensing by secondary users who has limitation in sensing capabilities, channels in the primary network are assigned in an ordered way, starting from a channel with lower index.
- As the channels are released by the primary users, full rearrangement of channels will happen at the beginning of next time slot moving the highest occupied channel to the lowest unoccupied channel.
- Secondary users are aware of channel assignment policy in the primary network.
- We assume state transition probabilities are not available for the secondary users, therefore random sensing strategies are used by these users.
- It is assumed that results of sensing action are error free.

- If the sensed channel is idle, the secondary user can transmit over that and all subsequent channels for duration of one time slot. Otherwise, it refrains from transmitting.
- It is assumed that all secondary users and primary users are in the same domain.

3.1 System Parameters

Arrival Rate of Primary Users. We assume that primary users enter system according to Poisson distribution with rate λ, the probability that k arrivals occur in a time slot with duration of T is given by [12]:

$$P_k^A = \frac{(\lambda T)^k . e^{-\lambda T}}{k!}. \tag{1}$$

Departure Rate of Primary Users. The session duration is exponentially distributed with mean $1/\mu$, the probability of a session departure in time slot t is [12]:

$$P^D = 1 - e^{-\mu T}. \tag{2}$$

The probability of having k out of m departures in a time slot is given by the binomial distribution [12]:

$$P_{K,m}^D = \binom{m}{k}(1 - e^{-\mu T})^k (e^{-\mu T})^{m-k}. \tag{3}$$

Markov Model. We model the system with a Discrete Time Markov Chain (DTMC). We consider a network which consists of N channels, each with same bandwidth. These channels are assigned to the primary users by a coordinator in an ordered manner. It is assumed that Primary users demand a single channel for transmission. The DTMC models occupancies of these channels by primary users. We observe system state at discrete time instants at the beginning of T second time intervals.

State Space. In fully ordered channel assignment, the system state can be represented by an scalar value s indicating the last busy channel in the network. In a network with N channels, the size of state space is $N + 1$.

State Transition Probabilities. Let $P_{i,j}^T$ be the transition probabilities from state i to state j, it can be defined as [13].

$$P_{i,j}^T = \sum_{k=max(0,i-j)}^{i} P_{j-i+k}^A . P_{k,m}^D \tag{4}$$

4 Random Sensing under Full Channel Reordering Strategy

In all proposed strategies, we assume that in addition of N channels of primary network a control channel also exists that it is used by secondary users for coordination purposes.

4.1 Pure Random Sensing

We first describe the time slot structure of both control and data channels. In the control channel, the first part of the time slot, T_s is dedicated for channel sensing and the rest part for negotiation. Through the negotiation phase, the users contend with each other and the winner of competition sends it's data in the next time slot. In the data channels, transmission will happen over some of the channels if the sensed channel in sensing phase is idle. The transmission starts after T_s. The time slot structure is illustrated in Fig. 1.

In pure random sensing strategy, at the beginning of each time slot, the winner of negotiation phase from previous time slot chooses one channel for sensing. If the sensed channel is idle, it will send it's data over the sensed channel and all subsequent after that. Otherwise, it refrains from transmission.

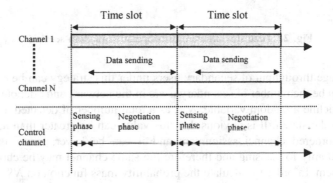

Fig. 1. Time slot structure in pure random sensing

Let π_i be the steady state probability of being in state i and R represents the bit rate of each channel, the average throughput per slot in secondary network can be calculated as follows:

$$\eta = \sum_{i=0}^{N} \sum_{j=1+1}^{N} \pi_i \cdot \frac{1}{N} \cdot (N - j + 1).(T - T_s).\,R. \tag{5}$$

4.2 Cooperative Random Sensing

The cooperative random sensing is based on the strategy proposed in [7]. It consists of three phases in the control channel. The first one is sensing phase. In this phase, each user whether it is transmitter or not, randomly chooses one channel for sensing. The second phase is called reporting. In this phase, mini slot protocol is run for gathering the channel states information. If the secondary user detects that channel i is idle, then it would send a beacon in the i-th mini slot. However, due to the ordered channel assignment property, this phase ends as the first beacon is sent. Thus, the length of this phase is not constant. The last phase, negotiation is the same as the corresponding one in the pure random sensing.

In the data channels, in case that at least one idle channel is detected, transmission begins after reporting phase. In Fig. 2 the time slot of this protocol is illustrated.

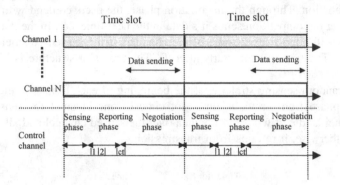

Fig. 2. Time slot structure in cooperative random sensing

The average throughput of secondary users under this strategy can be calculated as follows. Let u be the number of secondary users in the network and i denote the state of system. We define a random variable, $N_{u,i}$, as a total number of detected idle channels by u users in the state i. It is obvious that this value can be greater than u, due to the property of ordered channel assignment and it can be lower, since users choose channels randomly for sensing and therefore the same channel may be chosen by two or more of them. In order to calculate the probability mass function on NS, the number of channels sensed by secondary user, the sensing process is modeled by Markov chain with states range from 0 to $N - i$ for given system state i. The state transition probabilities, $q_i(l, l')$ of this Markov chain can be calculated as below:

$$q_i(l, l') = \begin{cases} \frac{i+l}{N}, & l' = l, \\ \frac{1}{N}, & l' > l, \\ 0, & otherwise. \end{cases} \tag{6}$$

Where l' denotes the number of sensed channel after sensing one more channel in comparison to the state l. Thus $P_{u,i}^S(NS = k)$, which denotes the propbability of k idle channels detected by u users under system state i, can be calculated after u step transition from state 0 to state k.

Now the average throughput under cooperative random sensing strategy can be derived by below formula.

$$\eta_u = \sum_{i=0}^{N} \pi_i \sum_{j=1}^{N-i} P_{u,i}^S(j) \cdot j \cdot (T - T_s - (N - j + 1)T_{ms}) \cdot R. \tag{7}$$

4.3 Reward Based Random Sensing

In this strategy, the control channel is divided into three phases: sensing, reporting and negotiating. In the sensing phase, the transmitter which is the winner of negotiation from previous time slot, randomly chooses one channel for sensing based on its observation in previous time slot. In the reporting phase, the state of sensed channel is reported by transmitter, through sending a packet in which the sensed channel and the state of the channel is denoted. Finally, the negotiation phase is the same as above random sensing strategies.

In the data channel, transmission begins after sensing phase, if the sensed channel is idle.

Now we discuss the sensing channel selection algorithm. We weight channels based on their estimation of reward. The reward is dependent on two parameters: the achievable bit rate in case the channel is idle and the probability of idleness of the channel. Since we don't have the exact value of the latter parameter, we use the fact that as the channel index increases the probability of idleness of the channel increases as well. Moreover, the user restricts it's selection based on it's observation in previous time slot. If the sensed channel in the previous time slot is busy, the user chooses it's sensing channel as below:

$$a(t) = argmax_{i=a(t-1),\dots,N} \left(\frac{i.(N - i + 1)}{\sum_{j=a(t-1)}^{N} j.(N - j + 1)} \right). \tag{8}$$

Otherwise, it would choose one of the channels in vicinity of $a(t-1)$. We consider channels with difference of $\pm N/4$ from i in the vicinity of i.

5 Numerical and Simulation Results

In this section, we present results to show the performance of our proposed strategies. We use throughput as a performance metric which represents the network throughput for the secondary users only.

We assume that the amount of time which is dedicated for reporting is negligible and secondary users earn 1 unit reward for transmission over each channel. Moreover, it is assumed that negotiation phase always has a winner which greedily looks for idle channels.

The results are obtained in MATLAB environment through simulations. Study the effect of CFN and channel sensing strategies on throughput of secondary network is depicted in Figs. 3 and 4. We compare the results of Pure Random Sensing, Cooperative Random and Reward based Random Sensing under fully ordered channel assignment, denoted by PrR-F, CoR, ReR-F, with Pure Random Sensing and Cooperative Random Sensing in not CFN scenario, denoted by PuR-NotCFN and CoR-NotCFN. Moreover, maximum obtainable throughput for secondary network is obtained which is shown by MAX. This can be calculated as

$$\sum_i \pi_i.(N - i + 1). \tag{9}$$

The considered values for system parameters are: $N = 16$, $\mu = 0.5$ in both figures. In order to show the performance of strategies over different network load, λ is considered to be 2 in Fig. 3 and 5 in Fig. 4. The results of these figures show that using ordered channel assignment in primary network leads to a significant increase in throughput of secondary network even if random sensing strategies are applied. Cooperative Random Sensing strategy can nearly achieve MAX throughput when number of secondary users are large enough. However, running mini slot protocol of this strategy needs high synchronization. Therefore Reward based Random Sensing can be used in situation that providing such synchronization is not possible. We can see that for low number of secondary users this strategy works better in comparison to Cooperative Random Sensing strategy. Moreover, we can observe that as the load of network decreases, the performance under ordered channel assignment increases more in comparison to not CFN scenarios. Therefore, it can be concluded CFN is more efficient in low load network scenarios.

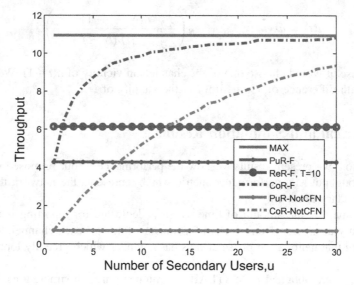

Fig. 3. Impact of random sensing strategies on throughput of secondary network for $N = 16$, $\mu = 0.5$ and $\lambda = 2$

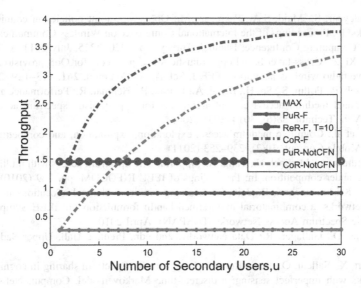

Fig. 4. Impact of random sensing strategies on throughput of secondary network for $N = 16$, $\mu = 0.5$ and $\lambda = 5$

6 Conclusion

In this paper, we investigated the performance of random sensing strategies in Cognitive Friendly Networks (CFN). The aim of CFN is to assist secondary users in process of detection of idle channels through assigning channels in somewhat ordered manner. We show that under fully ordered channel assignment common random sensing strategies: pure and cooperative one achieve much higher throughput in comparison to not CFN scenarios. Moreover we developed reward based random sensing strategy for CFN scenarios, which achieves higher throughput in comparison to random sensing strategy.

References

1. Akyildiz, I.F., Lee, W., Vuran, M.C., Mohanty, S.: NeXt generation dynamic spectrum access/cognitive radio wireless networks: A survey. Comput. Netw. **13**, 2127–2159 (2006)
2. Dalili Shoaei, A., Khorsandi, S.: A POMDP Model for opportunistic spectrum access under ordered channel assignment policy. In: Proceedings of the International Conference on Telecommunication, Jounieh, Lebonan, pp. 557–562 (2012)
3. Zhao, Q., Tong, L., Swami, A., Chen, Y.: Decentralized cognitive MAC for opportunistic spectrum access in Ad Hoc networks: A POMDP framework. IEEE J. Sel. Area Comm. **25**, 589–600 (2007)
4. Ahmad, S.H.A., Liu, M., Javidi, T., Zhao, Q., Krishnamachari, B.: Optimality of myopic sensing in multichannel opportunistic access. IEEE Trans. Inf. Theor. **55**, 4040–4050 (2009)
5. Xu, P., Gu, S., Gao, L., Yu, H., Wang, X., Gan, X., Dong, S.: Myopic sensing for multiple SUs in multichannel opportunistic access. In: Proceedings of International Conference Wireless Communications and Mobile Computing, New York, USA, pp. 256–260 (2010)

6. Salehkaleybar, S., Majd, S.A., Pakravan, M.: QoS aware joint policies in cognitive radio networks. In: Proceedings of the International Conference on Wireless Communications and Mobile Computing Conference, Istanbul, Turkey, pp. 2220–2225, July 2011
7. Su, H., Xi, Z.: Cross-layer based opportunistic MAC protocols for QoS provisionings over cognitive radio wireless networks. IEEE J. Sel. Areas Commun. **261**, 118–129 (2008)
8. Pawelczak, P., Pollin, S., So, H., Bahai, A., Prasad, R., Hekmat, R.: Performance analysis of multichannel medium access control algorithms for opportunistic spectrum access. IEEE Trans. Veh. Technol. **58**(6), 3014–3031 (2008)
9. Lai, L., et al.: Cognitive medium access: exploration, exploitation, and competition. IEEE Trans. Mobile Comput. **10**(2), 239–253 (2011)
10. Anandkumar, A., Michael, N., Tang, A.: Opportunistic Spectrum access with multiple users: learning under competition. In: Proceedings of IEEE INFOCOM, pp. 1–9 (2010)
11. Gai, Y., Krishnamachari, B., Jain, R.: Learning multiuser channel allocations in cognitive radio networks: a combinatorial multi-armed bandit formulation. In: IEEE Symposium on Dynamic Spectrum Access Networks (DySPAN), April 2010
12. Bertsekas, D., Gallager, R.: Data Networks, 2nd edn. Prentice Hall, Upper Saddle River (1992)
13. Gelabert, X., Sallent, O., Pérez-Romero, J., Agustí, R.: Spectrum sharing in cognitive radio networks with imperfect sensing: a discrete-time Markov model. Comput. Netw. **54**(14), 2519–2536 (2010)

Introducing the GBA Covert Channel
in IP Multimedia Subsystem (IMS)

Ghader Ebrahimpour$^{(\boxtimes)}$, Siavash Khorsandi, and Ali Piroozi

Computer Engineering and IT Department,
Amirkabir University of Technology, Tehran, Iran
{ebrahimpour.g,khorsand,falipiroozi}@aut.ac.ir

Abstract. IP Multimedia Subsystem (IMS) is an access-agnostic IP-based technology to provide a wide range of real-time communication and multimedia services for end-users. Security is one of the main challenges in large-scale deployment of IMS. In this paper, we have focused on a particular security hole in the authentication process in IMS. We introduce and discuss the application scenarios of a new covert channel in Generic Bootstrapping Architecture (GBA). GBA-based authentication is part of GAA standard based on shared-secret published by 3GPP. It is demonstrated that this vulnerability can be established to gain unauthorized access to unlawfully utilize the services.

Keywords: IMS · GBA · Covert channel · Authentication protocol · Boot-strapping procedure

1 Introduction

IP Multimedia Subsystem (IMS) is an international standard aimed to replace outgoing TDM-based technologies to provide multimedia communication and content on an access-agnostic basis. It is to unify digital communication infrastructures regardless of their access technologies (cellular, WiFi, PSTN and etc.) [2]. IMS is introduced in 3GPP release 5 to 8 in partnership with TISPAN as a realization of Next Generation Networks (NGN) concept [1]. IMS is defined on top of IP networks and is widely utilizing IP-based protocols published by IETF. Security is one of the main challenges facing IMS deployments. User authentication is one of the basic services needed to control user access to resources and services. A number of different approaches for authentication are proposed. GBA is the standard-based authentication approach based on shared secret used for authentication and key agreement.

Covert channel is a security threat where unauthorized information flow is estab-lished between two participating parties in a single system or a network of connected systems [5]. As the complexity of computer systems grows, various forms of covert channel have been proposed, such as covert channel in IP, SIP, and other network protocols [12, 13, 15].

Covert channel attacks can potentially create high security risk, because they create an illegal communication channel between processes that are not allowed to commu-nicate by the security policy. Although covert channel implementation in general is

© Springer International Publishing Switzerland 2014
A. Movaghar et al. (Eds.): CNDS 2013, CCIS 428, pp. 13–22, 2014.
DOI: 10.1007/978-3-319-10903-9_2

very difficult and sometimes quite complicated if implemented correctly it can lead to severe information leakage [14].

Research in covert channels can be placed in three categories: detection and explaining of covert channels, measuring the amount of information that is transferred through these channels and mitigating covert channels effects [11]. Since the security is one of the major challenges in IMS, therefore investigation of covert channels in these networks will also be important. To best of our knowledge, research on covert channels in IMS has so far been limited to IP and SIP protocols and other aspects of system operation and in particular the authentication process is not investigated.

In this paper we introduce a new covert channel that uses the GBA authentication process for transferring information. Unlike other covert channels, the GBA covert channel uses the user authentication protocol to transfer data. We will explain a scenario in which proposed covert channel has been used for impersonation, in order to gain unauthorized access to services.

The rest of this paper is organized as follows. The concept and various categories of covert channels are described in Sect. 2. In Sect. 3 we will take a glimpse to IMS and its architecture. Section 4 will discuss the GBA, a method for authentication in the IMS, components and reference points of it. We present the GBA covert channel, in Sect. 5. Finally, the last section concludes the paper.

2 Covert Channels

Covert channel refers to any communication channel that can be used by a process to illicitly transfer information that violates the system's security policy. In most cases resource sharing can be a potential vehicle to create a covert channel. There are many threats that should be considered. One of these threats that have not paid enough attention is covert channels [6]. The TCSEC defines two kinds of covert channels: covert timing channels and covert storage channels. These types of covert channels are further elaborated in the following sections.

2.1 Covert Storage Channels

Covert storage channel is a method of communication, in which one process writes in a storage location and another process reads it, these actions can be done directly or indirectly [4]. In other word, one process writes to a shared resource and another process reads from it. Storage channels can be established between processes that parties are in a single computer or networked computers [5]. Printer queue is an example of this type of channel. Two processes are running, when a process with a higher security level wants to sends 1 to a low level process fills up the printer queue, and when it wants to sends 0 leaves the queue. The other process pulls the printer queue to receive data [6].

2.2   Covert Timing Channels

Covert timing channels is a method of communication in which a process sends information to another process by timing modulation in its use of one resource, as such the second process would gain the information by observing the changes in the timings compared to the normal scenario [4].

3   IMS Architecture

In previous section we introduced covert channels. In this section we present IMS, its different layers and architecture. Figure 1 gives an architectural overview of the IMS. IMS has at least three different layers: transport, control and service. Each layer has a special purpose and interacts with its adjacent layer through abstract standard interfaces [2].

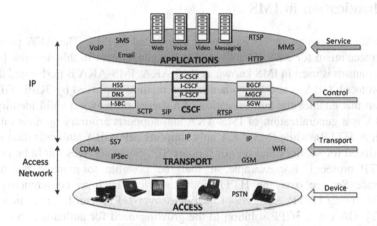

Fig. 1. IMS architecture [2]

The transport layer abstracts the actual access network's functions from the IMS architecture, i.e., it (transport layer) is the intersection point of access layer and the IP network layer. Every entity above the transport layer is based on IP, while the layer below this layer is not based on IP and can uses every protocol. The control layer is responsible for authentication, routing and distribution of IMS traffic between the transport and the service layer. The majority of the traffic in control layer is Session Initiation Protocol (SIP)-base. The main component of this layer is the Call Session Control Function (CSCF) which simplifies the correct interaction among the application server, media servers and the Home Subscriber Service (HSS). The HSS is a database of subscriber and multimedia session control information. Application services are provided by the service layer. New IMS-based service and applications are in this layer, too. This layer is the final layer that gives the IMS architecture the power and flexibility to develop new services.

The power of IMS architecture is that, the transport and control layers can effectively separate the provided services from the access networks, so the services can be provided without concerning about the access network details or how the service reaches the device. The IMS devices don't need to know the service's place and the access network that currently is used, because, the service is easily accessible. This disassociation is a key characteristic that give the next wave of IMS services the ability to transfer to any device [2].

The focus of the IMS is S-CSCF control layer's component that controls registration process, routing, storing session status and service's profiles. When a UE sends a registration request to a S-CSCF, it takes UE's authentication information from HSS and based on this information, produces a question for UE. The UE sends its answer to the S-CSCF. After verification of the UE's response, the S-CSCF accepts the registration and monitors UE's registration status. Subsequently, the user can use the IMS services.

4   Authentication in IMS

Several authentication protocols have been introduced in IMS. The AKA protocol is the main mechanism for authentication and key establishment in this network [3]. The AKA mechanism is used in IMS known as IMS-AKA. IMS-AKA is performed through the SIP protocol. GBA is another authentication method approved by 3GPP. GBA is a mechanism that enables the authentication of a user if they own a valid identity in an HSS. GBA is a generalization of IMS-AKA and supports arbitrary application protocols (such as HTTP), while IMS-AKA only supports SIP. GBA authentication method was introduced for services that do not support SIP. Some services might be available over HTTP protocol. For example, it shall be possible to manage the data on the Presence Service over the HTTP. Other services such as conferencing might be available using HTTP. So access to services over HTTP can be done in a secure manner [7]. GAA is a 3GPP solution to the growing need for authentication and key agreement between the UE and the network and the GBA is one of possible ways to use the GAA [17].

4.1   GBA

GBA performs authentication by creating a challenge and confirming that the UE responses is same with the calculated values in the HSS. The GBA consists of four entities: UE, NAF, BSF, and HSS, which are shown in Fig. 2 [8].

Network Entities of GBA. In this section we describe the network entities of GBA.

   User Equipment (UE): UE is a device used by user to access services that supports NAF-specific protocols. It is divided into two components: Mobile Entity (ME) and Universal Integrated Circuit Card (UICC) [16].
   Bootstrapping Server Function (BSF): BSF is hosted in a network element under the control of a Mobile Network Operator (MNO). BSF, HSS, and UEs participate in GBA in which a shared secret is established between the network and a UE by

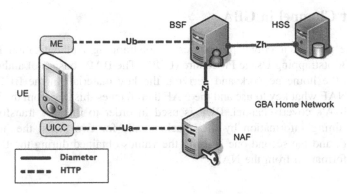

Fig. 2. Network entities of GBA

running the bootstrapping procedure. The shared secret can be used between NAFs and UEs, for example, for authentication purposes [8]. The BSF will restrict the applicability of the key material to a set of NAFs by using a suitable key derivation. The lifetime of the key material is set according to the local policy of the BSF [9]. Network Application Function (NAF): NAF is hosted in a network element. The UE requests a service by contacting a NAF. The NAF has the functionality to communicate with the subscriber's BSF. It should be able to acquire shared key material established between the UE and the BSF during the bootstrapping procedure [9]. After the bootstrapping procedure has been completed, the UE and the NAF can run some application specific protocol which the authentication of messages will be based on session keys generated during the bootstrapping procedure between the UE and the BSF [8].

Home Subscriber Server (HSS): HSS is a database that stores GUSSs (i.e. user authentication information).

GBA Reference Points. GBA's interfaces are as follows:

Ub: The reference point Ub resides in between the UE and the BSF and provides mutual authentication between them. It allows the UE to bootstraps the session keys based on 3GPP AKA infrastructure.

Ua: The Ua interface provides the application protocol and has been secured using the keys agreed between the UE and the BSF during the execution of bootstrapping procedure over reference point Ub.

Zh: The reference point Zh is used between the BSF and the HSS. It allows the BSF to fetch the required authentication information and all GUSSs from the HSS.

Zn: The reference point Zn is used by the NAF due to fetching the key material exchanges between the UE and the BSF during the bootstrapping procedure over the reference point Ub [8].

Zh and Zn Interfaces are based on the Diameter protocol and Ua and Ub Interfaces are based on the HTTP protocol.

5   Covert Channel in GBA

GBA can be divided into two procedures: Bootstrapping Authentication Procedure (BAP) and Bootstrapping Usage Procedure (BUP). The BAP consists of authenticating the client to the home network and deriving the key material. In the BUP, the UE informs the NAF what key to use and the NAF then fetches this key from the BSF [10].

In the GBA's covert channel, BUP is used in order to illegally transform information. Obtaining information by the attacker calls for two steps: the first one is running BAP, and the second one is using the values obtained during the BAP to get confident information from the NAF.

5.1   Bootstrapping Authentication Procedure (BAP)

Bootstrapping Authentication Procedure (BAP) is as follows:

Before the UE and the NAF start their communication, they should decide whether they want to use GBA or not. When the UE wants to interact with the NAF, starts a communication on the Ua interface with the NAF (without GBA parameters). If the NAF needs shared keys from GBA and UE's request does not have them, the NFA, responds with a bootstrapping initiation message.

When a UE wants to interact with a NAF and it knows a BAP procedure is required, it should first perform a bootstrapping procedure. Otherwise, the UE will perform the bootstrapping authentication, just if a bootstrapping initiation message has been received or if the lifetime of the key in UE has expired [8]. The UE sends a HTTP request to BSF and the BSF retrieves the complete user's GUSSs and an AV (Authentication Vector) from HSS (over the reference point Zh) [9].

After that, the BSF forwards RAND and AUTN to the UE in a 401 message (without the CK, IK and XRES) [9]. It should be mentioned that, every AV includes CK, IK, RAND, XRES and AUTN, as the following relation:

$$AV \ = \ RAND \parallel AUTN \parallel XRES \parallel CK \parallel IK$$

Where RAND is a random challenge, AUTH is a network authentication token, XRES is an expected authentication result, CK is a session key for encryption, and IK is a session key for integrity.

The UE checks the AUTN to verify that it comes from an authorized network. The UE calculates RES (user authentication result), IK and CK, too [17]. The result is two session keys, IK and CK in the BSF and the UE. The UE sends another HTTP request to the BSF containing the digest AKA response which is calculated using RES [9]. The BSF authenticates the UE by checking the digest AKA response. The BSF creates Ks by concatenation of CK and IK, it also produces B-TID which is used for binding subscriber identity to the key in reference points Ua, Ub and Zn. After, the BSF sends a 200 OK message to the UE which contains a B-TID to indicate the success of authentication and the key's lifetime. The UE produces Ks by concatenation of CK and IK. The BSF and the UE use Ks to create Ks-NAF which is used for securing the Ua reference point [9]. The Ks-NAF is computed as follows:

$$Ks\text{-}NAF = f_{KD}(Ks, \text{"gba-me"}, RAND, IMPI, NAF\text{-}ID)$$

f_{KD} is the key derivation function and is implemented in the ME. Key's derivation parameters consist of the user's IMPI, NAF-ID, and RAND. NAF-ID consists of the full name of the NAF's DNS concatenated with the Ua security protocol identifier. The BSF and the UE should store Ks for future use until the Ks' lifetime has expired or it is updated [9].

5.2   Bootstrapping Usage Procedure (BUP)

BUP is the second procedure for using GBA and starts with TLS handshake between the UE and the NAF. When NAF and UE decide to use GBA, whenever the UE wants to interact with the NAF, it starts a communication with NAF on the reference point Ua and sends B-TID to it. So, the NAF can receive related keys from the BSF. The NAF starts a communication with BSF over the reference point Zn. The NAF requests the key corresponding to the B-TID that the UE has sent to it. With this request, the NAF also sends its public hostname to the BSF, and the BSF shall be able to verify that the NAF is authorized to use that hostname.

The BSF creates the key required to protect the protocol used over the reference point Ua, using Ks and key derivation parameters; Afterwards, the BSF sends the key to the NAF for the requested key Ks-NAF, as well as the bootstrapping time and the lifetime of the key. If the key identified by the B-TID is not available in BSF, the BSF will notify NAF with its response and the NAF will send a request to the UE for a bootstrapping renegotiation. NAF will continue its communication with UE by the protocol used over the reference point Ua. When the run of the protocol over the reference point Ua is complete, the purpose of bootstrapping is satisfied because it allows the UE and NAF to use the reference point Ua in a secure way [9].

5.3   The GBA Covert Channel Operation

In the GBA covert channel, NAF sends information to UE illegally using the boot-strapping usage procedure (BUP). This covert channel has two steps: First, a user performs the bootstrapping usage procedure (BUP) and receives a B-TID from BSF. Second, the user communicates with the NAF and receives information over covert channel. The second step is as follows: the user sends an HTTP request with required parameters for authentication, received in the first step, to the NAF. The NAF sends a bootstrapping renegotiation message if it wants to transfer bit 1, and a "200 OK", which is used for success authentication, if it wants to transfer bit 0. Thus, the user can send requests and receive responses to obtain information from the NAF.

5.4   A Simple Scenario for Using GBA Covert Channel

Suppose the following scenario shown in Fig. 3. User A is a typical user and has their B-TID and Ks_NAF. To use services, if the user A has not been authenticated, they should perform the BAP and then send a request to the NAF to be authenticated. We suppose that the user A has already performed BAP, and now wants to use services. As shown in Fig. 3, in BUP, the user A sends a request to the NAF containing B-TID. The NAF receives this request and communicates with subscriber's BSF to acquire shared key material (such as Ks_NAF) established between the UE and the BSF during the bootstrapping procedure. At this point, the NAF has both A's B-TID and Ks_NAF. In the next step, the NAF sends an HTTP response with a "401 Unauthorized" status code to the user A and then receives and verifies the A's response. If the A's authentication succeeds, the NAF provides the services to the user A and stores A's B-TID and Ks_NAF for future connections.

Suppose M is an attacker that communicates with the NAF through the covert channel. The user M can use the covert channel to receive the A's authentication values from the NAF (Fig. 4). When the user M obtains the A's B-TID and Ks_NAF through the covert channel, they can use them for authentication and use of services. Now the user M can use services which has been provided for the user A as the identity of user A.

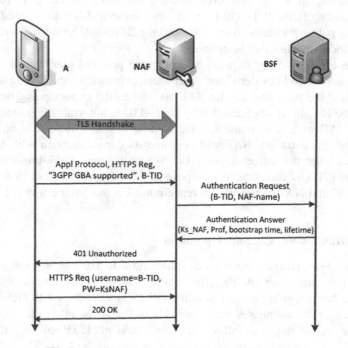

Fig. 3. Obtaining A's B-TID and Ks_NAF by NAF

5.5   Other Form of Covert Channel

The covert channel introduced in Sect. 5.1 can be done in other forms. In this subsection, another form of the GBA covert channel is introduced below:

The attacker (M) has two B-TIDs and their corresponding Ks_NAFs. One B-TID has expired, and the other one has not. The attacker establishes two distinct connections with NAF and sends the expired B-TID through the first connection and the other

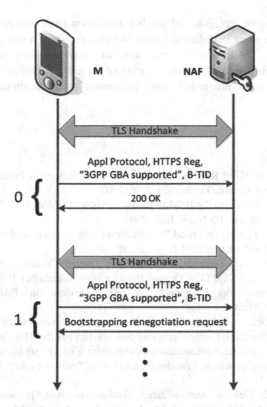

Fig. 4. Information transferring by covert channel

through the second. If the NAF wants to transfer bit 1, it sends an HTTP response with a "401 Unauthorized" status code to the M through the first connection and nothing through the other; and if the NAF wants to send bit 0 to the M, it will respond to the second connection and discards the first one. Thus, NAF will send information to M through the covert channel.

5.6 Elimination

One of the reasons that led to this covert channel is the lack of BSF in the user's authentication process between NAF and UE. On the other hand, for user authentication, both B-TID and Ks_NAF are provided for NAF. A user that has these two values can authenticate themselves to the NAF, so if the NAF sends B-TID and Ks_NAF to the attacker in an unintended manner, the attacker can impersonate themselves as a typical user. Therefore, if one of these values, which is probably Ks_NAF, is not provided for the NAF, the NAF cannot send those values to an unauthorized user.

6 Conclusion

In this paper we described one of the authentication procedures in IMS and introduced a new covert channel in the authentication process. This covert channel misuses the authentication procedure in GBA and sends information from one network's entity to another which can be done in different forms. We also designed a scenario that led to an impersonation attack. There can be some other scenarios resulting in severe information leakage which in turn causes other forms of attacks. Therefore, in order for the information leakage to be prevented, some prevention methods should be considered.

References

1. 3GPP, Overview of 3GPP Release 5 - Summary of all Release 5 Features. 3GPP - ETSI Mobile Competence Centre, Technical report (2003)
2. Salchow, K.: Introduction to the IP Multimedia Subsystem (IMS): IMS Basic Concepts and Terminology. Whitepaper F5 Netw. Inc. (2007)
3. 3GPP TS 33.102 V11.5.0., Technical Specification Group Services and System Aspects; 3G Security; Security architecture (2012)
4. Department of Defense. Department of Defense Trusted Computer System Evaluation Criteria, DOD 5200.28-STD (The Orange Book) edition (December 1985)
5. McFail, M.: Covert storage channels: A brief overview. In: PACISE Conference, Bloomsburg, PA (2005)
6. Pennington, E., Oblitey, W., Ezekiel, S., Wolfe, J.: An Overview of Covert Channels. Covert Channels Research Group Computer Science Department IUP, Indiana
7. 3GPP TS 33.222: Generic Authentication Architecture (GAA); Access to network application functions using Hypertext Transfer Protocol over Transport Layer Security (HTTPS), (Release 12) (2013)
8. 3GPP TS 33.220: Generic Authentication Architecture (GAA); Generic bootstrapping architecture, (Release 12) (2013)
9. Ilyas, M., Ahson, S.A.: IP Multimedia Subsystem (IMS) Handbook. CRC Press, Boca Raton (2008)
10. Olkkonen, T.: Generic Authentication Architecture. In: Security and Privacy in Pervasive Computing, Seminar on Network Security, Espoo 2006
11. Millen, J.: 20 years of covert channel modeling and analysis. In: Proceedings of the 1999 IEEE Symposium on Security and Privacy, pp. 113–114 (1999)
12. Mazurczyk, W., Szczypiorski, K.: Covert channels in SIP for VoIP signalling. In: Jahankhani, H., Revett, K., Palmer-Brown, D. (eds.) Global E-Security, pp. 65–72. Springer, Heidelberg (2008)
13. Cabuk, S., Brodley, C.E., Shields, C.: IP covert channel detection. ACM Trans. Inf. Syst. Secur. TISSEC 12(4), 22 (2009)
14. Gallagher, P.R.: A guide to understanding covert channel analysis of trusted systems, National Computer Security Center, USA (1993). http://fas.org/irp/nsa/rainbow/tg030.htm
15. Zander, S., Armitage, G., Branch, P.: Covert channels in the IP time to live field. In: Proceedings of Australian Telecommunication Networks and Applications Conference (ATNAC) (2006)
16. Kasera, S., Narang, N.: 3G Networks. Tata McGraw-Hill Education, New York (2004)
17. 3GPP TS 33.919; Generic Authentication Architecture (GAA); System description, (Release 11) (2012)

DCF/RCB: A New Method for Detection and Punishment of Selfish Nodes in IEEE 802.11

Maryam Chinipardaz$^{(\boxtimes)}$ and Mehdi Dehghan

Computer Engineering and Information Technology Department,
Amirkabir University of Technology, Tehran, Iran
{m.chinipardaz,dehghan}@aut.ac.ir

Abstract. The IEEE 802.11 standard protocol is one of the most popular standards for wireless networks and its widespread and growing use has led to numerous studies on its performance and improvement of its different mechanisms. The media access mechanism used in this protocol is designed with the assumption that all users will fully comply with its rules so it doesn't contain any approach for prevention and detection of any violation of the protocol that is called misbehavior. Selfish node misbehaves to obtain more network resources and this misbehavior can cause the loss of fairness among hosts and great reduction in the overall network performance.

Among different misbehavior, waiting for a smaller backoff period against other nodes is an efficient way to gain much more throughput in the network. Different methods have been proposed so far but all of them share some defects and have some limiting factors. We study backoff misbehavior in this paper and a new mechanism called DCF/RCB containing detection and punishment methods is presented to overcome this misbehavior. The mechanism is based on a new method of assigning backoff, using a deterministic pseudo random function. It can be shown that the proposed mechanism is resilient to colluding nodes and has not some limiting factors in previous proposed schemes. Simulation results are presented to show the success of our proposed mechanism in the presence of backoff misbehavior model.

Keywords: Wireless network · MAC layer · IEEE 802.11 · Misbehavior · Backoff

1 Introduction

Any violation of predefined protocol framework is called misbehavior. Misbehavior can occur in each layer of network protocol stack and it can be classified according its goal: malicious and selfish behavior. Malicious node misbehaves to disrupt the services of the network. Selfish node uses misbehavior to gain more network resources against other well-behaved nodes. Some possible benefits achieved by selfish behavior are as following:

© Springer International Publishing Switzerland 2014
A. Movaghar et al. (Eds.): CNDS 2013, CCIS 428, pp. 23–36, 2014.
DOI: 10.1007/978-3-319-10903-9_3

- Obtaining a large part of network capacity (as a result of improvement of its throughput)
- Reducing consumed energy
- Improving achieved Quality of service, for example, less delay

In the rest of the paper, "misbehavior" refers to selfish behavior and does not relate to security aspects of wireless network.

In this paper we concentrate on selfish behavior in accessing shared media in ad hoc network with the IEEE 802.11 DCF standard. Because (a) MAC layer is directly associated with wireless media, misbehaving in this layer is much more efficient for selfish node than misbehaving in the transport and network layer, (b) The detection mechanism used in higher layers cannot detect MAC layer misbehavior i.e. misbehavior in MAC layer is hidden from higher layers. Therefore it can be combined with the misbehavior of higher layer to improve them, (c) IEEE 802.11 is the most common protocol in local wireless networks, (d) its tools (access points and wireless adapters) are very cheap, (e) its simulation codes are widely available.

Different misbehaviors can be done by selfish node at MAC layer with the IEEE 802.11 DCF. For example, a node can scramble the packets send by other nodes to make them increase their contention window. Increasing the NAV value in RTS, CTS or DATA frame to make other nodes wait for a longer time, is another example. Manipulating the backoff value is one of the most important misbehaviors in this layer. A classification of MAC layer misbehavior can be found in [1].

Backoff manipulation is one of the easiest and most efficient ways for selfish goals. A selfish node can easily backoff for a smaller time and consequently gains much more throughput against well-behaved nodes. Concurrently, because of the random nature of backoff, it is one of the hardest ones for others to detect the manipulation. Therefore, this misbehavior has attracted a lot of studies and research.

In this paper we propose a new method that can detect and punish selfish nodes. In Sect. 2 there is a review of similar works and their defects. In Sect. 3 a review of IEEE 802.11 DCF is presented. Our proposed scheme and its specifications are presented in Sect. 4. Section 5 contains the advantages of our proposed scheme against other previous schemes in this area and all of them are analyzed. In the last section there are some simulations that all show the accurateness of our scheme.

2   Related Works

The first group of studies against misbehavior tries not to change the protocol and propose to locate a detection system in the network for monitoring nodes behavior [2,3]. Although it does not need to change the standard protocol, this group of methods has some significant disadvantages. One of the most important characteristics of ad hoc network is the lack of infrastructure and central node.

Because of the variety of network nodes and their movement, none of the nodes is completely stable and reliable. So, placing the detection system is itself a new problem. Another issue is how to use the information gathered by detection system for misbehavior prevention or penalization. As in ad hoc network each node communicates through its neighbors, implementing the punishment methods needs the change of protocol in each node.

In [2] a system called Domino is proposed, which is a program that can be placed in Access Point (AP) and tries to evaluate the behavior of nodes contacting the AP. This detection system can be used in networks with a central reliable node. Moreover, its diagnosis method for detecting backoff manipulation is based on comparison of the average backoff with a threshold value and that is a non-optimal method.

The second category of studies includes the methods that change the MAC protocol with the use of game theory mechanism for nodes to prevent them from misbehaving [4,5]. The goal in game theory is to design a distributed protocol that guarantees the existence, uniqueness and convergence to Nash equilibrium with acceptable efficiency. Since game theory protocols assume that all nodes are selfish (worst-case scenario), the efficiency of these protocol is significantly less than the protocols that assume the majority of nodes are well-behaved.

The third category of studies contains methods that alter the protocol to decrease its randomness and lack of monitoring so that misbehaving is harder and its detection is easier and most of the time led to misbehavior avoidance [6–8]. These methods usually include penalizing the selfish node or neutralizing its misbehavior. Due to the advantages of this group, the method presented in this paper fits in third category and completes the ideas in this group.

Kyasanur et al. in [6] propose a method that in each transmission the destination node assigns a random backoff for the sender to use for its next transmission to that destination. The destination node penalizes the sender by setting larger backoff in the case of misbehavior. Although in this method the backoff values are assigned by the destination node, the destination misbehavior is itself another problem. This method is suitable for a network with reliable destination that cannot be guaranteed in ad hoc network.

Cardenas et al. in [7] improve the previous idea. Sender and destination agree on a backoff value for sender's next transmission during current transmission. It ensures the randomness of backoff as long as at least one party is reliable. This method is vulnerable to collusion.

By extending the idea presented in [6], Shi et al. suggest that Local Most Trustworthy node (LMT node) assigns backoff values to neighbor nodes [8]. Finding LMT node imposes a lot of overhead to each node. Although LMT node can almost detect the sender's misbehavior but there isn't any reaction mechanism for misbehaving node.

Methods presented so far, are vulnerable to collusion, because there is always another node in network that participate in assigning a backoff. The method presented in this paper is resistant against collusion. It can be used in both two-way and four-way handshaking communication. It works in the case of node movement and collisions in the network. These are all analyzed in Sect. 5.

3   IEEE 802.11 DCF

The IEEE 802.11 DCF (Distributed Coordination Function) standard [9] uses CSMA/CA (carrier sense/multiple access with collision avoidance) algorithm with the purpose of decreasing collisions in network. There are two methods of communication in DCF: (1) two-way handshaking, the source and destination exchange DATA and ACK frames. This method is suitable for short DATA frames and (2) four-way handshaking, that an exchange of RTS/CTS comes before DATA frame transmission. This method is more suitable for long data frames. Because the shorter length of RTS frame (20 bytes) against long data frames (up to 2346 bytes) decrease the possibility of collision. In this section we describe the four-way handshake communication.

A station that has a new packet for transmission, first checks the channel. If the channel is idle for DIFS (Distributed Inter Frame Space) period, a small frame called RTS (Request To Send) is sent. If channel is detected busy during DIFS, the station delays sending until it detects the channel idle for DIFS time. In the situation that several stations are contending for accessing the channel, when they all sense the idle channel, for preventing the collision of their simultaneous transmissions, they must first choose a random number called backoff and after waiting for that time, in the case of idle channel they will send their RTS frame. Equation 1 gives the number of idle time slots, the sender must wait before its transmission.

$$backoff = integer(CW \times rand(0,1)) \qquad (1)$$

In (1) CW is the contention window, $rand$ is a random number between 0 and 1. Integer function converts its value to an integer. If the destination receives the RTS frame, it will respond it with a small frame called the CTS (Clear To Send). When the sender receives the CTS frame, it will begin sending DATA. After receiving DATA, the destination node sends an ACK frame to the sender for acknowledgement. Figure 1 shows the exchange of frames and some of time intervals between them.

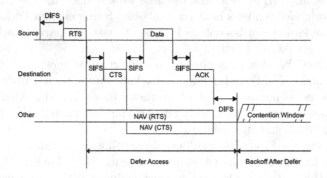

Fig. 1. RTS/CTS/DATA/ACK and NAV setting

If the sender does not receive the CTS frame or if it does not receive the ACK frame within their specified time, it will retry its transmission with a delay. The sender uses the BEB (Binary Exponential Backoff) algorithm to calculate a new contention window. The contention window for ith retransmission of a packet is shown by CW_i and is calculated in (2).

$$CW_i = \min(2^{(i-1)} \times (CW_{min} + 1) - 1, CW_{max}) \tag{2}$$

As the attempt number increases the CW get larger. So the backoff value is computed from a larger range and in result there is less probability of congestion.

Virtual sensing in each node is performed by NAV (Network Allocation Vector). NAV keeps predicted time for the current transmission and is set from the field in RTS and CTS frames showing the time needed for the transmission.

4   Proposed Scheme

Our goal is suggesting a mechanism for selecting backoff values that follows two properties: first, it must have the randomness property; second, it follows a deterministic function, so that it could be calculated and monitored by other nodes. In this paper we present a function called BKfunction that considers these two properties.

In the proposed method each node monitors its neighbors transmissions. By considering the BKfunction mechanism, a detection procedure is presented called CheckBackoff. Each node will perform this procedure after receiving a packet from a node in its neighborhood to evaluate the senders behavior for that transmission. The receivers will update the misbehavior degree of sender after the evaluation. The destination node will use misbehavior degree for its punishment mechanism for the sender. Our method is an extension to IEEE 802.11 DCF with some changes and extra parts. The new protocol is called DCF/RCB because it is an extension to DCF and RCB is the abbreviation of ReComputable Backoff. The description of this scheme is presented in detail in the following sections.

4.1   Packet Fields

In this method RTS and DATA frames include two more fields, previous backoff and attempt number. Sender sets the previous backoff, it has used and the attempt number of current transmission in these fields.

4.2   Table of Neighbors

Each node has a list for storing some information about its neighbor nodes, an example of this list is shown in Table 1. This information is needed for evaluating the behavior of senders and is used for punishment decision for misbehavior ones.

For each neighbor, the first value, misbehavior degree is the amount of selfishness distinguished for that neighbor and it is calculated from evaluating the behavior of neighbor in its previous transmissions. It has a value between 0 and 100. Other fields are attempt number, previous backoff and destination; extracted from the last packet that has been received from that neighbor node.

Table 1. Neighbor list example

	Stored Values			
Neighbors	Misbehavior degree	Attempt number	Previous backoff	Destination
Node 1	10	1	24	5
Node 2	45	3	4	3

4.3 BKfunction

BKfunction that has been proposed for calculating a new backoff follows the LCG (Linear Congruential Generator) pseudo random number generator. LCG represents one of the oldest and best-known pseudorandom number generator algorithm. BKfunction is recursive, i.e. previous backoff value is needed for calculating a new backoff. So the sender node must store the backoff value in each transmission for calculating its backoff for next transmission. Each node also must store the previous backoff of its neighbors in its neighbor list for evaluating the correctness of their new backoff. Equation (3) is an LCG function that produces random numbers in $[0, 32748]$.

$$backoffseed_i = (backoffseed_{i-1} \times 32719 + 3) \bmod 32749 \qquad (3)$$

Equation (4) shows how the new backoff is computed from $backoffseed$ in the range $[0, CW]$.

$$backoff_i = (backoffseed_i) \bmod (CW + 1) \qquad (4)$$

Different nodes must have different initial values to make diverse sequences of backoff. So, their unique id can be used for $backoffseed_0$ (5).

$$backoffseed_0 = sender\ id \qquad (5)$$

Since $CW_{min} = 7$ with the rewrite of (2) the contention window size is calculated as follows.

$$CW = \min(2^{attemptNumber+4} - 1, CW_{max}) \qquad (6)$$

$AttemptNumber$ shows the number of packet retransmissions for current frame. Previous backoff is the backoff calculated before for just previous sender's transmission.

For simplification we summarize the backoff process in a function called BKfunction (7). For calculating a new backoff, sender node needs its previous backoff and attempt number as the inputs of the function. The sender must wait for new backoff interval and then transmit its packet.

$$backoff_i = BKfunction(backoffseed_{i-1}, attemptNumber) \qquad (7)$$

Contention window is used for backoff calculation. The sender has the attempt number of its current frame and the receivers extract the attempt number from the frame, so they both can calculate and consider the contention window.

4.4 Evaluating the Received Frame

Each node that receives an RTS frame must evaluate the backoff of the sender in that transmission. So it will first perform the CheckBackoff procedure and due to its result, it will update the sender's misbehavior degree in its neighbor list.

CheckBackoff Procedure and Its Analysis. The description of CheckBackoff procedure along with its analysis is presented in this section. The formal analysis proves the capability of detecting selfish nodes in the procedure. The algorithm of CheckBackoff procedure is shown in Algorithm 1. The parameters used in the algorithm are described in Table 2.

Algorithm 1. CheckBackoff procedure

1: **if**   ((*packet_attempt_number*   =   *stored_expected_attempt_number*)   and   (*packet_privious_backoff = stored_privious_backoff*)) **then**

2:     *expected_backoff = BKfunction(packet fields)*

3:     **if** (*waited_slots ≤ expected_backoff*) **then**

4:         Deviation has occurred

5:     **end if**

6: **else**

7:     *aggregate_expected_backoff*   ←   *BKfunction(stored values)* + *ΣBKfunction(guessed parameters) + BKfunction(packet fields)*

8:     **if** (*waited_slots ≤ aggregate_expected_backoff*) **then**

9:         Deviation has occurred

10:     **end if**

11: **end if**

Selfish nodes try to backoff for smaller interval to access the channel faster and thus gain much more throughput against other nodes in the network. So there could be two kind of selfish behavior in the proposed method. First type: the sender sends the packet with correct fields but it does not wait for the correct backoff calculated from BKfunction. Second type: the sender will change the fields in the packet in such way that with the BKfunction, the calculated backoff value becomes smaller than the value with the correct fields. Then it waits for that smaller backoff. Now in this section, we will show that our method is capable of detecting these two kinds of misbehaviors caused by the selfishness of the node.

Table 2. Check backoff procedure parameters

waited_slots	The number of time slots between two successive transmissions of sender. Each node In the network, computes the waited slots of its neighbors according to the packets receives from them
packet_attempt_number	The number of sender's retransmission attempts that is extracted from the packet
stored_expected_attempt_number	The expected number of retransmission attempt of the sender that is stored in the receiver
packet_previous_backoff	The sender's previous backoff that is extracted from the packet
stored_previous_backoff	The sender's previous backoff that is stored in the receiver
expected_backoff	Time period expected from the sender to wait

As mentioned before all the neighbors receiving a packet will perform the CheckBackoff procedure to check the current transmission of the sender.

There is a condition set in line 1 of Algorithm 1. If the receiving packet matches the condition set, it means that the sender has the expected transmission and the current transmission can be checked for backoff. The backoff expected for this transmission is calculated in line 2. By comparing the waited slots of the sender with expected backoff, selfish behavior type 1 can be detected.

If the receiving packet doesn't match the condition set, two assumptions can be made.

1. There were some packets send by sender before the current one that we didn't receive.
2. The sender had committed the misbehavior type 2.

To further check, we suppose the first assumption and go on. So, we calculate the expected backoff with the consideration of the backoff of unsuccessful retransmissions as much as we can guess them correctly. An aggregate backoff is computed in line 7 of Algorithm 1 and it is considered as the expected backoff.

Now we prove that if the node had made misbehavior type 2, this procedure can detect it. If the selfish sender has misbehavior type2, it has changed its packet fields to obtain a smaller backoff than its current correct backoff, but the CheckBackoff procedure calculates an aggregate backoff as the expected backoff. This aggregate includes the backoff that is obtained from the BKfunction with stored values, i.e. the correct backoff that the misbehavior node must have been complying with it. This aggregated backoff is used for comparison with waited slots.

If the node had misbehavior type2, the followings are true about the sender.

$$correct\ backoff = BKfunction(correct\ values)$$
$$incorrect\ backoff = BKfunction(incorrect\ values)$$
$$incorrect\ backoff \leq waited\ slots < correct\ backoff$$

Correct backoff is calculated in receiver as follows.

$$correct\ backoff = BKfunction(stored\ values)$$

Due to the definition of aggregate expected backoff we have:

$$BKfunction(stored\ values) < aggregate\ expected\ backoff$$

So finally we can conclude:

$$waited\ slots \ll aggregate\ expected\ backoff$$

So as we saw, the misbehavior type 2 can also be detected in the algorithm.

4.5 Updating Misbehavior Degree

If the receiver detects selfish behavior for the sender in current transmission, it will increase the senders misbehavior degree; otherwise it will decrease the senders misbehavior degree. The increment value shown in (8) is a function of deviation amount. α has a value in $[0,1]$ and is used for preventing some misdiagnosis. If the misbehavior node carries on backoff manipulation, the neighboring nodes will increase its misbehavior degree until it reaches 100. At this point the sender is distinguished as a severe misbehaving node and its misbehavior degree doesn't decrease any more.

$$inc = f(\alpha \times expected\ backoff - waited\ slots) \qquad (8)$$

4.6 Punishment Mechanism

Whenever a node receives an RTS packet frame, it will first run the Check-Backoff procedure and updates the senders misbehavior degree. If this node is the destination of the packet, it performs punishment mechanism. The Punishment mechanism has two stages. If the senders misbehavior degree is below 100, the receiver will respond to the sender with a probability proportional to the misbehavior degree. For example, if the senders misbehavior degree is equal to 50, half of its packets are responded. This is the first stage of punishment. When the senders misbehavior degree has reached 100 in destination node list, the punishment stage 2 is occurred. In this case the senders packets will never be respond.

5 Analysis of Proposed Scheme

In this section we present and analyze the advantages of the DCF/RCB method against other proposed methods.

5.1   Thwart Colluding

Unlike the previous research that present a new method for assigning a back-off value to sender, discussed in Sect. 2, in DCF/RCB, the other nodes do not participate in assigning a backoff for the sender. The senders history and its current packet determine its current backoff. So there is no colluding for backoff assignment in this method.

Since the monitoring of sender is distributed, its misbehavior is not only detected by the destination node, it can also be detected by any neighbor node that receives the packet. So the selfish sender will receive punishment from any node that has detected its misbehavior. This kind of distributed monitoring and punishment will thwart the colluding of nodes for punishment.

5.2   Applicable for Mobile Networks

Some of the methods proposed in the previous research are not applicable for a mobile network; however, now we show that DCF/RCB can be used for mobile networks. Here we consider a mobile node that has been moved to another place in the network so it will have some new neighbors. After its first transmission after the movement, its old neighbors will monitor its transmission and evaluate its behavior as they did in the past. But other neighbors will add this new node in their neighbor list with initializing the list fields. Misbehavior degree is set to 0 and attempt number, previous backoff and destination are extracted from the packet.

Although new neighbors have no idea about the sender's misbehavior history, they can follow its behavior from the current time. This is somehow logical too, because a node that has been behaving selfishly in its past place and with its past neighbors is not necessarily a selfish node in its new condition. So new neighbors must evaluate the node from the behaviors they have seen.

5.3   Applicable for both Two-Way and Four-Way Handshaking Communication Method

Some previous research used RTS/CTS exchange as part of their backoff assigning procedure, so they cannot be used for two-way handshaking transmission. The DCF/RCB method can be used in both two-way and four-way handshaking transmissions. In the case of two-way transmissions the fields need for computing backoff in extracted from data frame in both sender and receiver.

5.4   Considering CW

In DCF/RCB method the contention window that is computed from attempt number is considered in BKfunction for calculating backoff both in sender and receiver; however, in some previous proposed methods that other nodes e.g. destination node participates in backoff assigning, the contention window is not considered because the other nodes do not know the exact attempt number of the transmission.

6   Simulation

The DCF/RCB is implemented by developing IEEE 802.11 DCF standard using ns2 simulator [10]. For showing how IEEE 802.11 with DCF/RCB method will behave against different nodes, we present some simulation and their result. But first we explain our selfishness simulation model.

6.1   Selfishness Simulation

For showing the amount and effect of selfishness we need to parameterize it. The selfish node manipulates its backoff value to wait for a shorter time to access the channel faster than other nodes. Manipulating backoff can be implemented in different ways.

Here the node's selfishness degree is a number between 0 and 100. A node with $selfishnessdegree = x$ will wait for the $(100 - x)/100$ of its backoff. For example a node with $selfishnessdegree = 0$ will wait all its backoff time and a node with $selfishnessdegree = 100$ won't wait any time.

6.2   Simulation Conditions

The ns2 is used for our simulations. We use UDP for transport layer protocol and CBR as the sender's traffic. The simulation includes 20 nodes that are randomly distributed in a 100×100 meter area. There are 10 flows in the network and 4 of them are sent by selfish nodes. The packet size is 512 bytes, and the data rate is 1 Mbps.

6.3   Simulation Results

First we test the proposed protocol in the absence of misbehavior to see if there is any throughput degradation against the base protocol i.e. DCF. Figure 2 depicts the average throughput of nodes in the absence of misbehavior. As we can see the throughput of DCF/RCB is almost the same as DCF.

We use two metrics, correct diagnosis and misdiagnosis in order to show the accurateness of the proposed mechanism. Correct diagnosis is the percentage of packets sent by a misbehavior node that is detected as a packet from a selfish node. Misdiagnosis is the percentage of packets sent by a well behaved node that is by mistake detected as a packet from selfish node.

Figure 3 shows the protocol accuracy in detecting selfish nodes. As we can see with the growing in sender's selfishness degree, the correct diagnosis is increasing. Misdiagnosis percentage is almost constant and independent from selfishness degree.

In Fig. 4 we can see the throughput of well-behaved and misbehaved nodes in a network with DCF and DCF/RCB protocol according to misbehavior percentage.

As it can be seen from Fig. 4 with the use of DCF protocol with the increase in selfishness degree of misbehavior senders, well-behaved nodes have a great

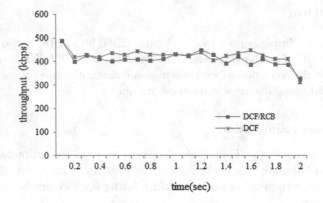

Fig. 2. Average throughput of nodes in the absence of misbehavior

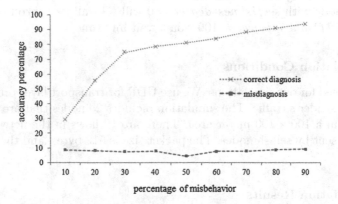

Fig. 3. Correct diagnosis and misdiagnosis percentage

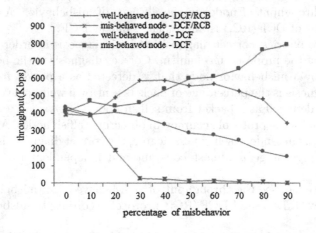

Fig. 4. Average throughput based on misbehavior percentage

reduction in the throughput and on the other hand misbehaved nodes have their throughput increased. With the use of DCF/RCB the result is opposite. Notice that by increasing selfishness degree in DCF/RCB above 50 percent, none of the nodes in the network can use the channel and that is because of the punishment of misbehaved nodes.

7   Conclusion and Future Work

A Selfish node in MAC layer can cause severe performance degradation and injustice among hosts. For ensuring service availability in MAC layer, different possible misbehaviors must be studied and evaluated.

Different solutions have been presented for overcoming selfish behavior in IEEE 802.11 DCF MAC layer. In this paper with considering previous solutions, we tried to propose a new idea for calculating backoff values. A pseudo random and deterministic function called BKfunction was presented. Based on this function we present a detection scheme called CheckBackoff that every node can perform it when receiving a packet to evaluate sender's behavior in that transmission. We show that the two possible selfish behaviors in this system can be detected by CheckBackoff procedure. The destination node can punish selfish senders by not responding to their packets with a possibility and thus making them to retransmit their packet. This punishment aims in neutralization of selfish node behavior (waiting for smaller backoff).

There are some plans to complete this scheme. Extending the proposed scheme to cover other MAC layer misbehaviors, is one of our plans. Selecting the proposed protocol parameters adaptively can improve the protocol performance. More detailed experimental results and game analysis of the proposed scheme are also our plan for future work.

References

1. Guang, L., Assi, C., Benslimane, A.: MAC layer misbehavior in wireless networks: challenges and solutions. IEEE Wirel. Commun. **15**, 6–14 (2008)
2. Raya, M., Aad, I., Hubaux, J.P., El Fawal, A.: DOMINO: detecting MAC Layer Greedy behavior in IEEE 802.11 hotspots. IEEE Trans. Mob. Comput. **12**, 1691–1705 (2006)
3. Zhang, Y., Lee, W.: Intrusion detection in wireless Ad hoc networks. In: 6th Annual International Conference on Mobile Computing and Networking, pp. 275–283. ACM (2000)
4. Konorski, J.: A game-theoretic study of CSMA/CA under a backoff attack. IEEE/ACM Trans. Networking 14(6), 1167–1178 (2006)
5. Cagalj, M., Ganeriwal, S., Aad, I., Hubaux, J.-P.: On cheating in CSMA/CA Ad hoc networks. In: IEEE INFOCOM 2005 (2004)
6. Kyasanur, P., Vaidya, N.H.: Selfish MAC layer misbehavior in wireless networks. IEEE Trans. Mob. Comput. 4(5), 502–516 (2005)
7. Cardenas, A., Radosavac, S., Baras, J.S.: Detection and prevention of MAC layer misbehavior in Ad hoc networks. In: 2nd ACM Workshop on Security of Ad Hoc and Sensor Networks, pp. 17–22. ACM (2004)

8. Shi, F., Baek, J., Song, J., Liu, W.: A novel scheme to prevent MAC layer misbehavior in IEEE 802.11 Ad hoc Networks. Telecommun. Syst. **52**(4), 2397–2406 (2011)
9. IEEE 802 LAN/MAN Standards Committee: Wireless LAN Medium Access Control (MAC) and Physical Layer (PHY) Specifications. IEEE Standard 802, 999 (1999)
10. Fall, K., Varadhan, K.: The ns Manual (formerly ns Notes and Documentation). The VINT Project (2002)

Wireless Sensor Networks

Wireless Sensor Network Lifetime Maximization Using Multiple Mobile Sink Nodes

Ghassem Samimi[1](✉), Ehsan Saradar Torshizi[2](✉),
and Ali Mohammad Afshin Hemmatyar[3](✉)

[1] School of Science and Engineering,
Sharif University of Technology, Kish Island, Iran
samimi@kish.sharif.edu
[2] Department of Computer Engineering, Urmia University, Urmia, Iran
st_e.saradar@urmia.ac.ir
[3] Department of Computer Engineering,
Sharif University of Technology, Tehran, Iran
hemmatyar@sharif.edu

Abstract. Sensors consume most of their limited energy on transmitting the collected information to the sink node. Therefore, the determination of the sensor-to-sink information flow routes becomes important for the survivability of sensor networks. Besides, using mobile sink node can extend the network lifetime by balancing the sensors energy consumption. In this paper, we studied lifetime maximization in wireless sensor networks (WSNs) by jointly considering sink mobility and routing. In addition, we take advantage of multiple mobile sink nodes to further improve the network lifetime. A Mixed Integer Linear Programming (MILP) formulation is proposed to find the optimal routing and sink mobility pattern. Besides, we proposed a heuristic approach to achieve a near optimal result in a polynomial time. The performance of the proposed formulation evaluated for both single and multi-sink networks. Numerical results indicated that by using the proposed approaches network lifetime increased significantly as compared to not only the fixed sink node model but also conventional mobile sink models.

Keywords: Wireless sensor network · Lifetime maximization · Sink mobility · Mixed integer linear programming · Multi-sink

1 Introduction

Recent advances in micro-electro-mechanical systems, low cost sensing devices and wireless communications have led to the emergence of WSNs. WSNs are comprised of a large number of low cost and energy limited sensing devices.

Due to the limited communication range of the sensor nodes, the data packets carrying the sensed information usually have to follow multi-hop transmission. As a consequence, sensors that are communicate directly (i.e. in one hop) with the sink tend to run out of energy faster than the others. The main reason is that they consume energy

© Springer International Publishing Switzerland 2014
A. Movaghar et al. (Eds.): CNDS 2013, CCIS 428, pp. 39–51, 2014.
DOI: 10.1007/978-3-319-10903-9_4

not only on transmitting their own data packets but also on relaying the information sent by other sensors to the sink node. This is the so-called "the sink neighborhood problem" [1], "crowded center effect" [2] or the "energy hole problem" [3], which decreases the network lifetime considerably.

Recent studies indicate that exploiting sink mobility can improve the network lifetime. In fact, a mobile sink node can distribute the heavy forwarding load on sensor nodes which are connected directly to the sink node [4, 5]. Having multiple mobile sink nodes will reduce the rate at which the sink neighbors deplete their energy and also result in shorter paths from sensor nodes to their closest sink node [6, 7]. As a consequence, we expect using multiple mobile sinks decrease the sensors energy consumption and improve the network lifetime. In this paper, we propose a framework to maximize the network lifetime of a WSN by jointly considering sink mobility and routing. A multi-sink scenario is assumed while each sink node can change its location from time to time. We assume that each sensor node generates data at a fixed rate while there is a sink node which is responsible for gathering its generated data.

The rest of this paper is organized as follows. Related work is surveyed in Sect. 2. The system model is stated in Sect. 3. Proposed approaches are presented in Sect. 4. Numerical results are given in Sect. 5. Finally, the paper is concluded in Sect. 6.

2 Related Work

Although early researches on the lifetime maximization problem mostly focus on routing protocols that strive to save energy mainly deals with the sensor nodes [8], it has recently been observed that sink mobility can be exploited to further improve the network lifetime [9]. Wang et al. formulated the lifetime maximization problem as a linear programming (LP) model to maximize the network lifetime [10]. Unlike the models we proposed in this paper, they did not consider the routing problem in their proposed optimization model. Instead, they applied shortest path algorithms in order to determine sensor to sink data flow paths which causes an imbalance in energy consumption in sensor nodes which results in shorter network lifetime [11]. Alsalih et al. proposed a mobile data collector placement scheme for extending the lifetime of the network [12]. They divided the network lifetime into equal length rounds. In contrast, in our proposed formulation rounds length are not required to be equal.

Some authors investigated the impact of single sink mobility on the network lifetime [13, 14]. They proposed LP formulation to maximize the network lifetime by jointly considering routing and sink mobility. In this paper, we consider not only sink mobility and routing but also investigate the multi-sink approach to maximize the network lifetime. Shi and Hou investigated the problem of lifetime maximization using a single mobile sink node when the sink mobility is unconstrained [15]. Note that the problem considered in this paper differs completely from the so-called delay-tolerant network (DTN) [16, 17]. In DTN network lifetime is not a major performance evaluation parameter. Instead, in DTN it is assumed that the network can tolerate frequent network long delays in data delivery.

3 System Model

We assumed a WSN consisting of N energy constrained sensor nodes and mobile sink nodes that harvest data from the WSN. Each sensor node i collects data from its surrounding environment at the rate of q_i and sends the collected data to the corresponding sink node directly or via the relays of other sensor nodes. Two sensors are connected, if they are located within each other's communication range. Let R_c indicates the communication range of each sensor node. Let $S = \{s_1, \ldots, s_N\}$ ($|S| = N$) and $R = \{r_1, \ldots, r_k\}$ denote the set of sensor nodes and sink nodes, respectively. Each sensor node i has limited energy indicated by E_i. Each sensor consumes a certain amount of energy for data transmission and reception. Let E_t denotes the energy consumed to transmit a bit of data from node i to node j. Then it would be

$$E_t = e_t + b \times R_C^\alpha \qquad (1)$$

Where e_t and b are constants [18]. α is path loss parameter. Let E_r denotes the energy consumed for receiving a bit of data. Without loss of generality, the network lifetime is defined as the time until the first sensor node runs out of energy.

4 Proposed Approaches

For given N sensors and $|R|$ mobile sink nodes, it is required to determine the data routing and mobility pattern of the sink node(s) in order to maximize the network lifetime. The mobile sink node can stop at any point in the sensing field as long as it is within the transmission range of at least of one of the sensor nodes. As an example, Fig. 1 shows a set of 4 sensor nodes and their transmission ranges. The intersection of the transmission range of sensor nodes divide the sensing field into 9 different subareas $A_1, A_2, \ldots, A_9$. The sink node can stop at each subarea for a certain amount of time.

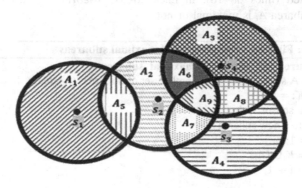

Fig. 1. An example of 4 sensor nodes and 9 subareas

Definition 1: For each subarea A_i, let $N(A_i)$ refers to the set of sensor nodes that A_i is located in their transmission range.

In Fig. 1, $N(A_1) = \{s_1\}$ and $N(A_2) = \{s_2\}$. In other words, when the sink node is located at A_1, it can receive data from s_1 and when it is placed at A_2 it can receive data from s_2. However, when the sink node stops at A_5, it can receive data from both s_1 and s_2 at the same time. In the same way, when the sink node stops at A_9, it can receive data from s_2, s_3 and s_4 simultaneously.

Definition 2: Each subarea A_i is maximal, if there is no subarea A_j where $N(A_i) \subset N(A_j)$.

In Fig. 1, A_5 and A_9 are two maximal subareas. In fact $N(A_1) \cup N(A_2) = N(A_5)$ and $N(A_2) \cup N(A_3) \cup N(A_4) \cup N(A_6) \cup N(A_7) \cup N(A_8) = N(A_9)$. In other words, when the sink node can stay at A_9, it is not efficient to put the sink node at A_2, A_3, A_4, A_6, A_7 nor A_8. Therefore, we assume the set of maximal subareas as the possible location for the sink placement.

Definition 3: Each set of maximal subarea M is complete, if for each subarea $A_j \notin M$ there exists a subarea $A_i \in M$ such that $N(A_j) \subset N(A_i)$.

For each subarea A_i, let $l_i^j = 1$, if subarea A_i is located in the transmission range of sensor s_j otherwise, $l_i^j = 0$.

Theorem 1: subarea A_i is not maximal, if there exist a subarea A_j such that $\exists k \in Sl_i^k \vee l_j^k \neq l_i^k$ and $\forall h \in Sl_i^h \vee l_j^h = l_j^h (i \neq j)$.

Proof: the proof of the above theorem can be directly derived from *Definition 2*. In other words, subarea A_i is not maximal, if there is a subarea A_j which is located in the transmission range of all sensor s_k that $l_i^k = 1$ and there exist at least one sensor node h that $l_i^h = 0$ and A_j is located in the transmission range s_h. As an example in Fig. 1, A_6 is not maximal because $l_6^3 = 0$ while $l_9^3 = 1$ and $\forall h \in Sl_3^h \vee l_9^h = l_9^h$. ∎

Algorithm 1 constructs a set of complete maximal subareas. In lines 02–07, we assume that transmission range of each sensor node creates a new subarea. Besides, for each two sensor S_i and S_j which their transmission ranges has intersection, a new subarea is created (lines 08–18). In lines 26–31, *Theorem1* is used to determine whether each subarea A_i is maximal or not.

Algorithm 1: Finding a complete set of maximal subareas

Procedure Find_complete_maximal_subareas()
Output: A set K which is a complete set of maximal subareas

01 $l := 0; K := \emptyset;$
02 **foreach** sensor s_i **do**
03   create a new subarea A_l
        $l_l^i := 1;$
04      $K := K \cup \{A_l\};$
05      $l := l + 1;$
06 **end**

```
07    foreach sensor s_i do
08       foreach sensor s_j (j ≠ i) do
09          if the transmission range of s_i has intersection with the transmission
10       range of s_j then
11             create a new subarea A_l
12             l_l^i := 1;
13             l_l^j := 1;
14             K := K ∪ {A_l};
15             l := l + 1;
16          end
17       end
18    end
19    foreach subarea A_i do
20       foreach sensor s_j do
21          if A_i is located in the transmission range of s_j then
22             l_i^j := 1;
23          end
24       end
25    end
26    foreach subarea A_i do
27       foreach subarea A_j do
28          if i ≠ j and ∃k ∈ S l_i^k ∨ l_j^k ≠ l_i^k and l_i^h ∨ l_j^h = l_j^h
29             K := K − {A_i};
30          end
31       end
32    end
```


4.1 Optimal Multiple Mobile Sink Placement (OMMSP)

We use R and S to indicate as the set of mobile sink nodes and sensor nodes respectively. We also denote K as the set of complete maximal subareas and $N(i)$ is used to indicate the set of sensor nodes which are located in the transmission range of sensor i. Besides, $A(i)$ shows the set of maximal subareas which are located in the transmission range of sensor i and $A(i) \subset K$. We also denote $x_{i,j}^{l,k}$ as the total information flow from sensor i to j which is generated by node l and is required to be delivered to the sink node k. Besides, $y_{i,p}^{l,k}$ is used to indicate the total information flow generated by node l and sent by sensor i to sink k while it dwells at subarea p. During the network lifetime T, each mobile sink node can dwell at each subarea for a certain amount of time. Let t_p^k denotes the sojourn time of the mobile sink node k at subarea A_p. $a^{l,k}$ is binary variable used to show whether sink k is selected as data gathering node for sensor l or not. In other words, if and only if $a^{l,k} = 1$ then sink node k is selected as data gathering node for sensor l and all data generated by node l should be forwarded to sink k during the network lifetime. Given these facts, the problem can be formulated as follows:

$$Max\ z = T \tag{2}$$
s.t.

$$\sum_{\forall j \in N(i)} x_{i,j}^{l,k} + \sum_{\forall p \in A(i)} y_{i,p}^{l,k} - \sum_{\forall j \in N(i)} x_{j,i}^{l,k} = 0 \qquad \begin{matrix} \forall i, l \in S, k \\ \in R, i \neq l \end{matrix} \tag{3}$$

$$\sum_{\forall j \in N(i), k \in R} x_{i,j}^{l,k} + \sum_{\forall p \in A(i), k \in R} y_{i,p}^{l,k} - \sum_{\forall j \in N(i), k \in R} x_{j,i}^{l,k} = q_l T \qquad \forall i, l \in S, i = l \tag{4}$$

$$\sum_{\forall j \in N(l)} x_{l,j}^{l,k} + \sum_{\forall p \in A(l)} y_{l,p}^{l,k} \leq M a^{l,k} \qquad \forall l, \in S, k \in R \tag{5}$$

$$\sum_{\forall i \in S} y_{i,p}^{l,k} \leq q_l t_p^k \qquad \begin{matrix} \forall l \in S, p \\ \in K, k \in R \end{matrix} \tag{6}$$

$$\sum_{\forall k \in R} a^{l,k} = 1 \qquad \forall l \in S \tag{7}$$

$$\sum_{\forall j \in N(i), l \in S, k \in R} (E_t x_{i,j}^{l,k} + E_r x_{j,i}^{l,k}) + \sum_{\forall p \in A(i), l \in S, k \in R} E_t y_{i,p}^{l,k} \leq E_i \qquad \forall i \in S \tag{8}$$

$$\sum_{\forall p \in K} t_p^k = T \qquad \forall k \in R \tag{9}$$

$$a^{l,k} \in \{0, 1\} \qquad \forall l \in S, k \in R \tag{10}$$

$$x_{i,j}^{l,k}, y_{i,p}^{l,k}, t_p^k \geq 0 \qquad \begin{matrix} \forall i, j, l \in S, p \\ \in K, k \in R \end{matrix} \tag{11}$$

The objective function (2) aims to maximize the network lifetime. Constraints (3) are flow balance constraint written for each sensor node i, l while $i \neq l$ and insure that each sensor node i relays all its incoming data flow. Meanwhile constraints (4) insure that each sensor node l generates data with the rate of q_l during the network lifetime and transmits the generated data to the other sensor nodes or a sink node. Note that for each sensor node l, there is a sink node k which is responsible for gathering its generated data and k is constant during the network lifetime (i.e., each sensor sends its data to the same sink node during the network lifetime). Constraints (5) insure that the data generated by each sensor node l is transmitted to its corresponding sink node. M is a big value that indicates the upper bounds of the generated data by a sensor node during the network lifetime. Note that M can be calculated easily using the following equation:

$$M = max_{\forall i \in S} \left(E_i / E_t \right) \tag{12}$$

Each sink node $k \in R$ dwells at the subarea $p \in K$ for t_p^k units of time. Meanwhile each sensor node l generates data with the rate of q_l. Constraints (6) indicate that each sink node k can gather at most $q_l t_p^k$ units of data generated by each sensor node l at each subarea p. Constraints (7) insure that for each sensor node l, there is a sink node which is responsible for gathering its generated data. Constraints (8) are energy constraint and indicate that the total energy consumed at each sensor node should not exceed its initial energy. Constraints (9) insure that the total sojourn time of each mobile sink node is equal to the network lifetime (i.e. sink mobility happens during network lifetime). $a^{l,k}$ is a binary variable that indicated by constraints (10) and $x_{i,j}^{l,k}$, $y_{i,p}^{l,k}$, t_p^k should take a non-negative value insured by constraints (11).

4.2   Heuristic Multiple Mobile Sink Placement (HMMSP)

The formulation given in Eqs. (2)–(11) is an MILP and determining the optimal value for the binary variables is the most time consuming part for solving the proposed MILP. If the optimal value for the binary variables is known, then the proposed MILP turns into a LP formulation which is solvable using the polynomial-time algorithms such as *ellipsoid* algorithm [19]. In this section a heuristic approach is used to efficiently find the values for $a^{l,k}(\forall l \in S, k \in R)$ and convert the proposed MILP into to a LP formulation.

In OMMSP formulation for $|R|$ mobile sink(s), there are $|S| \times |R|$ binary variables. We can assume the sensor network as $|R|$ different clusters. Each sensor which belongs to cluster k, should transmit its generated data to mobile sink node k. In other words, for each sensor i which belongs to cluster k, $a^{i,k} = 1$. HMMSP groups the set of sensor S into $|R|$ different clusters so as to minimize the maximum distance between each sensor and its cluster center. Note that we assume that sensor i is located at (x_i, y_i) and (X_k, Y_k) refers to the center of cluster k. In Fig. 2, the flowchart of the proposed heuristic approach is shown.

5   Numerical Results

In this section, we evaluate the performance of the proposed models by placing mobile sink nodes in several WSNs of typical topologies. To evaluate the performance of the proposed model, we investigate several metrics such as network lifetime, pause time distribution, average nodal residual energy and computation time. In particular, we have compared the performance of our proposed models with three different methods called static sink nodes placement (SELRP) [8], a single mobile sink node (MNL) [14] and multiple mobile sink node placement model (MILP) [12]. MOSEK [20] is used for solving the proposed formulations. We assume a homogeneous WSN. For each sensor node i, $E_i = 10$ J and $q_i = 1024$ bps. The values of other parameters are set to be $e_t = 50$ nJ/bit, $E_r = 50$ nJ/bit, b = 100 pJ/bit/m^3 and $\alpha = 3$. All sensors have the same communication range which is equal to 25 m ($R_c = 25$ m). Besides the sensing field is 100×100 m^2 area. We start with a simple scenario in which N = 81 sensor nodes are deployed in grid topology. Figure 3 shows the nodal residual energy at the end of network lifetime when fixed sink placement is used (SLERP). In Fig. 3 X and Y axis shows the sensor location while Z axis illustrates the sensors residual energy. Figure 3 confirms the uneven energy consumption in static sink networks.

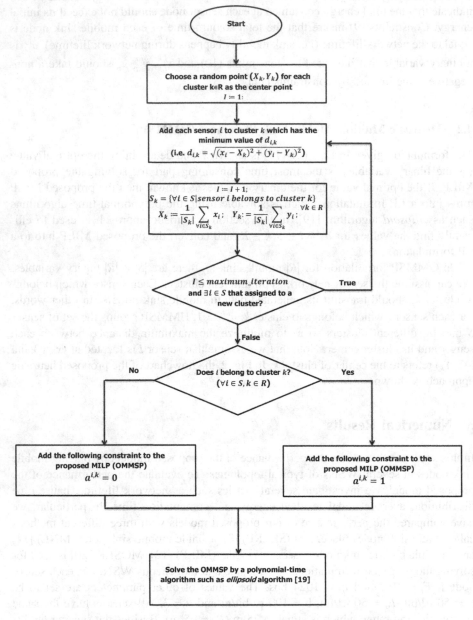

Fig. 2. The flowchart of the proposed heuristic approach (HMMSP)

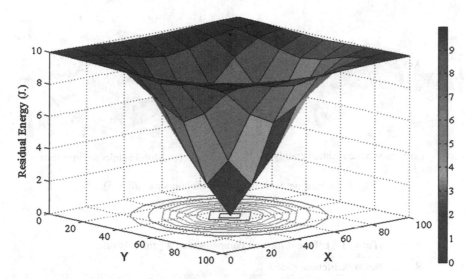

Fig. 3. Sensor nodes residual energy for gird network with static sink node placement

Figures 4 and 5 show sensors residual energy and sink sojourn time at the end of network lifetime for different number of mobile sink nodes when OMMSP method is used. Sensors residual energy become more balance at the end of network lifetime when mobile sink node is used. Besides, multi-sink can distribute the heavy forwarding load on sensor nodes. By increasing the number of mobile sink node, each sink node tends to move toward the periphery of a network.

Table 1 compares our proposed approaches (OMMSP and HMMSP) with the other three methods (SELRP [8], MNL [14] and MILP [12]) for different grid networks. The Number of sensor nodes varies between 36 and 81 while the number of sink nodes varies between 1 and 3. Unfortunately, the MNL method supports only single mobile sink networks. In mobile sink networks by increasing the network size, the number of alternative paths between a sensor and sink node is also increases. Consequently,

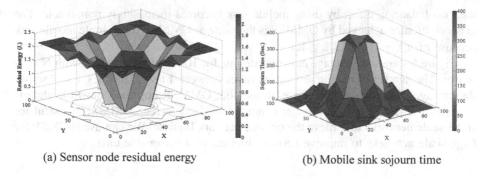

(a) Sensor node residual energy   (b) Mobile sink sojourn time

Fig. 4. A grid network with single mobile sink ($|R| = 1$)

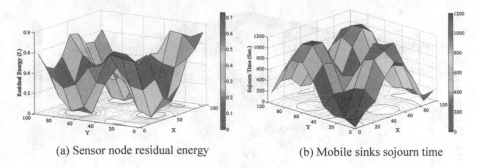

(a) Sensor node residual energy   (b) Mobile sinks sojourn time

Fig. 5. A grid network with three mobile sink ($|R| = 3$)

Table 1. Different method comparison in a grid network

N	R	Network lifetime (Sec.)				
		SELRP [8]	MNL [14]	MILP [12]	OMMSP	HMMSP
36	1	912.87	1056.45	1000.00	1265.01	1265.01
36	2	1713.98	–	2000.00	2479.40	2390.85
36	3	2604.73	–	2600.00	2985.40	2846.25
49	1	782.32	1208.80	1200.00	1315.60	1315.60
49	2	1495.27	–	2200.00	2578.58	2486.48
49	3	2309.19	–	2600.00	3134.67	2988.56
64	1	615.76	1353.15	1200.00	1468.22	1468.22
64	2	1154.34	–	2400.00	2630.15	2536.21
64	3	1799.65	–	2800.00	3260.06	3108.11
81	1	480.21	1502.34	1400.00	1689.27	1689.27
81	2	934.63	–	2400.00	2682.75	2586.94
81	3	1442.12	–	3000.00	3390.46	3232.43

the load-balancing effect by using mobile sink becomes increasingly remarkable. The network lifetime achieved by OMMSP is the same as HMMSP for a single mobile sink because of $a^{i,k} = 1 (\forall i \in S, k \in R)$.

Figure 6 shows the average network lifetime for 100 random networks with N = 60 sensor. The number of mobile sink nodes varies between 1 and 3. Besides, Fig. 7 shows the average computation time for each method. OMMSP improves network lifetime more than HMMSP but with longer computation time. In fact, OMMSP is useful for small-scale networks to achieve the optimal network lifetime. We can use HMMSP for large-scale networks to improve network lifetime in a reasonable time.

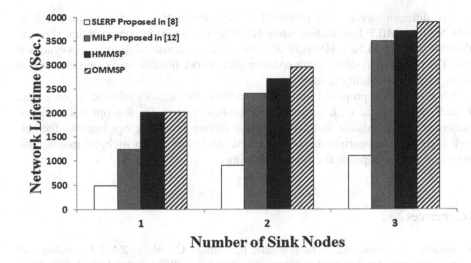

Fig. 6. Impact of multi-sink on the network lifetime

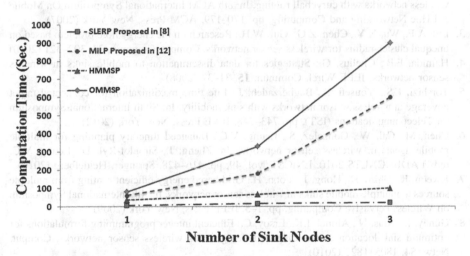

Fig. 7. Computation time comparison for different number of sink nodes

6 Conclusion

In this paper, we investigate the network lifetime maximization problem by jointly considering sink mobility and routing. Besides, we take advantage of a multiple sink nodes to improve the network lifetime. We use a multi-sink mobility model in which each sink node can move around within the sensor field and stop at certain locations to gather the generated data from the sensor nodes. Each sink node is responsible to gather the generated data of a set of sensor nodes during the network lifetime.

Two different methods are proposed to solve the lifetime maximization problem. OMMSP is an MILP formulation while HMMSP is a heuristic approach that converts OMMSP into LP. In fact, HMMSP achieves a near optimal solution in a polynomial time. The proposed models try to maximize the network lifetime by finding the optimal routing and sink mobility pattern.

The result of the proposed formulation includes the network lifetime, sojourn time of each sink node at each location and dataflow matrix for the optimal solution. Numerical results indicate that using a single mobile sink node can improve the network lifetime in comparison to the static sink. Moreover, using multiple mobile sink nodes can further improve the network lifetime.

References

1. Basagni, S., Carosi, A., Melachrinoudis, E., Petrioli, C., Wang, Z.M.: Controlled sink mobility for prolonging wireless sensor networks lifetime. Wirel. Netw. **14**, 831–858 (2008)
2. Popa, L., Rostamizadeh, A., Karp, R., Papadimitriou, C., Stoica, I.: Balancing traffic load in wireless networks with curveball routing. In: 8th ACM International Symposium On Mobile Ad Hoc Networking and Computing, pp. 170–179. ACM Press, New York (2007)
3. Liu, A.F., Wu, X.Y., Chen, Z.G., Gui, W.H.: Research on the energy hole problem based on unequal cluster-radius for wireless sensor networks. Comput. Commun. **33**, 302–321 (2010)
4. Hamida, E.B., Chelius, G.: Strategies for data dissemination to mobile sinks in wireless sensor networks. IEEE Wirel. Commun. **15**, 31–37 (2008)
5. Torshizi, E.S., Yousefi, S., Bagherzadeh, J.: Life time maximization for connected target coverage in wireless sensor networks with sink mobility. In: Sixth International Symposium on Telecommunications (IST), pp. 743–748. IEEE Press, New York (2012)
6. Chen, M., Cai, W., Gonzalez, S., Leung, V.C.: Balanced itinerary planning for multiple mobile agents in wireless sensor networks. In: Zheng, J., Simplot-Ryl, D., Leung, V.C. (eds.) ADHOCNETS 2010. LNICST, vol. 49, pp. 416–428. Springer, Heidelberg (2010)
7. Kweon, K., Ghim, H., Hong, J., Yoon, H.: Grid-based energy-efficient routing from multiple sources to multiple mobile sinks in wireless sensor networks. In: 4th International Symposium on Wireless Pervasive Computing, pp. 1–5. IEEE Press, New York (2009)
8. Güney, E., Aras, N., Altınel, İ.K., Ersoy, C.: Efficient integer programming formulations for optimum sink location and routing in heterogeneous wireless sensor networks. Comput. Netw. **54**, 1805–1822 (2010)
9. Tian, K., Zhang, B., Huang, K., Ma, J.: Data gathering protocols for wireless sensor networks with mobile sinks. In: Global Telecommunications Conference(GLOBECOM), pp. 1–6. IEEE Press, New York (2010)
10. Wang, Z.M., Basagni, S., Melachrinoudis, E., Petrioli, C.: Exploiting sink mobility for maximizing sensor networks lifetime. In: Proceedings of the 38th Hawaii International Conference on System Sciences (HICSS 2005), pp. 1–9. IEEE Press, New York (2005)
11. Papadimitriou, I., Georgiadis, L.: Maximum lifetime routing to mobile sink in wireless sensor networks. In: 13th IEEE SoftCom, pp 1–5. IEEE Press, New York (2005)
12. Alsalih, W., Hassanein, H., Akl, S.: Placement of multiple mobile data collectors in wireless sensor networks. Ad Hoc Netw. **8**, 378–390 (2010)
13. Li, X., Yang, J., Nayak, A., Stojmenovic, I.: Localized geographic routing to a mobile sink with guaranteed delivery in sensor networks. Sel. Areas Commun. **30**, 1719–1729 (2012)

14. Luo, J., Hubaux, J.P.: Joint sink mobility and routing to maximize the lifetime of wireless sensor networks: the case of constrained mobility. IEEE/ACM Trans. Netw. (TON) **18**, 871–884 (2010)
15. Shi, Y., Hou, Y.T.: Some fundamental results on base station movement problem for wireless sensor networks. IEEE/ACM Trans. Netw. (TON) **20**, 1054–1067 (2012)
16. Guo, Z., Wang, B., Cui, J.H.: Generic prediction assisted single-copy routing in underwater delay tolerant sensor networks. Ad Hoc Netw. **11**, 1136–1149 (2013)
17. Yun, Y., Xia, Y.: Maximizing the lifetime of wireless sensor networks with mobile sink in delay-tolerant applications. IEEE Trans. Mob. Comput. **9**, 1308–1318 (2010)
18. Heinzelman, W.R., Chandrakasan, A., Balakrishnan, H.: Energy-efficient communication protocol for wireless microsensor networks. In: 33rd Annual Hawaii International Conference on System Sciences, pp. 1–10. IEEE Press, New York (2000)
19. Bland, R.G., Goldfarb, D., Todd, M.J.: The ellipsoid method: a survey. Oper. Res. **29**, 1039–1091 (1981)
20. MOSEK. http://www.mosek.com

IRTP: Improved Reliable Transport Protocol for Wireless Sensor Networks

Parisa Bolourian Haghighi[1(✉)],
Mohammad Hossein Yaghmaee Moghaddam[2],
Maliheh Bahekmat[2], and Mahsa Bolourian Haghighi[3]

[1] Department of Computer Engineering, Faculty of Engineering,
Imam Reza International University, Mashhad, Iran
p.boloorian@gmail.com
[2] Department of Computer Engineering, Ferdowsi University, Mashhad, Iran
yaghmaee@ieee.org, info@bahekmat.ir
[3] School of Computer Sciences, Universiti Sains Malaysia, USM,
11800 Pulau Pinang, Malaysia
mbhll_ttm023@student.usm.my

Abstract. Environmental monitoring is determined as one of the leading applications in wireless sensor networks. In this application, every sensor node transmits a flow of sensed data to the sink periodically. Energy consumption is considered as a significant factor associated with the restriction in design of these specific purpose networks. To this end, we want one of the major sources of energy consumption, i.e. the number of message transmissions to be reduced. In this class, delay is not of so much importance. The transport layer is responsible for reliable and end to end delivery of the data among the sensors through the links. Due to energy, computing and storage limitation of wireless sensor networks, the traditional transport protocols cannot be applied to sensor network directly and without modifications. In this layer, certain operations are applied on the entire network to make it reliable for the application layer and reduce unnecessary retransmissions.

Keywords: Wireless sensor networks · Reliability · Retransmission · Energy efficiency · Transport layer · Link-quality

1 Introduction

The embedded computing systems (systems which are directly in connection to the physical world and support a few limited actions) established the concept of creation and expansion of networks called wireless sensor networks. The WSNs are networks that include self-configurable and low power nodes which are deployed densely in inaccessible environments. Sensors receive the data in their surrounding physical environment, and they convert them into data which can be processed and stored. These networks can be used to protect natural resources, increase in products, establish security, intelligent houses and in military environments. In the sensor networks, the main traffic is from sensor node towards sink. After a few hops, the sensed data reach

© Springer International Publishing Switzerland 2014
A. Movaghar et al. (Eds.): CNDS 2013, CCIS 428, pp. 52–65, 2014.
DOI: 10.1007/978-3-319-10903-9_5

the sink. Sink aggregates the data and relays the network to other connected wireless or wired networks.

One of the applications of sensor networks is monitoring. In this application of sensor networks, every node transmits a flow of sensed data to the sink in a cyclic form. The most important restriction in design of these specific purpose networks is deemed as energy consumption. To this end, one of the important sources of energy consumption in the sensor node, i.e. the number of message transmission is reduced. In this class, delay is not of so much importance.

2 Related Works

Transport layer protocols can be classified as follows. Some are based on IP (DTC [1], TSS [2]) and some are not, such as ERTP [3], RCRT [4]. Protocols can be also classified based on loss recovery method (end to end or hop by hop) and whether or not the middle nodes use cache, or which kind of messages they use to diagnose and recover loss (EACK [Explicit Acknowledgement], IACK [Implicit Acknowledgement], NACK [Negative Acknowledgement]). Whether this protocol is aware of energy, and whether a mechanism is predicted to diagnose and control the congestion.

In multipath networks, retransmissions based reliability is obtained on the basis of acknowledgement mechanism, i.e. the transmitter node is required to receive acknowledgement from the subsequent node on the path towards the sink. Among acknowledgement mechanisms, Explicit acknowledgement provides a traditional mechanism to ensure 100 % reliability of each packet. This mechanism is based on a control message that every node receiving a packet transmits it after full and flawless receipt of transmitted data. Just like explicit acknowledgement, negative acknowledgement is also a control message that allows the receiver to transmit the request for retransmission of a packet with a specific order number that has not been received. The aforesaid two mechanisms will result in significant overload transmission in the network, and also energy consumption that is not bearable by most of WSNs. In the implicit acknowledgement, after transfer of packet, the transmitter listens to the channel and interprets advancement of packet as an acknowledgement message, and thereby the superfluous overloads and energy consumption are avoided.

In [5] was the first person who introduced the concept of event reliability to the sink, by using event reliable protocol (ESRT). This protocol guarantees reliable and end to end transport of the event to the sink. This protocol fulfills reliability by the number of packets that transport data about an event towards the sink, i.e. within a time span, and by the number of packets the sink receives (frequency of received packets (f)), it finds out whether or not reliability is met for a certain event. This protocol assumes that the sink has a powerful radio range that can tell all the nodes in a broad cast message to adjust the f. A big significant restriction of this protocol is that it assumes that all the nodes are only one hop distant from the sink. In this protocol, it meets reliability by increasing transmission rate. This protocol, like hop by hop and loss recovery protocols, is not optimum from the aspect of energy consumption.

In [6], the reporting frequency rate f is defined as a function of statistical reliability β and a hop counter between a source sensing the data and the destination. Unlike ESRT which was the sink responsibility to estimate rate of transmitting the sensor nodes, in eESRT + ieACK, each node conducts it automatically. Here, at each hop, the reporting frequency f is on average reduced with the factor $1 - p$, in which the ratio of link packets failure is p. Thus, the reporting frequency f is increased with increase of path length in an exponential form, and the overall number of retransmissions is increased. The analyses demonstrate that from the energy aspect, the ESRT is not optimum for the paths longer than a threshold. Here ESRT energy efficiency is theoretically analyzed. In fact, LESRT is the least value determined for the reporting frequency of each sensor data so that it may provide for a successful transmission with β probability.

ERTP [3] is among other protocols of transmission with reliability and optimum energy consumption which is designed to produce data streaming applications in the WSNs. In this protocol, the sensor nodes transmit their sensor data from one or more sources to BS node or sink. This protocol uses statistical reliability metric to guarantee that the number of transmitted packets do not exceed a threshold. In this class, each sensor node cyclically senses some data and transmits them to sink. In this class, delay is not important, while energy consumption is considered an important category. In this protocol, quality of radio links channels is deemed unreliable, and the ratio of packets failure considerably changes over time. Reliability is computed by the number of packets that reach the sink, and not by reliability of each single one of packets. Use of statistical reliability has caused that during design of a safe transmission protocol, reaching of sufficient number of packets to the sink and also fewer transmissions are guaranteed. The statistical reliability approach in the works of [7, 8] also demonstrates that it considerably reduces the energy consumption.

3 Proposed Model

Estimation of radio communication quality in WSNs has a great impact on the efficiency of network and the higher layers. The reported works on the quality of communication are usually based on different hypotheses by considering different conditions which create quite different and sometimes contradictory results.

Dissemination of radio signals are affected by different elements, which result in the deterioration of its quality. Some of these elements are even effective on low power radio signals transmissions, which are usually used in WSNs. As a result, radio links in WSNs are often unpredictable. In fact, their quality changes over time and space. Spatial variation of link quality is due to constructive or destructive interferences. The impacts of multi paths can either be constructive, which causes the direct signal to be strengthened resulting in a high quality link, or can be destructive which interferes with the direct signal [9], and in the end, either constructive or destructive, disrupts quality of the link. To be either constructive or destructive, does not depend on the distance or path of receiver, but it depends more to the nature of physical path between transmitter and receiver (for instance existence of an obstacle) [10]. Srinivasan et al. [9] conducted researches by newer platforms such as Micaz and TelosB, and in different environments with different traffic load. They found out that the number of average links is between 5 % and 60 %, which constitutes a significant number of network links. Links of average quality which are located in the transition region were between 10 % and 90 % of packet receiving ratio. Links whose average packet receiving ratio is very low or very high which are located in connected and disconnected regions are subject to slight change over the time, and they are more inclined to stability.

Time variation in link quality is due to variations in the environment features. Many studies demonstrate that time variation in link quality is due to variation in the environment features such as, climate conditions (such as temperature, humidity), presence of human beings, interference, and obstacles [11, 12], in particular, [12] found out that time variation of LQI, RSSI (Received Signal Strength Indicator), in a clean environment (for instance, inside a building, without any moving obstacle and air conditioning) is not much significant.

In the WSNs, the LQEs[1] are classified into two categories: hardware based and software based.

There are three LQEs belonging to the family of hardware based link quality estimators: LQI, RSSI and SNR. These estimators read the value directly from radio transmitter/receiver (CC2420). The advantage of this group of estimators is that they do not need extra computations as software based does. Of course their worthiness in description of links has studied by research works.

RSSI gives a quick and precise estimation of network condition as to whether or not it is connected within the region. These observations are so explained that firstly, the empirical studies [13] demonstrate that for the RSSIs in excess of 87 dBm, the packet receiving rate exceeds 99 %, and the link is connected within the region. The least in this region, a variation at 2 dBm, also changes a qualified link into a disqualified link, and vice versa, it changes a disqualified link into a qualified link. This region is referred to as transitional region. These observations are shown hereunder (Figs. 1 and 2):

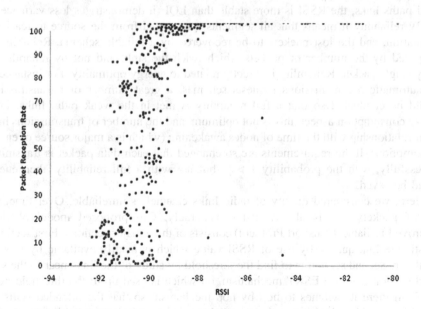

Fig. 1. Outdoor environment experiment [13]

---

[1] Link Quality Estimator.

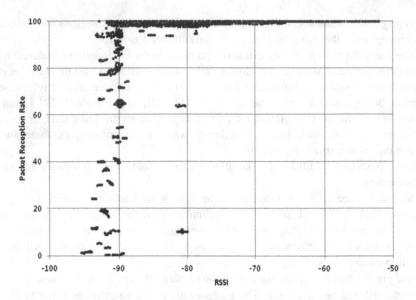

Fig. 2. Indoor environment experiment [14]

Secondly, RSSI is stable, and its standard deviation is less than 1 dBm within a span of 2 s. Accordingly, in order to determine the location of the link, reading the RSSI (by receiving a packet) will suffice. Meanwhile, [12, 14] also asserted that save multi paths links, the RSSI is more stable than LQI (it demonstrates less variance).

By reliability it means that all segments transmitted from the source to reach the destination, and the lost packets to be recovered by a reliable schema. Reliability is computed by the number of packets which reach the sink, and not by reliability of every single packet. Reliability is directly related to energy optimality. For instance, in the automatic retransmissions requests schemas, a great number of retransmissions should be conducted so that a full reliability is met in the weak radio links. From energy consumption aspect, this is not optimum, and the number of transmissions has a linear relationship with the time of nodes awakening (which is a major source of energy consumption). If the requirements are so changed that each data packet is transmitted successfully, with the probability $1 > \beta$, but not with a full reliability, then energy would be saved.

Here, we considered quality of radio links channel as unreliable. Over time, this rate of packets loss is also varied considerably. Our proposed model of IRTP (Improved Reliable Transport Protocol) consists of three major sections. First section is to estimate link quality by use of RSSI value which is readily available by Castalia simulator. Second section is to find the threshold by study of the links near to the sink. Third section is to use ESRT mechanism, on which is used up to the threshold node, and from there it switches to hop by hop mechanism so that the intended statistical reliability is achieved. Using statistical reliability leads to design a reliable transmission protocol, sufficient number of packets delivery to the sink, and also less number of transmissions is guaranteed. Statistical reliability approach in the works of [3, 6] demonstrates that it considerably reduces energy consumption. Meanwhile, in the concerned application, delay is not considered as an important parameter.

Nodes transmit their packets to the neighbors through wireless channel. In such links, probability of receiving a packet in the next node is not always 1, and certain reasons such as noise in channel and power of transmission ...etc. can make the possibility of receiving a packet by the two links different. In order to reach a node (threshold) wherefrom a hop by hop mechanism with transmission of implicit acknowledgement messages is used, the following procedure could be followed:

First, the value of packets loss in the sink node is assumed as zero, because sink transmits no packet to anywhere, and from there, there is no link to the next node. Sink gives zero to its previous node, which finds the probability of packet loss from itself to the sink based on the value it read from RSSI register. In some chips, this value can be found directly with regard to its hardware features. Method of finding packet loss ratio through RSSI value is as per following. First, with respect to noise floor, which is indicated in the Radio chip guide CC2420 [15], the value of SNR is found:

$$SNR = RSSI - noise\ floor \tag{1}$$

Then by taking into account the type of used modulation, which is PSK in this chip, the bits error rate is computed as follows:

$$BER = F(SNR, PSK) = 0.5 * erfc\left(sqrt\left(pow\left(10, \left(\frac{SNR}{10}\right)\right) * \frac{R_X(noise)}{R_X(data\ rate)}\right)\right) \tag{2}$$

In which erfc(X) is equal to:

$$erfc(x) = \frac{2}{\sqrt{\pi}} \int\limits_x^\infty e^{-x^2} dx \tag{3}$$

And it is an erroneous packet in which minimum one bit thereof is erroneous. Accordingly, based on probability of bit error, the probability of packet loss is computed as follows, i.e. the probability of packet loss of S bit long, is as per following:

$$p_p = 1 - (1 - BER)^S \tag{4}$$

The above value and the following formula are used to find the threshold:

$$\prod\nolimits_L^i = 1 - (1 - p_i)(1 - \prod\nolimits_L^{i+1}) \tag{5}$$

Sink node transmits this value of packets loss to its previous node. Based on the value of the packet loss that it finds, and the value that it computes for its link, this node also computes the loss probability value up to this node. In fact, the value of packet loss probability is the resulting sum of packet loss probabilities as a result of congestion, noise and failure, in which the other probabilities have not been considered for purpose of easiness, and only noise, was considered.

$$p_{h-1} = P_L^{h-1} = P_c^{h-1} + P_n^{h-1} + P_f^{h-1} \tag{6}$$

$$\prod_L^{h-1} = 1 - (1 - p_{h-1})\left(1 - \prod_L^h\right) = P_{h-1} \tag{7}$$

As it was already pointed out, in [6], the reporting frequency f is defined as a function of statistical probability β and counter of the hop between the source which senses the data and the destination. Unlike ESRT, in this mechanism, every node conducts this automatically. Also, In IRTP, in every hop, the reporting frequency f is on average basis reduced with 1 − p factor, in which p is the loss ratio of the link packets. Thus, reporting frequency f, is increased exponentially with increase in the path length, and the overall number of retransmissions is increased. Analyses demonstrate that ESRT is not optimum from energy aspect for the paths of more than some threshold. Here, ESRT is studied from the aspect of energy optimality theory. In fact, L_{ESRT} is the minimum determined value for reporting frequency of each sensed data so that to meet successful transmission with β probability.

$$L_{ESRT}(\beta) = \left\lceil \frac{\log(1 - \beta)}{\log(1 - \prod_{i=0}^{h-1} \bar{P}_i)} \right\rceil \tag{8}$$

$$E_{ESRT} = L_{ESRT}(\beta)\left(1 + \sum_{i=1}^{h-2} \prod_{k=0}^{i-1} \bar{p}_k\right) \tag{9}$$

In stop and wait hop by hop Acknowledgement Automatic Repeat request (SW HBH ACK ARQ) mechanism, reliability is met in each hop. If a transmitting node receives an acknowledgement message prior to reaching of time out from its subsequent node, it transmits a new packet; otherwise, it retransmits the current packet.

A receiver transmits acknowledgement message for each packet (even repeated ones) it receives. Once a packet is properly received, it is immediately transmitted to the next node. Here, it is agreed that the repeated packets should not be transmitted to the next node. As reaching reliability at β level is intended, the number of retransmissions in each hop is limited to $L_{ARQ}(i,\beta)$ which is indicated hereunder:

$$L_{ARQ}(i, \beta) = \left\lceil \frac{\log(1 - \beta^{\frac{1}{h}})}{\log(\bar{p}_i)} \right\rceil \tag{10}$$

$$E_{ARQ} = \sum_{i=0}^{h-1} \frac{1 - (1 - \bar{p}_i\bar{q}_i)^{L_{ARQ}(i,\beta)}}{\bar{p}_i\bar{q}_i}(1 + \bar{p}_i) \tag{11}$$

If energy consumed for the explicit acknowledgement messages is taken into account, using implicit mechanism in WSNs is more optimal. By increase in the path length, the number of transmissions in ESRT is increased in exponential form, but in the SW HBH ACK ARQ mechanism, the increase is in linear form. Unlike ESRT, this protocol acts better for the paths of less than some threshold. This limit is subject to the links loss ratio. Under a desired condition, if no error is made, ESRT has no overload, but it has a hop by hop acknowledgment.

In many sensors, in order to transmit data safely, the SW HBH ARQ mechanism is used, in which the acknowledgement is automatically transmitted by the middle access control layer. Acknowledgement messages are necessary for the wired links, but for the wireless links which include multi hop paths, these messages are not required to be used, because the transmitter is able to hear the transmission forwarding of the packet, and considers it as an implicit acknowledgement (iACK) message.

Like ARQ, in ieARQ protocol, the number of retransmissions is computed as follows:

$$L_{ieARQ}(i, \beta) = L_{oiARQ}(i, \beta) = L_{ARQ}(i, \beta) = \frac{\log(1 - \beta^{\frac{1}{h}})}{\log(\bar{P}_i)} \quad (12)$$

And because overhearing mechanism is used, compared to ARQ protocol, one less explicit acknowledgment message is transmitted at each node. Accordingly the following is resulted:

$$E_{ieARQ}(\beta) = E_{ARQ}(\beta) - (h - 1) = \left(\sum_{i=0}^{h-1} \frac{1 - (1 - \bar{p}_i \bar{q}_i)^{L_{ARQ}(i,\beta)}}{\bar{p}_i \bar{q}_i} (1 + \bar{p}_i) \right) - (h - 1)$$

$$(13)$$

In consequence, based on what was pointed out above, the proposed algorithm is presented as follows:

```
IRTP()
{
  For (i=sink;i=sink-4;i++)
  {
    ReadRSSI(i);
    Π_L^i = 1 - (1 - p_i)(1 - Π_L^{i+1});
  }
  If (Π_L i > 0.9)
    Hsw=0;
  Else
    Hsw=1;
For(i=0;i<Hsw;i++)
  {
    ReadRSSI(i);
    N_transmissions(i)= ciel(log(1-beta)/log(1-pi));
  }
For(i=Hsw;i<h;i++)
  {
    N_transmissions(i)= ceil(log(1-pow(beta,1/h))/log(1-pi));
    Timer();
  }}
```

Each sensor node compares the value $\prod_L^i$ with a predetermined value, and if they were equal, this node will be considered as a threshold for change of mechanism. Advantage of this protocol is unnecessariness to be aware of packet reduction ratio in all links, and only by knowing about the loss in the links near to the sink, this mechanism is able to identify the threshold value. After this threshold, the mechanism of packets transmission is changed and the packets are transmitted hop by hop. In this mechanism, as it was pointed out in earlier sections, the wireless channel feature is used, in which the nodes can hear the messages transmitted in the network, and transmission of an explicit acknowledgement message is not required, i.e. transmission forward of a packet is considered like an acknowledgement message to a node which is awaiting to hear the acknowledgement message, because once a packet is transmitted, the signal of packet transmission is spread in the air, and the node awaiting to receive acknowledgement message, can hear such message, and consider it as an implicit response from the node receiving the message.

As it was also pointed out, within a span that the network is active, and for different reasons, the sensor nodes links experience variations over time. Such variations are significant for the links that loss ratio is within transitional region. Therefore, in the proposed protocol, another effective factor to reach the intended reliability is to have the real loss to compute the number of retransmissions and the value of threshold in the network, i.e. in the previous protocol, the ratio of packet loss in the links is 0.45, but the number of transmissions that the nodes make in the network corresponds to the old value, which the link estimating protocol provided within the previous t seconds, but it is not the real value nor does it correspond to the current conditions of the network. This old value can be improved by benefitting from the feature of RSSI registers, and once the number of transmissions in the network is to be estimated, the value in this register would be used so that a condition like that of previous protocol has not taken into account.

Thus, by the number of transmissions it estimates, the hybrid protocol can meet the reliability defined for it via current RSSI values. In case of using eESRT + ieACK protocol with software base LQE, link qualities aren't accurate for an outdoor WSN. As a result no packet would generally reach the destination, i.e. it would possibly fetch the sensed data from node No.1 even up to the first half of network, but on the whole, it will not meet the target, i.e. to reach reliability with the number of transmissions determined for each node, namely from one hop onward, this number of transmissions is inadequate, and the packet would never reach the next node and ultimately to the destination so that by retransmission to provide for reliability.

4   Simulation Results

Simulation of proposed algorithm was implemented on Castalia 3.3 simulator of WSNs [16], and on OMNeT++ foundation. Modeling of average path loss uses log normal shadowing which is considered one of the most precise models for the WSNs. The radio model which is used, in fact simulates the behavior of the physical layer in the WSNs. Tunable MAC was used for simulation. This protocol was created for the tests conducted by multi access with CSMA-CA (Carrier Sense Multi Access with

Collision Avoidance), and allowing for parameters effective in identifying the carrier signal. By regulating the parameters, behavior of CSMA-CA can be held.

The routing protocol used is Bypass Routing, because the target was to hold the behavior of this algorithm apart from the routing layer. 10 nodes are arranged in linear form, and every node recognizes its prior and subsequent neighbors. This is the reason why routing is not used, and there are no overloads of transmission of packets in the routing layer. In the network, links are of different loss probability which is dependent on the environment and parameters pointed out before. The earlier studies demonstrate that in a network whose links are of high quality (85 %–100 %), such value remains nearly steady for a certain period. Also, in this simulation, the quality of the links are so regulated that there is a temporal variation after every 10 min, so that a network near to a real network is modeled. Of course as it was already pointed out before, the average quality of the links for a span, for instance 2 h, within which the simulation is performed, is so assumed that such parameters as environment temperature that have a great impact on simulation parameters, are considered as fixed.

As it was stated before, there are various radio propagation models, which their purpose is to predict the signal power of each received packet. In every node in physical layer, one threshold is so determined that if the signal power was less than the determined level, the packet receives an error label, and it is removed from transmissions queue by the MAC layer. One of these models is Log Normal Shadowing model. Shadowing model does not distinguish the communication range precisely. Extension of signal in several routes creates fading effect, and affects the power of received signal. In fact, the above models compute the average received power at a distance of d.

This model consists of two sections. The first section is called Path Loss Model, and it is assumed that the average receiving power is reduced in logarithm form, and it computes the average receiving power at a distance of d. In computing such average power, a reference average consumed power at a distance of d0 called PL (d0) is used, and its formula is as follows:

The purpose of the second section of Log Normal Shadowing is the reflection of variation in the received power at a certain distance. The shadowing model is generally computed as follows:

$$PL(d) = PL(d0) + 10n \log(\frac{d}{d0}) \tag{14}$$

n is the consumed power of the route. The consumed power of the route is found by using experimental methods. In this simulation which is an outdoor model, n is assigned 2 (n = 2).

$$PL(d) = PL(d0) + 10n \log(\frac{d}{d0}) + X_{dB} \tag{15}$$

X_{dB} is the Gaussian Random Variable with a zero mean and standard deviation 6_{dB}. 6_{dB} is empirically estimated. In this simulation, the values obtained in the outdoor environment by past studies were also used. Nodes sense temperature from the environment, and if it was in excess of a threshold, they will be transmitted in packets to the sink. To this end, the physical model provided in this simulator is used.

It has to be pointed out that as it was already stated in the previous sections, for transmission, messages are located on the channel, and message signal reaches all nodes, of course in different powers, and it reaches a node that its destination is set to. For the implicit acknowledgments, this approach was benefited from. If a packet destination is two packets farther, it will be deemed like an implicit acknowledgment message, and because in the last node, it does not transmit a packet forward so that an implicit message is transmitted to the transmitting node, the explicit acknowledgement message was used.

Results obtained from simulation are shown in the following diagrams. First, the previous work was tested by using passive values which the estimator of the link provided, and because those values were changed in the network, the number of computed retransmissions is not sufficient for this link, and from node 4 onward, packets forwarding towards destination fails. Of course as it is also shown in the diagram, even the number of packets which were to be transmitted up to the node in the half way of network, might be less than the one designated to reach the target reliability. But, ultimately it will reach a certain part of the network that the insufficiency of the maximum number of retransmission is identified, and from a hop forward, it is entirely closed and it is not transmitted towards the sink (Figs. 3, 4, 5, 6, 7, 8 and 9).

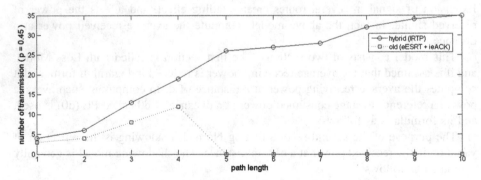

Fig. 3. Number of retransmissions in hybrid (IRTP) and base protocol

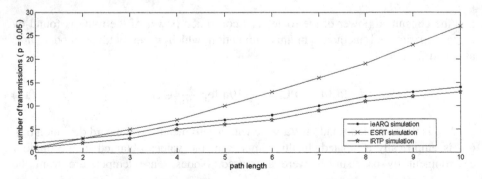

Fig. 4. Number of retransmissions in links with loss probability = 0.05

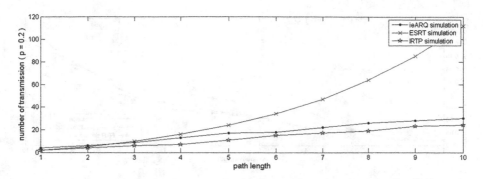

Fig. 5. Number of retransmissions in links with loss probability = 0.2

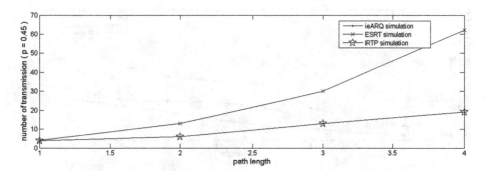

Fig. 6. Number of retransmissions in links with loss probability = 0.45

In the following figures the base protocol ESRT, and ieARQ are compared and all the results are obtained of a network where loss rates are for the current network, because RSSI gives accurate and agile estimate of the links.

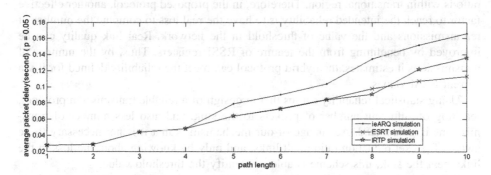

Fig. 7. Average delay of packet in the links with loss probability of 0.05

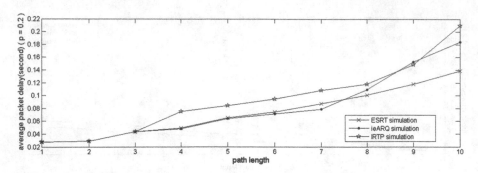

Fig. 8. Average delay of packet in the links with loss probability of 0.2

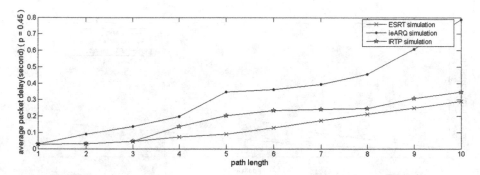

Fig. 9. Average delay of packet in the links with loss probability of 0.45

5   Conclusion

As mentioned, in outdoor WSNs for different reasons, the sensor nodes links experience variations over time. Such variations are significant for the links that loss ratio is within transitional region. Therefore, in the proposed protocol, another effective factor to reach the intended reliability is to have the real loss to compute the number of retransmissions and the value of threshold in the network. Real link quality can be improved by benefitting from the feature of RSSI registers. Thus, by the number of transmissions it estimates, the hybrid protocol can meet the reliability defined for it via current RSSI values.

Using statistical reliability causes that in design of a reliable transmission protocol, reaching of sufficient number of packets to the sink, and also less number of transmissions is guaranteed. Advantage of our mechanism is that it is not necessary to be aware of packet reduction ratio in all links, and only by knowing about the loss in the links near the sink, this scheme is able to identify the threshold value.

Future works can be done on the delay of the protocol. Reducing time out of not receiving an implicit acknowledgment would be challenging to some applications.

References

1. Dunkels, A., Alonso, J., Voigt, T.: Distributed TCP caching for wireless sensor networks. In: 3rd Annual Mediterranean Ad-Hoc Networks Workshop (2004)
2. Braun, T., Voigt, T., Dunkels, A.: TCP support for sensor networks. In: Proceedings of Fourth Annual Conference on Wireless on Demand Network Systems and Services (2007)
3. Le, T., Hu, W., Corke, P., Jha, S.: ERTP: energy-efficient and reliable transport protocol for data streaming in wireless sensor networks. Comput. Commun. 32(7–10), 154–1171 (2009)
4. Paek, J., Govindan, R.: RCRT: rate-controlled reliable transport for wireless sensor networks. In: Proceedings of the 5th International Conference on Embedded Networked Sensor Systems, New York (2007)
5. Akan, O.B., Akyildiz, I.F.: ESRT: event-to-sink reliable transport in wireless sensor networks. IEEE/ACM Trans. Netw. 13(5), 1003–1016 (2005)
6. Rosberg, Z., Liu, R., Dinh, T., Dong, Y., Jha, S.: Statistical reliability for energy efficient data transport in WSN. Wirel. Netw. 16(7), 1913–1927 (2010)
7. Rosberg, Z., Liu, R., Tuan, L.D., Jha, S., Dong, A.Y., Zic, J.: Energy efficient statistically reliable hybrid transport protocol for sensed data streaming. CSIRO ICT Centre Pub, June 2007
8. Dinh, T.L., Hu, W., Sikka, P., Corke, P., Jha, S.: Design and deployment of a remote robust sensor network: experiences from an outdoor water quality monitoring network. In: 32nd IEEE Conference on Local Computer Networks (LCN), Dublin, 15–18 October 2007
9. Srinivasan, K., Dutta, P., Tavakoli, A., Levis, P.: An empirical study of low power wireless. ACM Trans. Sens. Netw. 6(2), 49 (2010)
10. Goldsmith, A.: Wireless Communications. Cambridge University Press, Cambridge (2005)
11. Lin, S., Zhou, G., Whitehouse, K., Wu, Y., Stankovic, J.A., He, T.: Towards stable network performance in wireless sensor networks. In: 30th IEEE Real-Time Systems Symposium. IEEE Computer Society (2009)
12. Tang, L., Wang, K.C., Huang, Y., Gu, F.: Channel characterization and link quality assessment of IEEE 802.15. 4-compliant radio for factory environments. IEEE Trans. Indust. Inf. 3(2), 99–110 (2007)
13. Baccour, N., Koubaa, A., Jamâa, M.B., do Rosário, D., Youssef, H., Alves, M., Becker, L.B.: RadiaLE: a framework for designing and assessing link quality estimators in wireless sensor networks. Ad Hoc Netw. 9(7), 1–18 (2011)
14. Srinivasan, K., Dutta, P., Tavakoli, A., Levis, P.: Understanding the causes of packet delivery success and failure in dense wireless sensor networks. In: 4th International Conference on Embedded Networked Sensor Systems. ACM (2006)
15. CC2420 Product information and data sheet, chipcon
16. Castalia-3.3. http://castalia.research.nicta.com.au/index.php/en/

A Perturbation-Proof Self-stabilizing Algorithm for Constructing Virtual Backbones in Wireless Ad-Hoc Networks

Amirreza Ramtin[✉], Vesal Hakami, and Mehdi Dehghan

Department of Information Technology, Amirkabir University of Technology,
Tehran, Iran
a_ramtin@aut.ac.ir

Abstract. Self-stabilization is a key property of fault-tolerant distributed computing systems. A self-stabilizing algorithm ensures that the system eventually converges to a legitimate configuration from arbitrary initializations without any external intervention, and it remains in that legitimate configuration as long as no transient fault occurs. In this paper, the problem of virtual backbone construction in wireless ad-hoc networks is first translated into its graph-theoretic counterpart, i.e., approximate minimum connected dominating set construction. We then propose a self-stabilizing algorithm with time complexity $O(n)$. Our algorithm features a perturbation-proof property in the sense that the steady state of the system gives rise to a Nash equilibrium, effectively discouraging the selfish nodes from perturbing the legitimate configuration by changing their valid states. Other advantages of this algorithm include increasing accessibility, reducing the number of update messages during convergence, and stabilizing with minimum changes in the topological structure. Proofs are given for the self-stabilization and perturbation-proofness of the proposed algorithm. The simulation results show that our algorithm outperforms comparable schemes in terms of stabilization time and number of state transitions.

Keywords: Self-stabilization · Wireless ad-hoc network · Virtual backbone · Selfishness · Perturbation · Nash equilibrium

1 Introduction

It is a well-established fact that the fundamental source of energy consumption in wireless ad hoc networks (WANETs) is the exchange of packets between nodes. Hence, when it comes to the design of routing mechanisms for WANETs, a key measure of efficiency is low communication overhead. A communication-efficient structure for supporting routing and multicast in WANETs is the virtual backbone architecture [1]. The virtual backbone approach to routing consists of two phases: (a) creation and update of a virtual backbone substrate, (b) finding and updating the paths. In this paper, we focus on the first phase. With regards to virtual backbone creation and maintenance, the two foremost desirable properties are stability and self-configuration without external intervention, given the dynamic and unstable topology of WANETs

© Springer International Publishing Switzerland 2014
A. Movaghar et al. (eds.): CNDS 2013, CCIS 428, pp. 66–76, 2014.
DOI: 10.1007/978-3-319-10903-9_6

and the multi-hop nature of communications [4]. A promising approach to realize stability and self-configuration is to rely on the notion of self-stabilization in distributed fault-tolerance [8]. A self-stabilizing algorithm guarantees that the system eventually converges to the desirable state regardless of its initial configuration, and that it remains in the desirable configuration as long as no transient fault occurs. Hence, designing virtual backbones with the self-stabilization property has the advantages of automatic structuring, and robustness against: transient faults, node failures, changes in their internal states, and occasional breakages in the communication structure of the system [8].

However, in the majority of self-stabilizing protocols for wireless ad-hoc networks, it is routinely assumed that the network nodes will cooperate with each other so that the overall stabilization of the system is guaranteed. This is while in most practical settings, the nodes neither belong to the same authority, nor do they operate under a single administration domain. Hence, it might be the case that the nodes pursue some private goals that may be in conflict with the system-wide objective. Consider, in particular, virtual backbone construction using a self-stabilizing algorithm. Obviously, once the protocol stabilizes, the nodes serving in the backbone have to sacrifice more processing and communication resources to the benefit of the entire network. Hence, each backbone node faces a dilemma as to whether maintain its serving role in the constructed backbone, or alternatively, perturb the system hoping that the algorithm would re-stabilize this time into a new configuration where the node is a backbone client rather than a server.

Motivated by the impact of node selfishness on protocol stabilization in ad-hoc networks, in this paper, we deal with perturbation-proneness in the context of virtual backbone construction in WANETs. The problem is first translated into minimum connected dominating set (MCDS) construction in the topological graph of the network. We then propose a self-stabilizing MCDS algorithm that prevents selfish nodes from post convergence perturbation of the system. A byproduct of our proposed scheme is faster recovery from all single-fault configurations with reduced message complexity, lower number of state transitions, and minimal topological re-structuring, which contributes to saving energy and increasing network life.

The rest of the paper is organized as follows: We briefly introduce the basic concepts and review the previous studies in Sect. 2. In Sect. 3, the proposed algorithm is discussed and proofs are given to establish its correctness. Section 4 deals with the numerical evaluation of the algorithm and comparisons are made to contrast its performance against prior art. The paper ends with conclusions.

2 Theoretical Background and Relevant Works

A system is self-stabilizing, if and only if, two conditions are satisfied starting with any arbitrarily initial state and with non-deterministically executing algorithm rules, as follows: (a) system converges to a legitimate global configuration (*convergence*) after finite moves, (b) and system remains in that legitimate configuration (*closure*) until no transient faults happens [2]. In graph theory, a connected dominated set (CDS) of graph G is a set D of nodes if two conditions are met: (a) D is a connected sub-graph from G.

(b) Any node of G is in D or adjacent to at least one node of D. A CDS of G is a MCDS, if it has the minimum members among all CDSs of G.

In the recent years, several self-stabilizing algorithms have been proposed for constructing CDS, but a majority of them has been designed based on central daemon (scheduler) which is practically impossible to implement in wireless ad-hoc network [3]. Furthermore, most of these works solely construct a CDS and their final product is not an approximation of MCDS [6]. Another drawback of all such algorithms is that they do not differentiate faults management with respect to their spread.

The self-stabilizing algorithm proposed in [7] which works under distributed scheduler with $O(n^2)$ time complexity is chosen among the relevant research works. We refer to this algorithm as MCDS*ss* in the rest of this paper. CDS Constructed by this algorithm is based on a sequential algorithm [7] that produces an $8opt + 1$ approximation of MCDS in graph.

It is not unlikely to consider a selfish self-stabilizing system under the assumption that nodes deviate from valid states and change their state to increase their utility by re-convergence to a different valid state. Nash equilibrium, a criterion for termination of a game, in self-stabilizing systems is discussed in [5] aiming at checking if it is possible to use it to prevent from selfish node perturbation in such systems. Fixed points in a game could be considered identical with final states in self-stabilizing systems. Distributed self-stabilizing systems are divided into four categories considering if fixed points are in Nash equilibrium or not. The main category is absolutely perturbation-proof. A system is absolutely perturbation-proof, if every system fixed point is in Nash equilibrium for any set of utility functions.

Nash equilibrium is a strategy per player in which none of the players intends to deviate from equilibrium strategies unilaterally i.e. it does not gain any profit by unilateral deviation from strategy and adopting another one under the condition that other players remain in their equilibrium states.

3   Proposed Algorithm

In this section, a high-level description of self-stabilizing and perturbation–proof virtual backbone construction algorithm based on MCDS abbreviated as MCDS*pp* will be explained.

3.1   Discussion on Design and Functionality of Algorithm

MCDS*pp* is designed based on marathe et al. algorithm [7]. This algorithm first constructs a breadth-first spanning (BFS) tree in network graph. Then, there is a repeated loop from root to the last depth of tree. In each loop, a maximal independent set (MIS) forms in the same depth nodes, not dominated by nodes of lower depths. Integration of all these sets produces a MIS in network graph. It is proven that this MIS is a WCDS. Finally, a fully connected set is established by adding connecting nodes to that set. Connecting nodes are the father of members of MIS in BFS tree. The final fully connected set is a CDS-tree. It is proven that a CDS-tree is an 8opt + 1 approximation of MCDS.

We assume that the tree T is formed in network graph through a self-stabilizing BFS tree algorithm. The distance of each node from root is determined by "l" variable. The validation of tree state and accuracy of "l" variable are the basic assumptions in MCDS*pp* algorithm implementation.

The state of each node is specified by two variables of *ind* and *dom* in MCDS configuration. These variables may hold two statuses: IN and OUT. Each node in legitimate configuration holds one of three states (IN, IN), (IN, OUT) and (OUT, OUT) based on the values of two variables (*dom*, *ind*). Set of nodes having state (IN, IN) are members of MIS. Union of nodes in state (IN, IN) and (IN, OUT) is a CDS. In legitimate configuration, state transition between four possible states is a transient fault.

In a legitimate configuration of self-stabilizing system, 1-fault situation is the occurrence a fault in a node like *v* that is generated by an undesirable change in its variables. It can be shown that two conditions apply (a) one of the rules is active in *v*. (b) it's possible to reach stability by execution of only one rule in *v*. The aim of designing the proposed algorithm is to detect and resolve 1-fault states by applying rules only in that faulty node and prevention from error propagation by unwanted execution of rules in neighboring nodes of *v*, $N(v)$.

For simplification of understanding our proposed algorithm, we first define some terms that are preconditions of state transition operations in nodes and some sets for better readability of algorithm pseudo-code (Fig. 1).

Sets of PN, BN, MN, and CN refer to parent nodes (lower depth neighbors), brother nodes (same depth neighbors), mature nodes (union of PN and BN), and child nodes (higher depth neighbors) of a node in T tree respectively. Fifth term specifies father of a node. Father of a node is one of parent neighbors that has the lowest *id*. The 6th and 7th terms specify whether a mature or parent neighbor is member of MIS or not. The 8th term specifies if a node is pending. If neither a node nor its mature neighbors are members of MIS, that node is pending. The 9th term specifies if a node conflicts. If a node and at least one of its mature neighbors are members of MIS, conflict term will

1. $BN(v) := \{w \in N(v) | l.w = l.v\}$

2. $PN(v) := \{w \in N(v) | l.w < l.v\}$

3. $CN(v) := \{w \in N(v) | l.w > l.v\}$

4. $MN(v) := \{w \in N(v) | l.w <= l.v\}$

5. $father(v) := \min\{id.w | w \in PN(v)\}$

6. $inMatureNeighbor(v) \equiv \exists w \in MN(v) : ind.w = IN$

7. $inParentNeighbor(v) \equiv \exists w \in PN(v) : ind.w = IN$

8. $Pending(v) \equiv ind.v = OUT \wedge \sim inMatureNeighbor(v)$

9. $conflict(v) \equiv ind.v = IN \wedge inMatureNeighbor(v)$

10. $inBrotherWithLowerId(v) \equiv \exists w \in BN(v) : ind.w = IN \wedge id.w < id.v$

11. $conflictWithParent(v) \equiv ind.v = IN \wedge inParentNeighbor(v)$

Fig. 1. Set and predicate definitions

$R1.$ $l.v = 0 \land (ind.v = OUT \lor dom.v = OUT) \to ind.v := IN,\ dom.v := IN$

$R2.$ $l.v = 1 \land ind.v = IN \to ind.v := OUT$

$R3.$ $l.v \neq 0 \land l.v \neq 1 \land ind.v = OUT \land \sim inParentNeighbor(v) \land \forall w \in$
$PN(v): \sim pending(w) \land \Big(\forall w \in BN(v): id.w > id.v \lor \big(ind.w = OUT \land$
$(inParentNeighbor(w) \lor inBrotherWithLowerId(w))\big)\Big) \to ind.v :=$
$IN,\ dom.v := IN$

$R4.$ $l.v \neq 0 \land l.v \neq 1 \land conflictWithParent(v) \land \big(\forall w \in PN(v): \sim conflict(w)\big) \to$
$ind.v := OUT$

$R5.$ $l.v \neq 0 \land l.v \neq 1 \land ind.v = IN \land \sim conflictWithParent(v) \land \big(\forall w \in$
$BN(v): ind.w = IN \land \sim conflictWithParent(w) \land \sim inBrotherWithLowerId(w) \land$
$id.w < id.v\big) \to ind.v := OUT$

$R6.$ $\sim R2 \land \sim R4 \land \sim R5 \land ind.v = IN \land dom.v = OUT \to dom.v := IN$

$R7.$ $\sim R3 \land ind.v = OUT \land dom.v = OUT \land (\exists w \in CN(v): ind.w = IN \land$
$\sim conflict(w) \land father(w) = v) \to dom.v := IN$

$R8.$ $\sim R3 \land ind.v = OUT \land dom.v = IN \land (\forall w \in CN(v): father(w) \neq v \lor$
$(ind.w = OUT \land \sim pending(w))) \to dom.v := OUT$

Fig. 2. Rules of MCDS*pp* algorithm

hold in that node. The 10th term is active in a node if at least one of its brother is a member of MIS and its *id* is lower than that node. Activity of 11th term indicates conflict between node and one of its parent neighbors.

Rules of MCDS*pp* are depicted in Fig. 2. The process of constructing MIS in T tree proceeds from root towards the last depth according to rules of 1–5. First rule determines root state. This node must become a member of MIS. Second rule determines the membership of root neighboring nodes (first depth). Rules 3, 4, and 5 specify remained nodes membership in MIS. One node becomes a member by performing rule 3 and cancels its membership by performing rule 4 or 5. While MIS forms, deeper nodes states has no effect on upper nodes states in T. The state of deeper nodes has no effect on the shallower ones. We give priority of MIS membership to the nodes that have lower *id* than their brothers in each same depth level of tree, in order to break symmetry of nodes. To detect 1-fault situations, each node needs to know its 2-hop neighbors membership, too. This information guarantees that if 1-fault occurs in a neighbor of parent or brother of the node, in a legitimate configuration, no rules will become active on the node. According to rule 6, members of MIS i.e. the nodes for which the *ind* is in IN state, join MCDS. Rule 7 or 8 checks membership or none-membership of remained nodes in CDS respectively. Nodes that are fathers of members of MIS, become members of MCDS by executing rule 7.

3.2 Proof of Correctness

Lemma 1. Assuming that spanning tree T is valid up to i[th] depth and MIS is constructed up to $(i - 1)^{th}$ depth by MCDS*pp* rules and exists in valid state, MIS is constructed after maximum of m rounds up to i[th] depth and exists in valid state. No node changes its membership of MIS as long as no transient fault happens.

Proof. The root becomes a member of MIS by executing rule 1 at the first round. It is obvious that this membership is permanent because rules 2–5 are not executed in the

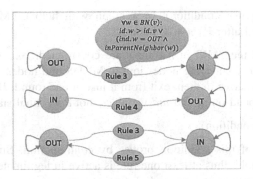

Fig. 3. *ind* variable state transition diagram regards to validation of shallower levels of tree

root. Similarly, neighbors of root (1 = 1) leave membership of MIS via rule 2 at the first round and this decision will be permanent. It is clear that the membership of deeper nodes has no effect on the membership of ith depth in MIS according to rules 1–5. The diagram of *ind* variable state transition of ith depth nodes (i > 1) is depicted in Fig. 3 assuming that MIS is already formed by rules 1–5. It can be shown in Fig. 3 that if a node passes path 1 or 2 it will be permanent i.e. those paths are traversed just once. The reason is that all predictions in paths 1 and 2 are related either to lower depth nodes for which the validation and stability are assumed, or to the base information like *id*. There is a predicate (inbrotherwithlowerid) in paths 3 and 4 which is also related to the state of the same depth nodes. At the first round, *ind* variable becomes equal to OUT by running rule 4 in all nodes that can traverse path 2. It is obvious that OUT state (non-membership in MIS) is permanent in these nodes. Following the first round, in the second round, all nodes which can traverse path 1 are activated and *ind* variable in those nodes become equal to IN. Consequently, no node traverses path 1 or 2 by traversing this round. After the second round, either *ind* variable value is permanently OUT in all nodes of ith depth or at least there is one node (v) that is in IN state, a permanent state, through path 1. In the third round, neighboring nodes with the same depth of node v which are in IN state switch to OUT state (rule 5). It can be shown that this state is permanent in those nodes and does not change in following rounds. In the next round, nodes that rule 5 is active in them travers path 3 and it is permanent. Then, rounds 3 and 4 will be repeated until there is still some nodes in which rules 3 or 5 are active. So, a number of rounds up to a maximum equal to the number of ith depth nodes are traversed until MIS is constructed at this depth.

Lemma 2. MIS structure in T is formed after n rounds. n is number of tree nodes.

Proof. We use induction to proof this lemma. In Lemma 1, it has been shown that root and second depth nodes of T enter to valid state of MIS just in one round (basis: statement holds for d = 1, 2). Using Lemma 1 inductive step will be proven for d > 1. Dou to Lemma 1 if MIS is formed up to i^{th} depth, after m_i round, it is formed up to $i + 1^{th}$ depth. Therefore time complexity of MIS construction is $o\left(\sum_{i=2}^{D} m_i\right)$ which is equal to $o(n)$. D is depth of T.

Lemma 3 (convergence condition). In a graph with help of MCDS*pp* algorithm, MCDS is constructed after $R_T + n + 1$ rounds.

Proof. T in R_T and then MIS in n rounds are constructed. According to rules 6–8, members of MIS and connecting nodes join to MCDS and nodes that are member of MCDS and rule 8 is active in them exit from it just in one round. Because all terms of those three rules depend on *id* and *ind* variables, not *dom*, final states are permanent.

Lemma 4 (closure condition).

Proof. Correctness of this condition proves by contradiction. Suppose that closure condition does not hold, thus at least one rule is active in legitimate configuration, but referring to demonstrations in Lemma 1–3, final states are permanent and no rules will be executed in the legitimate configuration.

3.3   Proof of Absolutely Perturbation-Proof Feature

Lemma 5. Happening 1-fault in *ind* variable of a ith depth node has no effect on the state of upper or lower depth nodes.

Proof. MIS had been formed before 1-fault incident in the legitimate configuration, therefore it causes one of pending or conflict predicates holds. State of parents effects on the preconditions of rules 3–5 in a node. To be sure that those rules do not activate by 1-fault incident in lower depth nodes, some terms are added to them in order to checking that pending or conflict predicates are active in parent neighbors or not. Similarly in rules 7–8, those predicates are checked for upper depth nodes, because state of children effects on preconditions of those rules. It is obvious that preconditions of rules 1, 2 and 6 have no connection to states of neighbors.

Lemma 6. Happening 1-fault in *ind* variable of a ith depth node has no effect on the other i^{th} depth nodes.

Proof. It is obvious that *ind* variable change in a node has no effect on the *dom* variables of its brothers. Hence, we investigate effect of 1-fault in node v on *ind* variables of the ith depth 1-hop neighbor z and 2-hop neighbor k.

If 1-fault (IN to OUT) happens in v, the only rule that might be active in z is rule 3. Note that state of z is OUT. If node z has a parent in IN state or its *id* is greater than v, rule 3 does not activate. Otherwise it is evident that in the valid states, rule 3 did not execute in z because of another brother like w that had a lower *id* than z and was in IN state. Because 1-fault happens in z, not w, rule 3 still do not activate in z. If state of k is IN, the only rule that might be active in that node is rule 5. However, in rule 5, even if term '∼inbrotherwithlowerid' is active, term '*ind*.w = IN' must be active concurrently either, but in the previous paragraph we show that 1-hop brother of v remains in OUT state. If node k is in OUT state, rule 3 certainly cannot be active in it, because there is no preconditions in that rule that holds with occurrence of 1-fault.

Assuming that 1-fault (OUT to IN) happens in v, if state of z is OUT, it cannot activate any rule in z. If state of z is IN, the only rule that might be active is rule 5. Because valid state of v had been OUT, there were some preconditions of rule 3 that had not hold. It is not possible that node v can activate rule 5 in another node because of those preconditions. In legitimate configuration, MIS membership states in two-hop neighborhood of v (k z v) is one of these three cases: (010, 100, 000). In the first case, the only rule that might be active is rule 3, but term '$ind.w = OUT$' must hold if rule 3 is active. Therefore 1-fault cannot activate rule 3 in k, because state of z is still IN. In the second case, the only rule that can be active is rule 5, but as the term '$ind.w = IN$' exists in rule 5, it cannot activate, because z is in OUT state. In the last case, although it seems that rule 3 can activate in node k, but a brother or a parent in IN state has existed and they still do not allow rule 3 being active in node k.

Lemma 7. Happening 1-fault in *dom* variable of a ith depth node has no effect on the states of neighbors.

Proof. Since in preconditions of rules 1–8 do not refer to *dom* variables of neighbors, So it is obvious that change of *dom* variable in a node has no effect on the others.

Theorem 1. If 1-fault occurs in a system based on MCDS*pp* algorithm, faulty node and only that node by executing just one rule enters to the valid state that it was in before.

Proof. Convergence feature of algorithm explains that system converges from an illegitimate configuration to a legitimate one. We also showed in Lemma 5–7 that occurrence of 1-fault has no effect on neighbors. Considering these two explanations, it is proven that with execution of self-stabilizing rules in the faulty node, system will return to legitimate configuration. Investigating algorithm rules shows that it will be done by just one rule execution.

Theorem 2. If self-stabilizing rules cause that after perturbation of any selfish node in a legitimate configuration, system returns to that legitimate configuration, that configuration is in Nash equilibrium.

Proof. According to definition of Nash equilibrium, a legitimate configuration of a self-stabilizing system is in Nash equilibrium, if no node can obtain profit by unilateral deviation from its state and going to a different state. Incentive of a node from perturbation in a self-stabilizing system is convergence to another legitimate configuration so that its utility in new configuration is more than pervious. In a legitimate configuration of a self-stabilizing system, perturbation of a node models with occurrence of 1-fault in that node. If self-stabilizing rules cause that after 1-fault or perturbation of a node, system again converges to the previous legitimate configuration, no nodes will have perturbation incentive and thus that configuration is in Nash equilibrium.

Theorem 3. A system based on MCDS*pp* algorithm is absolutely perturbation-proof.

Proof. According to Theorem 1, in a system based on MCDS*pp* algorithm, after 1-fault incident in legitimate configuration, system will return to that legitimate configuration again only by one move. In Theorem 2, we said that if self-stabilizing rules force system to return to the previous legitimate configuration after perturbation of a selfish node, that configuration is in Nash equilibrium. Therefore, stable states of a self-stabilizing system based on MCDS*pp* algorithm are in Nash equilibrium for any utility functions. It means that the MCDS*pp* algorithm is absolutely perturbation-proof.

4 Performance Analysis

In this section, we conduct a number of experiments to compare the performance of our virtual backbone construction algorithm MCDSpp with that of MCDSss [7]. The comparisons are made in terms of the number of state transitions and stabilization time. We simulate the algorithms under two operational scenarios: arbitrary configuration (*ind* and *dom* variables are randomly equal to IN or OUT) and multiple fault configuration. All experiments are implemented with OMnet++ simulator under an unfair scheduler, and the reported data points are the average of 100 tests in each scenario. Each node periodically notifies its neighbors of its current state by broadcasting beacon packets. The MAC configuration adheres to IEEE 802.11 and the channel model is simple path loss.

In Figs. 4 and 5, the number of state transitions and stabilization time of MCDSpp and MCDSss are reported, respectively. Average connectivity degree is 8 and we have varied the number of nodes. The number of state transitions is equal to the total number of *ind* and *dom* variable changes. From these two diagrams, it can be deduced that the performance superiority of MCDSpp over MCDSss becomes even more apparent as the number of nodes increases.

In another scenario, performance of these two algorithm is compared by fault injections to the legitimate configuration. In this test (see Fig. 6), the number of fault injections is variable from 1 to 20. Topology is formed from 20 nodes with average connectivity degree 3. MCDSpp stabilizes from single faults by only one state transition (move). While MCDSss needs on average 5 state transitions. With more fault injections, the performance gain of MCDSpp over MCDSss decreases and reaches 1.5.

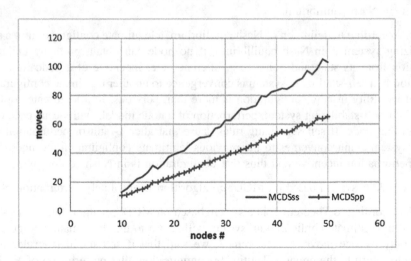

Fig. 4. The impact of the number of nodes on the number of state transitions.

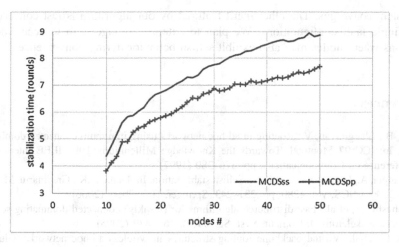

Fig. 5. The impact of the number of nodes on stabilization time.

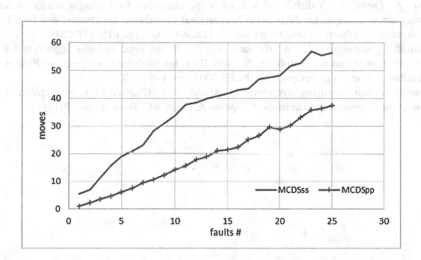

Fig. 6. The impact of the number of fault injections on the number of state transitions.

5   Conclusion

In this paper, a distributed virtual backbone construction algorithm has been proposed for wireless ad-hoc networks based on the notion of MCDS in graph theory. The proposed algorithm is self-stabilizing against transient faults and topology changes. We also proved that the algorithm's stable configuration gives rise to a Nash equilibrium, and thus, selfish nodes have no motivation to perturb the constructed backbone once the system converges. The other merit featured by our algorithm is fast convergence from single fault configurations. We plan to extend this algorithm to accommodate situations where nodes may also exhibit selfish behavior during convergence.

References

1. Das, B., Bharghavan, V.: Routing in ad-hoc networks using minimum connected dominating sets. In: ICC 97 Montreal, Towards the Knowledge Millennium. 1997 IEEE International Conference on Communications, pp. 376–380 (1997)
2. Dasgupta, A., Ghosh, S., Tixeuil, S.: Selfish stabilization. In: Datta, A.K., Gradinariu, M. (eds.) SSS 2006. LNCS, vol. 4280, pp. 231–243. Springer, Heidelberg (2006)
3. Dubhashi, D., et al.: Fast distributed algorithms for (weakly) connected dominating sets and linear-size skeletons. J. Comput. Syst. Sci. 71(4), 467–479 (2005)
4. Gao, L., et al.: Virtual backbone routing structures in wireless ad-hoc networks. Global J. Comput. Sci. Technol. 10(4), 21 (2010)
5. Gouda, M.G., Acharya, H.B.: Nash equilibria in stabilizing systems. In: Guerraoui, R., Petit, F. (eds.) SSS 2009. LNCS, vol. 5873, pp. 311–324. Springer, Heidelberg (2009)
6. Jain, A., Gupta, A.: A distributed self-stabilizing algorithm for finding a connected dominating set in a graph. In: 2005 Sixth International Conference on Parallel and Distributed Computing, Applications and Technologies, PDCAT 2005, pp. 615–619 (2005)
7. Kamei, S., Kakugawa, H.: A self-stabilizing distributed approximation algorithm for the minimum connected dominating set. In: 2007 IEEE International Conference on Parallel and Distributed Processing Symposium, IPDPS 2007, pp. 1–8 (2007)
8. Tixeuil, S.: Self-stabilizing algorithms. In: Atallah, M.J., Blanton, M. (eds.) Algorithms and Theory of Computation Handbook. Chapman & Hall/CRC, Boca Raton (2010)

Security

Security

PPayWord: A Secure and Fast P2P Micropayment Scheme for Video Streaming

Zahra Ghafoori$^{(\boxtimes)}$, Mehdi Dehghan, and Majid Nourhoseini

Computer Engineering Department, Amirkabir University of Technology,
Tehran, Iran
{zahra.ghafoori,dehghan,majidnh}@aut.ac.ir

Abstract. A practical payment scheme for peer to peer video streaming is an essential component toward commercialization of such systems. This component, on the other side, contributes to solve the free-riding problem and challenges on the copyright issue in peer to peer video streaming applications. In this paper, we propose a new peer to peer micropayment scheme for video streaming services, which is called PPayWord and is based on PayWord micropayment scheme. Considering features of video streaming services, we add transferability property to hash chains in PPayWord scheme, which results in payments with high performance and lower broker load. Furthermore, we study workload of peers and brokers together with analyzing PPayWord resistance against different frauds of peers. Performance results of the proposed scheme against PayWord verify its considerable load reduction on the payment system.

Keywords: Peer to peer video streaming · File sharing · Free-riding · Incentive mechanism · Hash chain · Micropayment

1 Introduction

Although, in the preliminary stage, video streaming was widely performed by client-server model, success of peer to peer (P2P) file sharing systems motivated academia as well as industry to use scalability and low cost features of P2P architecture to provide video streaming services for larger population of users. Achieving satisfaction of this scalability is closely related to the cooperation level of peers. However, most of the peers try to use the system resources without contributing their own resources. This problem is named as free-riding and the peers as free-riders. For example, in Gnutella P2P file sharing service, only 30 % of the users contribute their resources and most of requests are responded by only 1 % of hosts [1]. This small fraction of hosts are not able to provide a suitable quality in P2P video streaming [2]. A solution to encourage peers to cooperate is to create financial drive in peers through a payment scheme. In this way, each peer receives charges from other peers in turn of uploading content to them and can use the resulted income to get service from the system. On the other side, P2P video streaming systems tend to be more commercialized in the near future and in this movement, copyright issues should be considered. These requirements necessitate designing a convenient payment scheme for P2P video streaming.

© Springer International Publishing Switzerland 2014
A. Movaghar et al. (Eds.): CNDS 2013, CCIS 428, pp. 79–91, 2014.
DOI: 10.1007/978-3-319-10903-9_7

An appropriate payment scheme for P2P video streaming, beside providing a suitable level of security and rapidity, should have high efficiency and low overhead. Micropayment schemes, which are payments of smaller quantity or near to the credit card transaction fees, can fulfill these requirements efficiently. They, usually, use an electronic coin that is typically a hash chain or a signed message, to do the payments. In such schemes, detecting and penalizing cheater users usually prevent fraud. Considering the high number of financial transactions in P2P micropayment systems, designing should be done in a way to reduce broker workload. Broker is a trusted third party in micropayment and its online presence in every transaction makes its load in order of $O(T)$, where T is the number of transactions. However, P2P micropayment scheme should decrease this load to $O(M)$, where M is the number of generated coins [3].

In this paper, we present PPayWord[1], a fast and secure P2P micropayment scheme based on PayWord [4] which addresses timeliness requirement of video streaming applications. This is achieved through adding transferability property to hash chains. Hash operations are much faster and cheaper against asymmetric key operations and applying them makes payments secure, fast, and efficient. Furthermore, executing hash chains in a transferable manner reduces workload on the broker considerably. When partnership links between peers in P2P system are more stable, average length of transferred chains becomes larger, and since only transaction parties are involved meanwhile a chain is being spent, the proposed method causes higher reduction on broker load. PPayWord robustness against overspending is much higher than PayWord. Furthermore, double spending fraud is detectable by both broker and the cheated peer. Accordingly, punishment against such a fraud can be done more severely in our scheme.

The rest of this paper is organized as follow: In Sect. 2, a number of previous P2P micropayment schemes are briefly reviewed. In Sect. 3, PayWord micropayment scheme is reviewed. After expressing system model in Sect. 4, we describe PPayWord scheme together with discussion on its security and performance in Sect. 5. In Sect. 6, performance of PPayWord has been evaluated against PayWord scheme through simulations. This paper ends with conclusion and expression of future works in Sect. 7.

2   Related Work

Up to the current state, successful micropayment systems such as NetBill [5], Micromint and PayWord [4] have been proposed. In spite of their good performance in some situations, unique features of P2P systems have stimulated researchers to design other micropayment schemes that fit to these features. In this section, we have reviewed some of these studies.

PPay [3] is a P2P micropayment scheme that uses a self-managed floating currency. Payment with a purchased coin is done when the owner of the coin assigns it to a provider peer. Hereafter, the provider peer becomes holder of the assigned coin and can use it to pay another provider. Every new assignment transfers the coin to a new holder and needs coin owner participation. The coin owner accepts an authorized coin transfer

---

[1] P2P PayWord.

request from correct holder and reassigns the coin. Next, it informs two transaction parties about this transference. Thus, PPay reduces load of the broker and gives over the task of evaluating payments to peers themselves. These studies presented in [6–8] are based on the PPay scheme. WhoPay [6] was designed to act as a P2P micropayment scheme with high scalability and anonymity features. In [7] the copyright issue is discussed. The proposed mechanism guarantees that the author of a file is paid even if she/he does not participate in any transaction. In the lottery-based pricing scheme in [8] discount in prices is used to increase the level of peers' cooperation. Equal amounts of upload and download, do not undo effects of each other and peers must upload more to obtain revenue.

In KARMA [9], a distributed approach is proposed that keeps a history of uploads and downloads of each peer with a value, namely karma. The karma value for each peer is managed by a set of peers, called bank set. In the payments between two peers, their two bank sets are involved to transfer funds between their karma values. There are also other schemes such as [10] for using global currency in P2P networks. Authors of [11] formulate a layered topology and use an adaptive taxation strategy to incentivize peers to share their upload capacity.

Because of the timeliness requirement of the video streaming applications, the payments must be done relatively fast. Previous studies, which use expensive asymmetric key operations for all payments, do not realize this requirement. In this paper, we aim to design a secure and fast P2P micropayment scheme with low overhead. We provide a more detailed description of the PayWord mechanism in the next section as the basis of the proposed method.

3   PayWord Micropayment Scheme Overview

PayWord [4] is a credit-based micropayment scheme that uses hash chains to show the credit of each user in its providers. Each user opens an account in a broker who issues and signs the user's digital certificate. The Certificate assures vendors that the generated chains by the user are redeemable by the broker. Certificates are renewed monthly to help the broker to penalize users that have spent credits more than their money.

Each user, U, to pay a new vendor, V, needs to generate a new hash (payword) chain. Henceforth, U generates a random value, w_n, and each time computes the hash of w_{i+1} to produce the next payword, i.e. w_i for $i = n - 1, \ldots, 1, 0$. Ultimately, U reaches the root of the payword chain, w_0. Then it signs a commitment message for this chain and sends it to V. The commitment message contains the identifier of V, the value of w_0 and the certificate of U to prove that U has used the chain to pay V. The Vendor, V, checks for the accuracy of U's certificate and the commitment message signatures. Hereafter, U can pay V with the paywords of this chain in the reverse order of their production, i.e. the i-th payment (for $i = 1, 2, \ldots, n$) is done with pair (w_i, i). To accept this payment, V checks hash of w_i to see whether it is equal to the last spent payword, w_{i-1} and if so, it stores w_i for evaluating the next payment.

Each vendor at the end of day sends the last spent payword with its index, (w_l, l), together with corresponding commitment message to the broker for redeeming each received chain.

4 System Model

We assume a video source, and N peers, $P1, P2, \ldots, PN$, that are placed in an arbitrary structured or unstructured topology. Bandwidth of the video source is enough to serving N' number of peers such that $N' \ll N$; thus, peers must cooperate and upload received chunks to each other to be able to see the video. Video stream is divided into segments with equal size, called chunks, and is stored in the video source. The peers download and upload the video chunks according to a streaming protocol. Each peer pay for any received chunk and is paid when uploads a chunk to another peer. The payment system has k servers, namely brokers, as $B1, B2, B3, \ldots, Bk$ which are authentic entities that act as third parties of financial transactions.

All entities, except the video source, must have a key pair. The key pair of the brokers is assigned by the payment system moderators and has high security. Brokers' public key is accessible for peers in a secure manner such as payment system website. The key pair of each peer is assigned to it by a certificate when it registers in the payment system. Each peer additionally receives a unique identifier, at the time it registers in the system. The public key of each entity E is showed as PK_E. For example, PK_{Bi} is the public key of broker B_i. SK_E is the private key of entity E and its sign on message Msg is showed with $\{Msg\}SK_E$. An asymmetric cryptography scheme is used to sign messages. Hash operations are done by a powerful cryptography hash function h, such as MD5 or SHA. Important features of h are one-wayness and collision-resistancy. These two features imply that finding the input of h from its output or producing a same output from two different inputs are impossible in practice. Furthermore, we use $h^y(x)$ to point y recursive hash operations started at x.

5 PPayWord Micropayment Scheme

In this section we introduce our micropayment mechanism for P2P video streaming, namely PPayWord. This scheme is appropriate when the communication between two peers is not limited to one or a few transactions but lasts at least the typical length of hash chains. This communication continuation, commonly, exists in video streaming. Any peer, in video streaming, is communicating each time with its neighborhood peers and tries to keep the best ones as its partners to keep the quality of video displaying. Accordingly, each peer can, most probably, spend its hash chain totally within its partners. Therefore, the ownership of hash chains, which are not inherently transferable, can be transferred from a peer to another peer. We use this property in design of PPayWord.

In PPayWord, hash chains have been applied as each peer's credit when they getting service. Each hash value, called chunkpay, can be used to pay for one (or more) streaming segment(s). As the PPayWord is credit-based, peers need to be assured that chunkpay chains that they receive as payment are redeemable or transferable by a given broker. This assurance is obtained through certificates that peers receive from the brokers at the beginning of registration in the system. Certificate of peer P_i, which is as follow:

$$C_{p_i} = \{B_i, P_i, PK_{P_i}, exp\}SK_{B_i} \tag{1}$$

This certificate is signed by B_i as the broker of P_i and contains public key of P_i. The *exp* value is the expiration date of the certificate.

A chunkpay chain is generated similar to a payword chain except that it has a unique identifier called *chainId* and its length is limited by Ch_{minLen} and Ch_{maxLen}. The latter values are system parameters explained in the next section. Uniqueness of *chainId* must be commensurate among all present chain identifiers in the system. For instance, each peer can add the chain generation date to its own identifier, and use the hash of the resulted string as the generated chain identifier. At the initial stage, each peer signs a commitment message to pay with a chain. The content of the commitment messages depend on the type of the chain, which can be produced or transferred, is discussed in subsects. 5.2 and 5.3, respectively.

5.1 Brokers Chain Database

Brokers are the banking servers in PPayWord scheme. They sit between peers and provide a secure media for transferring and redeeming the chains. They additionally issue peers' certificates such as PayWord scheme. To add transferability characteristic to the chains, every broker has a chain database including transferred chains with length between Ch_{minLen} and Ch_{maxLen}. These chains are produced by peers who have received their certificates from that same broker. Ch_{minLen} indicates minimum acceptable length of chains that can be stored in the database of every broker. The value of this parameter maintains the online load of broker bellow a given level which is related to the number of broker's database entries. In fact, it guarantees that most of transferred chains are used at least in Ch_{minLen} transactions without broker involvement. This is an important property that increases scalability of PPayWord micropayment scheme. Ch_{maxLen} is the upper bound value that restricts probability of losing the credit of peers in partial transference of a chain.

5.2 Payment Through a New Hash Chain

In PPayWord each peer makes payments through the application of chains it produces or chains that it gets their ownership. Suppose that peer P_i wants to pay peer P_j and has no chain. Thus, it must generate a new chain, *ch*, and send a commitment message to P_j to make its payments with chain *ch*. This commitment message is as (2):

$$comm_{form1} = \{P_j, B_i, C_{P_i}, chainId, w_0, e\}SK_{P_i} \tag{2}$$

The information of chain producer and its responsible broker, P_i and B_i respectively, are extracted from this commitment message in case of chain transference. Inclusion of P_j information verifies that this commitment message is to pay P_j. Signature of Peer P_i verifies that this message has been given to P_j by P_i. To check the authenticity of this signature, P_j should obtain, in a secure manner, public key of the broker which has issued C_{P_i}. e is expiration date of commitment message.

Peer P_i, starting from w_1, can pay peer P_j via the chunkpays of this chain until all or most of chunkpays are spent. Now it does a redemption procedure in a completely different manner from PayWord scheme. In this procedure, P_j can take ownership of the chain, when its length is bigger than or equal to Ch_{minLen}. Peer P_j sends the ownership transference request of the chain to B_i. Thus ownership transference request is always sent to the broker that has signed the certificate of the chain producer. This request has the following format:

$$\text{transform}_1 = \{\text{comm}_{\text{form1}}, PK_{P_j}, 1\} \tag{3}$$

where $comm_{form1}$ is the commitment message that the producer of chain, P_i, has given to the provider peer, P_j. PK_{P_j} is the public key of P_j and is needed when the broker, B_i, inserts information of this chain to its database. l is length of chain and is equal to the index of the last spent chunkpay of it.

Broker B_i, as mentioned before, has a database in which each entry of it corresponds to a transferred chain and has fields explained in Table 1. When a chain is transferred for the first time, its corresponding entry is inserted in database.

Broker B_i after receiving chain transference request of P_j, checks if the index of the last spent chunkpay, l, is greater than or equal to Ch_{minLen}. Next, it verifies the certificate of P_i and its signature on the commitment message. If both of them are verified, it searches the chain in its database with the chain identifier as key. If there is no chain with this identifier, it stores the chain in its database, else there is a fraud: If the information of P_j exists in the Previous Owners field, it has cheated and has retransmitted an old commitment message. Otherwise, P_i has cheated and spent its self-generated chain in more than one peer, concurrently. In these cases, the cheater peer can be punished according to policies of payment system. This procedure is showed in Fig. 1.

Table 1. Entry fields at broker's chain database

Field Name	Comment
ChainId	Identifier of the chain
Producer	Producer of the chain
Previous Owners	Previous owners of the chain
PK_{owner}	Public Key of the current owner of the chain
Owner	Current owner of the chain
W_0	Root of the chain
L	Length of the chain

```
Upon receiving a transform₁ message with chain length l:
if l < Ch_minLen or verification of a signature fails then
        discard the message
else
        if there is no corresponding entry in chain database then
            store the chain in the database
        else
                if P_payee ∈ Previous Owners then
                        punish the cheater peer, P_payee
                else
                        punish the cheater peer, P_payer
                end if
        end if
end if
```

Fig. 1. Inserting a new chain in the database of the broker

In case that the last spent chunkpay index is less than Ch_{minLen}, the chain is partially used and the payee stores the last index and the value of the corresponding chunkpay to redeem it later.

5.3 Payment Through a Transferred Chain

Suppose the consumer peer has the ownership of a transferred chain, hence there is no need to generate a new one and it can pay the provider peer with the transferred chain. For clarity, we have followed the latter example: peer P_j decides to pay peer P_r with chain ch that has transferred to it from P_i. P_j signs a commitment message as (4), to do the payment with chain ch:

$$\text{comm}_{\text{form2}} = \{P_r, B_i, PK_{P_j}, \text{chainId}, e\} SK_{P_j} \tag{4}$$

Including P_r in the commitment message and existence of signature of P_j on it, assure that this commitment is given by P_j to P_r. B_i is the responsible broker and *chainId* is the searching index in the database of B_i.

Upon reception of this commitment message, Peer P_r checks signature of P_j with the announced public key inside the commitment message and only in case of signature verification it queries broker B_i about accuracy of chain ch. Broker B_i, in response to this query, searches the database with chainId as key and sends the corresponding entry if exists, and an error message otherwise. In the case of receiving a message contained with the corresponding entry of the database, peer P_r checks equality of PK_{owner} and Owner fields of response with PK_{P_j} and P_j values of the commitment message, respectively. To finalize acceptance of the payment with chain ch, it checks the absence of itself in the Previous Owners set. Next the value of w_0 is extracted from the message. Peer P_j, hereafter and with chunkpays of chain ch, can pay peer P_r in the same way as paying with a new chain.

As payment with a new chain, when the length of the spent chain is bigger than or equal to Ch_{minLen}, peer P_r can transfer this chain to itself by the related broker. To this end, P_r sends a transference request to B_i as follow:

$$transform2 = \{comm_{form2}, PK_{P_r}, 1\} \tag{5}$$

Broker B_i upon receiving this request checks the chain length. Next searches its database to find an entry with this *chainId*. If there is such an entry it checks equality of PK_{owner} field of this entry with PK_j value of the commitment. In case of equality, it checks signature accuracy of the commitment and transfers the chain. Otherwise there is a fraud that can be detected as mentioned in subsect. 5.2. This procedure is showed in Fig. 2.

```
Upon receiving a transform₂ message with chain length 1:
if 1 < Ch_minLen  or there is no corresponding entry then
      discard the message
else
    if PK_owner = PK_payer  then
        if payer's signature verified then
            transfer the chain
        else
            discard the message
        end if
    else
        if P_payee ∈ Previous Owners then
            punish P_payee
        else
            punish P_payer
    end if
end if
```

Fig. 2. Transferring a chain by the database of the broker

5.4 Brokers Operations at the End of Day

All peers send Information of transferred but not spent chains and partially used chains to the responsible brokers. In the former case only the value and length of the chain together with its identifier is enough, therefore, size of the redemption message is reduced. This information in the latter case includes commitment message and the value and index of the last spent chunkpay. Broker, at the end of day, processes all redemption requests of chains with length l that contain commitment message and acts as follows:

1. If the request contains a commitment message as (2), broker searches its database. If there is an entry with the *chainId* of this commitment, it is a fraud that can be detected as mentioned before. Otherwise, the broker does signature verification of the commitment message and then checks for equality of w_0 and $h^l(w_l)$ to transfer funds between accounts of two transaction parties.

2. If the request contains a commitment message as (4), the broker searches its database to find the corresponding entry. If there is not a related entry, the request is discarded. Otherwise, it checks for fields correctness and next verifies a signature accuracy and equality of w_0 and $h^l(w_l)$. If these results are true, it transfers funds between accounts of two transaction parties.

After processing all redemption requests that contained commitment, the broker checks other requests that have no commitment. For each of these messages, it searches the database to find an entry with *chainId* of the redemption request. If such an entry exists, it checks equality of w_0 value field and $h^l(W_l)$ to pay l units into chain owner's account.

Each broker, at the end of day, can detect fraud and punish cheater peers. As these operations are offline toward payments, they do not affect efficiency of payment transactions.

5.5 Brokers and Peers Load

PPayWord has good properties toward reducing the load of brokers, some of which are inherited from PayWord scheme, e.g., the cost of purchasing coins from broker has been eliminated and only transaction parties are involved meanwhile a chain is being spent. In addition, PPayWord has some other properties that increase its performance against the PayWord scheme. As a result of chain transference and decreasing chain generation demand in PPayWord, much lower amount of hash operations are needed by the brokers at the end of day. Signature verification operations have been decreased considerably, as well. In PPayWord, three situations may occur: (1) Two signature verifications are needed when redemption request contains commitment and corresponds to a partially used chain that has not transferred. (2) Only one signature verification is needed when redemption request contains commitment and corresponds to a transferred chain that has spent partially. (3) There is no need to verify any signature when redemption request does not contain commitment. Higher stability of relations in P2P video streaming system results in a higher chance of chains transference. In such a case, most of redemption requests will fall into two latter categories and considerable reduction in computational cost of the broker is yielded.

Broker, in an online manner, is involved only during chain transference and in the primary checking of payment accuracy with a chain. During chain transference between peers, except the first one that takes two signature verifications, only one signature verification is done by a broker. Other operations related to this transference including checking conditions and probably searching and inserting in the database have much lower overhead in comparison with signature verification. Let T denote the total number of transactions, ρ as a fraction of them that have been made with transferred chains and L_{avg} as the average length of chains. The broker approximately has checked $\frac{2 \times (1-\rho)T + \rho T}{L_{avg}}$ signatures and has answered $\frac{\rho T}{L_{avg}}$ chain accuracy queries, in an online manner. Obviously, load reduction and convenience of the broker database size is dependent on the L_{avg} value. On the other hand, this value is dependent to the extent of communication stability among peers. Hence, in a stable topology within which peers partnership links are subject to change to a lesser degree, PPayWord efficiency is higher.

Moreover, PPayWord reduces the required computations by peers. In a same scenario, the number of signature generations by peers in PPayWord and Payword schemes is nearly the same. However, chain generation demand reduction in PPayword causes lower hash operations in peers. In addition, nearly most of the transferred commitment messages between peers have the form of (4) and need only one signature verification.

5.6   Security

Robustness of PPayWord against *overspending* is similar to the PayWord scheme. Such a fraud is detected at the end of day when the broker balances accounts. Cheater peers can be punished according to policies of payment system. However, reducing effects of overspending is one of the important benefits of chain transference. This is due to the existence of offered services that have been turned to credit. In other words, a transferred overspent chain gets credit of services that are the reason of its transference and further payments with it become legal. Henceforth, reducing the chain production demand that is achieved by chain transferring also reduces possible volume of overspending by peers.

The PPayWord scheme prevents *double spending* fraud by previous owners of a chain. Suppose that peer P_i is one of the chain ch previous owners that have transferred it. P_i acts to double spend chain ch on peer P_j. In this case, verifying the accuracy of payment by P_j fails because of inequality of the Owner field of chain ch in broker's database and information of P_i.

Double spending fraud by owner of a chain succeeds but is detectable and does not bear profit. If P_i acts to spend a chain simultaneously in more than one peer, examining accuracy of the chain by the cheated peers succeeds but there are two cases:

1. The Cheated peers keep the chain for redemption and do not detect the fraud when the length of the spent chains by P_i is less than Ch_{minLen}. This case occurs when partnership between P_i and the cheated peers fails for any reason. Thus, to spend a chain with a smaller length than ch_{minLen} multiple times, peer P_i needs to change its partners repeatedly and this action decreases its service quality. On the other hand, this fraud is detectable and punishable by the broker at the end of day.
2. If the spent chain length in the cheated peers is more than Ch_{minLen}, one of them that firstly acts to transfer the chain to itself succeeds and the other cheated peers that act later fail. In such a case, both of broker and cheated peers can detect the fraud. Therefore, cheated peers discard P_i from their partners list and keep it in their blacklist for a while. Accordingly, P_i in addition to being punished by the payment system is dismissed by its partners and faces quality degradation.

PPayWord is robust against *replaying* commitment message to broker. If peer P_i replays an old commitment massage of chain ch, it cannot transfer chain ch to itself again. This is due the applied change in the Owner field of chain ch in the database of the related broker. If peer P_i tries to cheat in this way, this behavior is detected and punished by the payment system because P_i is one of the previous owners of chain ch.

Finally, if peer P_i cheats and announces length of a transferred chain more than reality, it gets no profit. Considering one-wayness property of hash function, P_i cannot produce the next hash values of the chain and use or transfer them to itself.

6 Experimental Evaluation

To give a performance evaluation of the proposed micropayment scheme, we present simulation results of PayWord and PPayWord schemes as well as a comparison of their computational and communicational costs. Computational cost is considered as the overall needed CPU cycles at broker and communicational cost is overall the transmitted payment messages volume. The OverSim simulation framework [12] is used to simulate a multi-tree P2P network for video streaming service with one video source and one broker. Video is divided to a number of substreams and is distributed over the constructed forest. Size of the network is altered between 100 and 1600 peers in an exponential manner and simulation time in all scenarios is 30 minute. Let us suppose that there is no churn and all participating peers are in the network from the beginning. It is worth mentioning that applied tree construction protocol causes parent failure and partial use of chains, even if there is no churn in the network. Every peer must join four trees to see video with full quality. Results are showed in two typical fixed lengths of chains, 10 and 20 and a chain is considered as partially used and is not transferable if its spent length is less than the configured chain length.

6.1 Computational Cost of Broker

Figure 3 shows the comparison of broker load for PPaWord with PayWord. As it seems, when most of the payments are made with transferred chains, load of the broker is divided by two, approximately. For both of the chain length configurations, results confirm the latter claim since the load of the broker in PPayWord is reduced about 40 %. We use semi-online term to point the load of a broker in case of transferring chain between peers due to the fact that this transference is online but offline against payments and do not affect their performance. Semi-online load of broker for *chain length = 20* is showed in Fig. 3. This figure shows that most of the broker workload is semi-online and there is a few job of broker in case of online checking payment accuracy and offline balancing accounts. We can adjust offline load and semi-online load of broker according to the system requirements. To this end, an upper bound for transferring every chain must be applied by adding a new column to broker's database. The value of this column is incremented one unit per chain transference and when it reaches to the considered upper bound, the chain cannot further be transferred.

6.2 Communicational Cost

Figure 4 shows that in PPayWord communication cost increases based on the length of the chains because lesser chain length means we need more commitment messages. On the other hand, unlike PayWord scheme wherein most of the messages are sent to broker at the end of day, in PPayWord this cost is distributed over time and does not make the broker as a bottleneck of the payment system. Higher stability of peers' links in the overlay structure results higher length of transferred chains which can reduce communication costs by decreasing needed commitment messages.

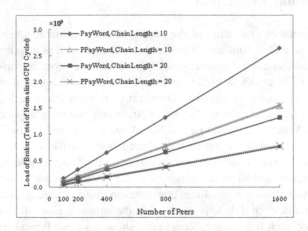

Fig. 3. Broker workload in PayWord and PPayWord schemes

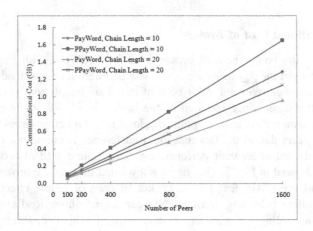

Fig. 4. Communication costs in PayWord and PPayWord schemes

7 Conclusion and Future Works

In this paper, we proposed an efficient and scalable micropayment scheme, called PPayWord. Performance of this scheme is investigated through the analytic discussion and simulations experiments. We discussed various probable risks and robustness of PPayWord against them. Simulation results verify our analysis on the load of broker and show that PPayWord causes more than 40 % reduction on the broker load. On the other side, using hash operations to do payments causes high speed of financial transactions. These two properties make PPayWord a convenient payment scheme in P2P video streaming.

PPayWord converts cooperation level of peers to some credit. Hence, this scheme can be used in designing an incentive mechanism in an efficient way. We aim to design an appropriate incentive mechanism for P2P video streaming which applies PPayWord micropayment scheme as a mean of measuring peers cooperation level. We additionally intend to tailor PPayWord for P2P streaming systems that have lower amount of communication continuation in peers' links.

References

1. Karakaya, M., Korpeoglu, I., Ulusoy, O.: Free riding in peer-to-peer networks. IEEE Internet Comput. **13**(2), 92–98 (2009)
2. Habib, A., Chuang, J.: Service differentiated peer selection: an incentive mechanism for peer-to-peer media streaming. IEEE Trans. Multimedia **8**(3), 610–621 (2006)
3. Yang, B., Garcia-Molina, H.: Ppay: micropayments for peer-to-peer systems. In: Proceedings of the 10th ACM Conference on Computer and Communication Security, pp. 300–310 (2003)
4. Rivest, R., Shamir, A., Lomas, M.: PayWord and MicroMint: two simple micropayment schemes security protocols. In: Crispo, Bruno (ed.) Security Protocols 1996. LNCS, vol. 1189, pp. 69–87. Springer, Heidelberg (1997)
5. Sirbu, M.A., Tygar, J.: NetBill: an Internet Commerce System Optimized for Network-Delivered Services, Tepper School of Business, p. 452 (2005)
6. Wei, K., Smith, A.J., Chen, Y.F.R., Vo, B.: WhoPay: a scalable and anonymous payment system for peer-to-peer environments. In: 26th IEEE International Conference on Distributed Computing Systems, pp. 13–13 (2006)
7. Catalano, D., Ruffo, G.: A fair micro-payment scheme for profit sharing in P2P networks. In: International Workshop on Hot Topics in Peer-to-Peer Systems, pp. 32–39 (2004)
8. Zghaibeh, M., Harmantzis, F.C.: A lottery-based pricing scheme for peer-to-peer networks. Telecommun. Syst. **37**(4), 217–230 (2008)
9. Vishnumurthy, V., Chandrakumar, S., Sirer, E.G.: Karma: a secure economic framework for p2p resource sharing. In: Proceedings of the Workshop of the Economics of P2P Systems (2003)
10. Aperjis, C., Freedman, M.J., Johari, R.: Peer-assisted content distribution with prices. In: 2008 Proceedings of the ACM CoNEXT Conference (2008)
11. Li, A., Liang, Y., Wu, D.: Utilizing layered taxation to provide incentives in P2P streaming systems. J. Syst. Softw. **85**(8), 1749–1756 (2012)
12. Baumgart, I., Heep, B., Krause, S.: OverSim: a scalable and flexible overlay framework for simulation and real network applications. In: Ninth IEEE International Conference on Peer-to-Peer Computing, pp. 87–88 (2009)

Missing a Trusted Reference Monitor: How to Enforce Confidential and Dynamic Access Policies?

Leila Karimi, Seyyed Ahmad Javadi, Mohammad Ali Hadavi[✉],
and Rasool Jalili

Department of Computer Engineering,
Sharif University of Technology, Tehran, Iran
{l_karimi,ajavadi,mhadavi}@ce.sharif.edu,
jalili@sharif.edu

Abstract. Popularity of data outsourcing and its consequent access control issues such as dynamism and efficiency is the main motivation of this paper. Existing solutions suffer from the potential unlimited number of user keys, inefficient update of policies, and disclosure of data owner's access control policies. Using Chinese remainder theorem and proxy re-encryption together, in this paper, we propose an efficient access control enforcement mechanism based on selective encryption that addresses all the shortages. The overall architecture, required algorithms, and access control policy update are discussed. The mechanism is evaluated through simulation and, the given results are satisfactory.

Keywords: Access control · Selective encryption · Chinese remainder theorem · Proxy re-encryption

1 Introduction

Due to reducing communication costs and increasing volume of data, Database-As-a-Service (DAS) model, in which an organization outsources its data to a database service provider, becomes a popular paradigm. Although data outsourcing provides many benefits, it introduces new security concerns. The main concern is the storage of sensitive data on a site that is not under the direct control of the data owner. As a result, the data confidentiality and integrity can be compromised. Additionally, the enforcement of access control restrictions on the outsourced data is of main concerns; the issue on which we have concentrated in this paper. In fact, access control enforcement cannot be delegated to a server, which is not trusted enough to be aware of access policies and to enforce them. A promising solution is selective encryption, which couples authorization and encryption. It translates an access policy into an equivalent encryption policy so that only legitimate users are able to retrieve the decryption key of a protected resource.

In addition to maintaining a user hierarchy and a key derivation process, enforcing access control through selective encryption faces a couple of challenges. Firstly,

© Springer International Publishing Switzerland 2014
A. Movaghar et al. (Eds.): CNDS 2013, CCIS 428, pp. 92–104, 2014.
DOI: 10.1007/978-3-319-10903-9_8

updating access policies may cause high overhead to the data owner. It needs acquiring granted/revoked resources from the server, re-encryption of them, and resending them to the server. Secondly, privacy of access control policies may be violated due to the untrustworthiness of the remote server.

In this paper, we propose a solution to overcome the above shortcomings. In particular, we address the problem of key management using the Chinese remainder theorem, and of efficiently supporting policy changes using the proxy re-encryption scheme. Using these two schemes together also ensures the privacy of authorization policies, as it is an important requirement for the data owner.

The rest of this paper is organized as follows. Section 2 reviews the related work. Section 3 is dedicated to some preliminaries and basic concepts to our solution. Section 4 describes the proposed solution for efficient access control enforcement in detail. This section also demonstrates how changes in the access control policies can be handled efficiently. Section 5 describes our proposed prototype architecture. Section 6 analyzes our solution from the security and efficiency perspectives. Finally, Sect. 7 concludes the paper.

2 Related Work

Damiani et al. [1] proposed an access control mechanism for an outsourced database using selective encryption, where they reduced the number of user keys through key derivation. Vimercati et al. [2] proposed a two-layer data encryption to enforce access control for dynamic policies. In their scheme, a public token catalogue expresses key derivation relationships. However, the catalogue could leak information about the policies and data. To solve the problem, they proposed adding an encryption layer on the public catalogue of tokens [3]. There are several shortcomings related to their scheme. The algorithm of building key derivation structure imposes high computing overhead to the data owner. An update to the access control policy requires the users to obtain new keys derived from the rebuilt key derivation structure and also requires data re-encryption with the new keys. As the consequence, the scheme is not scalable. Tian et al. [4] introduce a new DSP re-encryption mechanism, which provides an efficient policy update and management approach. Ateniese et al. [5] proposed a secure distributed storage scheme based on proxy re-encryption. Their scheme depends on the existence of a semi-trusted server. Moreover, the system data security can be compromised due to the collusion of a malicious server and any single malicious user.

In 2005, Sahai et al. [6] proposed an access control scheme, referred to as threshold encryption, based on their introduced concept of Attribute Based Encryption (ABE). In the scheme, the owner encrypts his data and specifies an attribute set and a number d. Only a user with at least d attributes of the given attribute set can decrypt the retrieved data. Wang et al. [7] combined techniques of ABE, proxy re-encryption, and lazy re-encryption to delegate most of the computation tasks involved in the revocation of authorizations to an untrusted server without disclosing data content.

Chinese Remainder Theorem (CRT) was used to propose a general access control structure when the policy enforcement point is not trusted [8]. Tourani et al. [9] then used above idea and proposed a CRT-based access control enforcement mechanism for data outsourcing scenario. Their solution allows updating policy changes, and access control policies are protected from being revealed to the server or the users.

3 Preliminaries

Let us review basic concepts and preliminaries, including CRT and proxy re-encryption before the introduction of our proposed access control enforcement mechanism.

3.1 Chinese Remainder Theorem (CRT)

Definition 1. *Chinese remainder theorem: for the system of simultaneous congruences in (1), in which $k \geq 2$, the positive integers $n_1, n_2, \ldots, n_k$ are pairwise relatively prime, and $a_1, a_2 \ldots, a_k \in \mathbb{Z}$, there exists a unique solution x, such that $0 \leq x < n = n_1 n_2 \ldots n_k$.*

$$\begin{cases} x \equiv a_1 \bmod n_1 \\ x \equiv a_2 \bmod n_2 \\ \cdots \\ x \equiv a_k \bmod n_k \end{cases} \tag{1}$$

Kong et al. [8] used CRT and proposed a scheme to share a key with k users. Suppose K_r is the key we want to share it with users $u_1, u_2, \ldots, u_k$. K_{s_i} is the private key of user u_i. Then, x_{K_r}, the solution of simultaneous congruences in (2), can be used as a shared key of K_r.

$$\begin{cases} x_{K_r} \equiv E_{K_{u_1}}(K_r) \bmod n_{u_1} \\ x_{K_r} \equiv E_{K_{u_2}}(K_r) \bmod n_{u_2} \\ \cdots \\ x_{K_r} \equiv E_{K_{u_k}}(K_r) \bmod n_{u_k} \end{cases} \tag{2}$$

When a user u_j is given a shared key x_{K_r}, he can compute K_r as follows:

$$E_{K_{u_j}}(K_r) = x_{K_r} \bmod n_{u_j} \tag{3}$$

$$K_r = D_{K_{u_j}^{-1}}(E_{K_{u_j}}(K_r)) \tag{4}$$

3.2 Proxy Re-Encryption

Definition 2. *Proxy re-encryption: Proxy re-encryption is a solution in which the data owner securely delegates the re-encryption mechanism to a proxy. The proxy re-encrypts the data without the need to decrypt any parts of the data.*

Syalim et al. [10] proposed a proxy re-encryption scheme for the symmetric ciphers, which is used in our mechanism to efficiently manage policy updates. Below, we introduce some primitive functions in symmetric proxy re-encryption scheme. Please refer to [10] for further details.

- *All or nothing transform (AONT)*: the algorithm converts a s-block message $M = m_0, \ldots, m_{s-1}$ to a pseudo message $M' = m'_0, \ldots, m'_{n-1}$ with n blocks, such that $n > s$ and any block of the original message cannot be retrieved if any block of the pseudo message is lost.
- *Perm*: the permutation algorithm *Perm* takes two sequences with the same size n as inputs and changes the order of the second sequence according to the first sequence, called "the permutation key." For example, the output of *Perm((3, 1, 2, 0),(a, b, c, d))* is *(d, b, c, a)*.
- *DePerm*: the algorithm takes two sequences as an input and changes the order of the second sequence to the form before being permuted by the *Perm* function using the first sequence as the permutation key. For example, the output of *DePerm((3, 1, 2, 0),(d, b, c, a))* is *(a, b, c, d)*.
- *FindCK*: the algorithm generates a conversion key CK, which can be used to convert a permuted sequence $POUT_A$ to another permuted sequence $POUT_B$. If $POUT_A$ is the permuted form of *InSeq* with the permutation key KP_A and $POUT_B$ is the permuted form of *InSeq* with the permutation key KP_B, then the conversion key CK has the property: $Perm(KP_B, InSeq) = Perm(CK, Perm(KP_A, InSeq))$
- *PGen*: the permutation generator function *PGen* takes a key k and an integer n as inputs and generates a permutation key A with n elements. It is implemented using the encryption function $E(k, p)$ that encrypts the plaintext p using the key k.
- *RandGen:* giving an integer n as an input, it generates an n-bit size random key.

4 Access Control Enforcement Mechanism

This section represents our proposed mechanism. At first, we describe a generic architecture for access control in the DAS model. Then, we describe our proposed mechanism based on the architecture.

4.1 Overall Framework

Figure 1 shows the system architecture for enforcing access control in the DAS model that involves following entities:

- Data owner: an organization that produces data and delegates its maintenance to the untrusted server.
- Server: an expertise database organization that receives encrypted data, is responsible to maintain it, responds to user queries, and helps the data owner in updating access control policies.
- User: an entity, whose queries are translated into queries over the encrypted data and sent to the server.

We assume that the server is honest-but-curious. It is honest in executing the protocols but is not trusted with the confidentiality of data and access control policies.

4.2   Initialization Phase

The following actions are performed by the data owner to outsource its data:

- For each user u_i of the system, the data owner generates a pair of keys $(K_{u_i}, K_{u_i}^{-1})$ and a modulus n_{u_i}.
- For each resource r of the system, the data owner generates a key K_r by which the resource is encrypted.

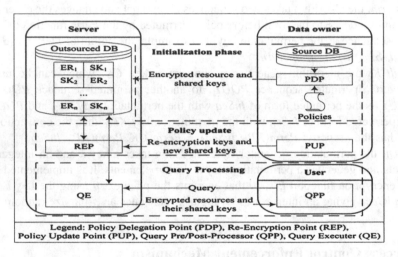

Fig. 1. Overall architecture of the proposed mechanism

- For each resource r of the system with access control list $\mathrm{ACL}(r) = \{u_1, u_2, \ldots, u_k\}$ and encryption key K_r, the data owner calculates the CRT solution x_{K_r} for the simultaneous congruences in (5).

$$
\begin{cases}
x_{K_r} \equiv E_{K_{u_1}}(K_r) \bmod n_{u_1} \\
x_{K_r} \equiv E_{K_{u_2}}(K_r) \bmod n_{u_2} \\
\quad \cdots \\
x_{K_r} \equiv E_{K_{u_k}}(K_r) \bmod n_{u_k}
\end{cases} \tag{5}
$$

For each resource r, the data owner calculates $c_r = \mathrm{SE}_{K_r}(r)$ and sends c_r and x_{K_r} to the server. Detailed explanation of the SE function is provided in Sect. 5.

4.3 Query Processing Phase

When a user u_i needs to retrieve a resource r from the server, he needs to perform the following steps with the server:

- User u_i generates a query and request r from the server.
- The server processes the query and sends c_r and x_{K_r} to u_i.
- If $u_i \in \mathrm{ACL}(r)$ then he computes K_r as follows:

$$E_{K_{u_i}}(K_r) = x_{K_r} \bmod n_{u_i} \tag{6}$$

$$K_r = D_{K_{u_i}^{-1}}\left(E_{K_{u_i}}(K_r)\right) \tag{7}$$

- User u_i accesses r using its key: $r = \mathrm{SD}_{K_r}(c_r)$. The function SD is further explained in Sect. 5.

If $u_i \notin \mathrm{ACL}(r)$, he cannot retrieve the key K_r, so he cannot access r.

4.4 Policy Update

Policy update operations can be restricted to granting and revoking an authorization. Here we describe general steps of our mechanism for updating policies.

1) Grant: Granting a new user u_i an access to a resource r does not require the key of the resource to be changed but it needs the shared key x_{K_r} to be updated. Kong et al. [8] suggest an efficient way for this purpose. Consider simultaneous congruence equations in (8) with x_{K_r} as the solution and the simultaneous congruences in (9) which contain a congruence equation for the new user u_i with x_{k_r}' as the solution.

$$\begin{cases} x_{K_r} \equiv E_{K_{u_1}}(K_r) \bmod n_{u_1} \\ x_{K_r} \equiv E_{K_{u_2}}(K_r) \bmod n_{u_2} \\ \quad\cdots \\ x_{K_r} \equiv E_{K_{u_k}}(K_r) \bmod n_{u_k} \end{cases} \tag{8}$$

$$\begin{cases} x_{k_r}' \equiv E_{K_{u_1}}(K_r) \bmod n_{u_1} \\ x_{k_r}' \equiv E_{K_{u_2}}(K_r) \bmod n_{u_2} \\ \quad\cdots \\ x_{k_r}' \equiv E_{K_{u_k}}(K_r) \bmod n_{u_k} \\ x_{k_r}' \equiv E_{K_{u_i}}(K_r) \bmod n_{u_i} \end{cases} \tag{9}$$

According to [8], the value of x_{k_r}' can be easily obtained by solving (10).

$$\begin{cases} x_{k_r}' \equiv x_{K_r} \bmod n_{u_1} n_{u_2} \ldots n_{u_k} \\ x_{k_r}' \equiv E_{K_{u_i}}(K_r) \bmod n_{u_i} \end{cases} \tag{10}$$

2) Revoke: Authorization revocation is more complicated than grant and requires changing the key of the resource. Consider a situation in which the data owner wants to revoke access to a resource r (encrypted with K_r) from a user u_i. The data owner and the server must go through following steps:

- The data owner updates ACL(r) by removing user u_i.
- The data owner generates re-encryption key REK_r using RKG function with K_r as an input.
- The data owner calculates the CRT solution x'_{k_r} according to the new ACL(r).
- The data owner sends REK_r and x'_{k_r} to the server and asks him to re-encrypt r.
- The server calculates c'_r using RE function with c_r and REK_r as inputs.

Preserving the confidentiality of r, this method re-encrypts r with a new key without imposing high computational overhead to the data owner.

5   The System Architecture

For implementing our proposed access control enforcement mechanism, we suggest the architecture shown in Fig. 2. According to Fig. 2, the proposed architecture consists of four main components discussed in the subsequent sections.

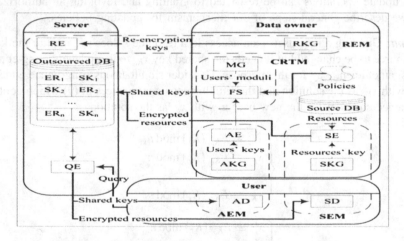

Fig. 2. The architecture of our implemented prototype

5.1   Symmetric Encryption Module

Symmetric Encryption Module (SEM) provides a symmetric key cryptosystem to encrypt resources in our system. There are three functions in this module:

1. Symmetric Key Generator (SKG): in this function three random k-bit keys K_1, K_2, and K_3 and a random b-bits key K_X are generated using *RandGen* function. Here, k is the size of key in *Pgen* algorithm and b is the size of each block of original message M in *AONT* algorithm. The resulted key is $K = (K_1, K_2, K_3, K_X)$, which is used in SE function, SD function, and REM.

2. Symmetric Encryption (SE): the function encrypts message M using the keys K_1, K_2, K_3, and K_X. Algorithm 1 shows the *SE* algorithm.
3. Symmetric Decryption (SD): the function decrypts ciphertext C using the keys K_1, K_2, K_3, and K_X. The SD algorithm is shown in Algorithm 2.

5.2   Asymmetric Encryption Module

The aim of Asymmetric Encryption Module (AEM) is to provide a public-key cryptosystem used for sharing the keys of resources. It contains three functions including, Asymmetric Key Generator (AKG), Asymmetric Encryption (AE), and Asymmetric Decryption (AD). The module can be implemented using a public-key cryptosystem such as RSA.

5.3   Re-Encryption Module

Re-Encryption Module (REM) consists of two functions to provide a proxy re-encryption mechanism for access control policy updates:

1. Re-encryption Key Generator (RKG): the function generates re-encryption keys sent to the server when policy is updated. It is implemented using Algorithm 3.
2. Re-Encryption (RE): the function is used when the data owner needs to update his policies by re-encrypting the cipher-text with the new key. Details of this function are shown in Algorithm 4.

Algorithm 1. SE algorithm

| Input: | keys K_1, K_2, K_3, and K_X, |
| | message $M = m_0, m_1, \ldots, m_{s-1}$ |
Output:	ciphertext $C = c_0, c_1, \ldots, c_{n-1}$
1.	$M' = AONT(M)$ $(M' = m'_0, \ldots, m'_{n-1})$
2.	$P_1 = PGen(K_1, b)$
3.	$P_2 = PGen(K_2, b)$
4.	$P_3 = PGen(K_3, n)$
5.	$M' = Perm(P_3, M')$
6.	$c_0 = Perm(P_1, m'_0) \oplus Perm(P_2, K_X)$
7.	From i = 1 to n-1:
	7.1 $c_i = Perm(P_1, m'_i) \oplus Perm(P_2, c_{i-1})$
8.	Return C

Algorithm 2. SD algorithm

| Input: | keys K_1, K_2, K_3, and K_X, |
| | ciphertext $C = c_0, c_1, \ldots, c_{n-1}$ |
Output:	message $M = m_0, m_1, \ldots, m_{s-1}$
1.	$P_1 = PGen(K_1, b)$
2.	$P_2 = PGen(K_2, b)$
3.	$P_3 = PGen(K_3, n)$
4.	From i = n-1 down to 1:
	4.1 $m'_i = DePerm(P_1, c_i \oplus Perm(P_2, c_{i-1}))$
5.	$m'_0 = DePerm(P_1, c_0 \oplus Perm(P_2, K_X))$
6.	$M' = DePerm(P_3, M')$ $(M' = m'_0, \ldots, m'_{n-1})$
7.	$M = AONT^{-1}(M')$
8.	Return M

Algorithm 3. RKG algorithm

Input:	keys K_1, K_2, K_3, and K_X
Output:	re-encryption key REK

1. $K_1' = RandGen(k)$
2. $K_2' = RandGen(k)$
3. $K_3' = RandGen(k)$
4. $K_X' = RandGen(b)$
5. $CK_1 = FindCK(PGen(K_1, b), PGen(K_1', b))$
6. $CK_3 = FindCK(PGen(K_3, n), PGen(K_3', n))$
7. $REK = (CK_1, CK_3, K_X, K_X', K_2, K_2')$
8. Return REK

Algorithm 4. RE algorithm

Input	re-encryption key REK=$(CK_1, CK_3, K_X, K_X', K_2, K_2')$,
	ciphertext$C = c_0, c_1, ..., c_{n-1}$
Output	ciphertext$C' = c_0', c_1', ..., c_{n-1}'$

1. $P_2 = PGen(K_2)$
2. $P_2' = PGen(K_2')$
3. From i = n-1 down to 1:
       3.1 $c_i' = Perm(CK_1, c_i \oplus Perm(P_2, c_{i-1}))$
4. $c_0' = Perm(CK_1, c_0 \oplus Perm(P_2, K_X))$
5. $C' = Perm(CK_3, C')$
6. $c_0' = c_0' \oplus Perm(P_2', K_X')$
7. From i=1 to n-1:
       7.1 $c_i' = c_i' \oplus Perm(P_2', c_{i-1}')$
8. Return C'

5.4 Chinese Remainder Theorem Module

Chinese Remainder Theorem Module (CRTM) is used by the data owner for key management. It contains two functions:

1. Modulus Generator (MG): for every user u_i, this function generates a modulus n_{s_i} such that $n_{s_1}, n_{s_2}, ..., n_{s_l}$ are pairwise relatively prime. These moduli will be used as CRT moduli.
2. Find Solution (FS): the function is used for computing the solution of simultaneous congruences in (1).

6 Theoretical and Experimental Analysis

Three main requirements for an access control enforcement mechanism in the DAS model are as follows:

1. The mechanism requires keeping a few numbers of secret keys by each user. Generally, mechanisms in which users keep a small set of secret keys are more feasible and manageable than those in which the number of keys is unlimited.

2. Efficiency of operations, especially policy updates should be acceptable. In fact, data outsourcing should not lead to unacceptable computational and storage overheads for the data owner.

3. Privacy of access control policy should be preserved. We assume that the server is honest-but-curious. The server may get some information about the content of data, if access control mechanism reveals access control policies.

We show that our proposed solution addresses these requirements, appropriately.

6.1   Number of User's Secret Keys

In our approach, each user needs to keep only a key pair (secret and public keys) to access all of her authorized resources. This advantage is a result of using CRT to compute a shared key value for each resource (x_{K_r}). Thereby, the authorized user can compute the decryption key of the resource and easily access the content of the resource. The second column of Table 1 compares our proposed mechanism with some other known solutions from this point of view. Compared to the proposals in [2, 11], and [12], in our approach the user does not need to derive lots of keys to access her permitted resources. So, accessing the resources is more efficient here and does not need several interactions with the server to drive proper keys.

Table 1. Comparison of our mechanism with some other solutions

Mechanism	Number of keys for each user	Are access policies kept confidential?
Key-derivation based mechanism [1]	More than one (based on the users hierarchy and ACLs)	Yes
Two-layer mechanism [2]	Two	No
Two-layer mechanism with encrypted tokens [14]	Two	Yes
Two-layer mechanism [15]	More than one (based on user membership in the groups)	Yes
Proposed mechanism	One pair (public and secret key)	Yes

6.2   Efficiency of Operations

In a typical selective encryption based access control enforcement mechanism, changing policy may need the update of some resources' encryption keys. Therefore, these resources should be re-encrypted using new encryption keys. Reaching this purpose necessitates conducting the three steps of receiving the resource from the server, decrypting it with the old key and re-encrypting it with the new key, and finally, sending the encrypted resource to the server.

In addition, data owner should inform the users about the key changes. Clearly in such a case, a lot of computational overheads are imposed to the data owner.

Our mechanism transfers a large portion of such computations to the server relying upon the CRT and re-encryption together. Let us investigate the computational cost of grant and revoke operations for the data owner in our solution.

Grant: as we discussed before, a data owner should find the new shared key as the solution of (10) and send it to the server to be replaced by the old one.

Revoke: re-encryption key generation and finding CRT solution x'_{k_r}, according to the new $ACL(r)$, are two main operations in a revoke process. According to the analysis in [10], re-encryption key generation needs two operations of finding conversion key (*FindCK*), four permutation key generations (*PGen*), and four random bits generations (*RandGen*). *FindCK* is cheap and *PGen* and *RandGen* are linear to a symmetric cipher operation. Thus, the re-encryption key generation function is linear to a symmetric cipher operation. On the other hand, computing the CRT solution, using an efficient algorithm suggested in [13], takes $O(tk^2)$ bit operations, where k is the number of bits of each modulus n_{u_i}, t is the number of users in $ACL(r)$, and kt is the number of bits for the CRT solution in (5). Now, we investigate on the relation between the number of users, the required bits for n_{u_i}, and the CRT solution.

Recall that a user u_i has its own modulus n_{u_i} and if $ACL(r) = \{u_1, u_2, ..., u_k\}$, then $0 \leq x_{K_r} < n_{u_1} n_{u_2} ... . n_{u_k}$. On the other hand, users' moduli are co-primes. Therefore, the maximum number of users in a system with m bits for each modulus n_{u_i} is equal to the number of prime numbers between 0 and 2^m. For a resource r whose ACL is the set U of all users, the maximum number of bits required for x_{K_r} is $m * l$ where $l = |U|$. Table 2 represents the maximum number of users and required bits for x_{K_r} based on some possible number of bits of a modulus. We use the Prime Number Theorem which proves that the number of prime numbers less than an integer n is approximately equal to $\frac{n}{\ln n}$. Therefore, finding the CRT solution in (5) takes approximately $O(k * k * \frac{2^k}{\ln k})$ bit operations where k is the size of modulus in bit. For instance, in a system with about 5900 users, finding CRT solution takes $O\left(16 * 16 * \frac{2^{16}}{\ln 16}\right)$ bit operations, in worse case, that is not an expensive process for the data owner.

Table 2. The relation between the number of users and the imposed storage cost of storing x_{K_r}

Size of user modulus	Maximum number of users	Size of x_{K_r} (in bits)
8 bit	$(2^8/ \ln 2^8) = 46$	8 * 46
16 bit	$(2^{16}/ \ln 2^{16}) = 5909$	16 * 5909
32 bit	$(2^{32}/ \ln 2^{32}) = 193635335$	32 * 193635335

6.3   Confidentiality of Access Control Policies

In our approach confidentiality of security policies is preserved against both the server and users. When the server receives a request, it sends the cipher-text and the shared key of the requested resources to the requester. However, the server cannot understand whether the user can decrypt the resource or not. Therefore, users' privileges are not revealed in the query processing scenario. Moreover, policy change in our approach does not reveal access policies to the server.

6.4 Experimental Results

We performed two series of experiments. We ran our programs on Java 2 Standard Edition (J2SE) 1.6.0 and Windows 7 with an Intel(R) Core i5 2.5 GHz processor and 6 GB of main memory. In both series, we used RSA as a public-key cryptosystem.

At first, we evaluated the efficiency of finding a CRT solution in terms of the required time for the data owner with different ACL sizes for a resource. Such a metric allows us to estimate the load on the data owner in the initialization phase as well as for the policy update. The graph in Fig. 3 illustrates the time of finding a CRT solution for a set of congruence equations. We observe that the growth is somehow linear to the size of ACL.

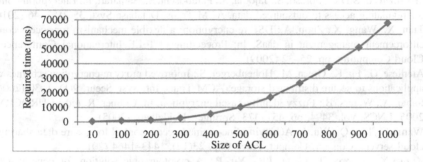

Fig. 3. Required time to find a CRT solution

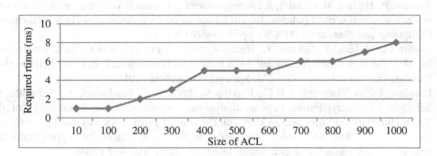

Fig. 4. Required time to drive a resource encryption key

Then, we evaluated the performance of calculating a resource key in terms of the required time for a user to derive the decryption key from a shared key (Fig. 4). Such a metric allows us to estimate the load on the user in the query processing phase. We observe in Fig. 4 that the growth is nearly linear to the size of ACL. Moreover, the time remains low for a reasonable size of ACL, e.g., 8 ms for 1000 users in an ACL.

7 Conclusions

In this paper, we address the problem of enforcing access control policies in database outsourcing scenario. Our mechanism uses Chinese remainder theorem and proxy re-encryption that results in a limited number of users' keys, the efficiency of policy changes, and the protection of access control policies from the untrusted server.

References

1. Damiani, E., di Vimercati, S.D.C., Foresti, S., Jajodia, S., Paraboschi, S., Samarati, P.: Key management for multi-user encrypted databases. In: Proceedings of the 2005 ACM Workshop on Storage Security and Survivability, pp. 74–83 (2005)
2. di Vimercati, S.D.C., Jajodia, S., Foresti, S., Paraboschi, S., Samarati, P.: Over-encryption: management of access control evolution on outsourced data. In: VLDB, pp. 123–134 (2007)
3. di Vimercati, S.D.C., Foresti, S., Jajodia, S., Paraboschi, S., Samarati, P.: Encryption policies for regulating access to outsourced data. ACM Trans. Database Syst. 35(2), 1–46 (2010)
4. Tian, X., Wang, X., Zhou, A.: DSP re-encryption: a flexible mechanism for access control enforcement management in daaS. In: Proceedingsof IEEE International Conference on Cloud Computing, pp. 25–32 (2009)
5. Ateniese, G., Fu, K., Green, M., Hohenberger, S.: Improved proxy re-encryption schemes with applications to secure distributed storage. ACM Trans. Inf. Syst. Secur. 9(1), 1–30 (2006)
6. Sahai, A., Waters, B.: Fuzzy identity-based encryption. In: Cramer, R. (ed.) EUROCRYPT 2005. LNCS, vol. 3494, pp. 457–473. Springer, Heidelberg (2005)
7. Wang, G., Liu, Q., Wu, J.: Achieving fine-grained access control for secure data sharing on cloud servers. Concurr. Comput. Pract. Exp. 23(12), 1443–1464 (2011)
8. Kong, Y., Seberry, J., Getta, J.R., Yu, P.: A cryptographic solution for general access control. In: Zhou, J., López, J., Deng, R.H., Bao, F. (eds.) ISC 2005. LNCS, vol. 3650, pp. 461–473. Springer, Heidelberg (2005)
9. Tourani, P., Hadavi, M.A., Jalili, R.: Access control enforcement on outsoured data ensuring privacy of access control policies. In: 2011 International Conference on High Performance Computing and Simulation (HPCS), pp. 491–497 (2011)
10. Syalim, A., Nishide, T., Sakurai, K.: Realizing proxy re-encryption in the symmetric world. In: Abd Manaf, A., Zeki, A., Zamani, M., Chuprat, S., El-Qawasmeh, E. (eds.) ICIEIS 2011, Part I. CCIS, vol. 251, pp. 259–274. Springer, Heidelberg (2011)
11. Damiani, E., di Vimercati, S.D.C., Foresti, S., Jajodia, S., Paraboschi, S., Samarati, P.: Selective data encryption in outsourced dynamic environments. In: Proceedings of the Second International Workshop on Views on Designing Complex Architectures, pp. 127–142
12. Zych, A., Petković, M., Jonker, W.: Efficient key management for cryptographically enforced access control. Comput. Stand. Interfaces 30(6), 410–417 (2008)
13. Menezes, A.J., Van Oorschot, P.C., Vanstone, S.A.: Handbook of Applied Cryptography. CRC, Boca Raton (1996)
14. di Vimercati, S.D.C., Foresti, S., Jajodia, S., Paraboschi, S., Pelosi, G., Samarati, P.: Preserving confidentiality of security policies in data outsourcing. In: Proceedings of the 7th ACM Workshop on Privacy in the Electronic Society, pp. 75–84 (2008)
15. Lanovenko, A., Guo, H.: Dynamic group key management in outsourced databases. In: Proceedings of the World Congress on Engineering and Computer Science, USA (2007)

An Improved Distributed Intrusion Detection Architecture for Cloud Computing

Hamid Reza Ghorbani[✉] and Mahmoud Reza Hashemi

School of Electrical and Computer Engineering,
College of Engineering, University of Tehran, Tehran, Iran
{ghorbani.it, rhashemi}@ut.ac.ir

Abstract. In recent years, cloud computing has provided a framework for dynamic and saleable use of a wide range of services. Despite the advantages of cloud, security is still one of its most challenging issues. Intrusion detection systems, as a common security tool, can be used to increase the level of security in cloud environments. However, some of the inherent features of the cloud, such as being highly distributed, the variety and dynamism of its services, and difference security needs of each user or cloud service has made conventional IDSs inefficient for this environment. In this paper, an efficient architecture for intrusion detection has been proposed for cloud computing. For this purpose, we classify services, in terms of their security requirements, into groups of services with similar security constraints. This way the intrusion detection process can be customized according to the specific attacks that usually target the services of each group. The proposed architecture has been evaluated using Snort and by customizing it for each cloud service security requirement. Simulations indicate that the proposed architecture has been able to decrease the total time of traffic analysis against attacks by 17.5 % on average, while having the same detection rate and not losing the accuracy.

Keywords: Cloud computing · Intrusion detection system · Snort · Distributed intrusion detection

1 Introduction

With the constant growth of internet processing and communication requirements of individuals and organizations, cloud computing (CC) has emerged as an effective approach to address this demands by efficiently exploiting technologies such as virtualization, distributed computing and communication networks. CC provides a scalable infrastructure and can dynamically, effortlessly, and instantly accommodate to any user computing and software need with minimum cost. Due to its inherent advantages such as high performance, availability, mobility, variety of services at affordable prices, pay as you go, improved energy efficiency and ease of use, CC has significantly expanded its market. According to a study by IDC, the number of industries that rely on public cloud service platforms will increase tenfold by 2016 [1].

A CC that is based on the public internet is subject to trust, privacy, and other security concerns [2, 3]. Unlike some distributed environments, data storage and

© Springer International Publishing Switzerland 2014
A. Movaghar et al. (Eds.): CNDS 2013, CCIS 428, pp. 105–116, 2014.
DOI: 10.1007/978-3-319-10903-9_9

processing may happen in different locations in CC, and user usually is not concerned and cannot control it. Scalability, mobility and high diversity in user's needs are other challenges of CC. These characteristics make the cloud environment vulnerable in terms of availability, confidentiality and integrity [4].

Intrusion detection systems (IDSs) are one of the main components of any network security. Network intrusions are series of unauthorized actions that attempt to compromise the confidentiality, integrity or availability of the network and computing resources [8]. As businesses rely on CC increases for a majority of their services, the risks and damages of an intrusion increases as well, so does the importance of efficient security policy. As mentioned above, another inherent feature of CC is the large amount of data generated in this environment, generally due to the large number of users and high volume of transactions between them. This can challenge the performance and efficiency of conventional intrusion detection systems. Furthermore, the distributed nature of cloud and the variety of its users and services is target of a wide range of threats and intrusions. Finally, energy consumption is another concern of cloud providers. Optimizing computational complexity and as a result reducing power requirements by using an efficient and optimized intrusion detection system can help in this regard [5].

In this paper, we propose a distributed IDS architecture for CC (DIDSCC) based on multifarious service security requirements. The proposed architecture categorizes services according to their security aspects, and identifies the threats facing each service. As a result, it can customize the intrusion detection process according to the needs of each category which can lead to a more efficient processing cost. Although, in this paper we focus on signature based IDSs, especially in our simulations, but the proposed architecture can be extended to anomaly based IDSs with minimum effort.

The paper is organized as follows. Related works are introduced in Sect. 2. Section 3 introduces the proposed architecture. Simulation results are presented in Sect. 4. Finally, the paper concludes in Sect. 5 with the concluding remarks and future works.

2 Related Work

In recent years, many researches have addressed intrusion detection, and security in CC. Some of them have worked on improving the efficiency of the IDSs.

When users and their services are known, we can customize the intrusion detection operation accordingly. Some approaches have improved efficiency by categorizing user threats or IDS alerts in terms of their severity. The objective of this categorization is to choose the most appropriate action when an alarm is raised or an attack is detected [5, 9]. Lee et al. [5] have developed a multilevel system event log management and intrusion detection system for cloud computing environment. The authors believe that various risk levels for users based on an abnormal degree specified for each user can improve the overall system performance. This level is represented by a number between one to four, and is measured based on factors such as user's behavior while using a service or the effect of a potential attack performed by this user. A central unit that acts as a decision maker determines the appropriate level of security for each user. The authors have failed to provide any quantitative results, but it seems that the proposed method does not scale well.

Roschke et al. [9] proposed to categorize services into three layers of system, platform and application. Each of these layers has its own characteristics and security concerns. They also use a central control unit to receive information from all IDSs and detect possible correlations between alarms and prevent distributed attacks. This method suffers from a single point of failure.

Some papers have improved efficiency by focusing on specific types of attacks and have proposed application-driven IDSs [8, 11]. Lo et al. [8] have suggested a cooperative framework for network intrusion detection using agents. This article focuses only on Denial of Service attack (DoS). In this framework, several intrusion detection systems have been deployed in a distributed structure. These IDSs share their knowledge bank. The disadvantage of this method is that it has focused on just one particular category of attacks.

Sander et al. [11] introduced a novel type of DDoS attack referred to as Economic Denial of Sustainability (EDoS) in cloud services and introduced a framework for defense against this attack. Due to the importance of full time availability of CC services, authors believe that traditional DoS attacks can be transformed into an Economic DoS attack in CC. This paper is focused on just DoS, as well.

Improving the efficiency of IDS has always been a concern. Some papers in this category have improved conventional IDS efficiency by determining the most important features that can detect intrusion using feature reduction methods [12]. These methods try to reduce the number of attributes and computational complexity while not significantly affecting detection rate [7, 10]. Chebrolu et al. [7] extracted the most effective features using data mining techniques before the intrusion detection process. Although data mining based intrusion detection systems aim to address the issues of processing big data, but some of the mentioned aspects of CC has made these approaches to be less efficient in terms of processing time, performance, and accuracy [21].

To summarize, as it has been stated in [2, 3, 6], most existing methods have either failed to consider the specific requirements of CC in terms of security, or have neglected the diversity in user security requirements. In this paper, a distributed IDS architecture for CC has been proposed that has improved IDS efficiency while maintaining accuracy. The proposed DIDSCC architecture is explained in more details in the next section.

3 Proposed Architecture

In this section, we present the proposed architecture. First, we provide the observations that have led to the new architecture, and then we will describe each of its components.

3.1 Observations

As mentioned before, our first observation indicates that CC environments is faced with a wide range of users, each requesting a different service, and consequently having different security requirements. These requirements not only vary from one user to the next for the same service, but also from one service to another. Applying the same security policy for all users, services and attacks may not be the most efficient approach.

In this paper, our focus is on signature based IDSs. These IDSs analyze each incoming packet against predefined rules. Clearly, some of the rules may be irrelevant to user, service, or attack. In a CC environment, where the number of users, network traffic, and number of services increases, efficient resource utilization is a major concern [13]. Efficient resource utilization, such as processing power, CPU utilization, and memory consumption has a direct impact on detection time and indirectly effect on detection rate [14].

As mentioned in [16], different services have different security concerns and priorities. For each concern, a specific set of attacks has been identified. By properly categorizing services and determining their corresponding set of attacks and rules, we can customize the IDS for each CC service category. Although a service might be more susceptible to a certain attack, and an attack may have more destructive effect on single kind of service, but it still should be protected from the remaining ones with a lower priority or importance. In other words, in a signature based IDS we need to check the rules corresponding to the former attacks first and address the lower priority rules next.

The second observation indicates that a simple but widely-applicable security model is the CIA triad; standing for Confidentiality, Integrity and Availability. Confidentiality refers to limiting information access and disclosure to authorized users, Integrity refers to preventing unauthorized modification of data and systems, and Availability refers, to the availability of information resources. Almost all network attacks can be traced to one or several of CIA elements [17, 18]. Hence in this paper we only consider these three security concerns.

In the next section we use the these two observations and present a new distributed IDS architecture to address them.

3.2 Proposed Approach

In this paper, an improved distributed IDS architecture has been proposed. In this architecture the cloud is segmented into three server groups. According to the second observation of the previous section, these three groups correspond to Confidentiality, Integrity, and Availability attacks, respectively.

For each cloud customer, according to its requested service and the attacks that this service is subject to, it will be hosted in one of these three server groups. The relation between services and attacks can be determined and announced by the CC provider or be left to the customer to select.

For example, consider a customer who wants to host its Personal Health Record service on a cloud provider. On a high level view, this service consists of two main component; namely, a portal for the introduction and delivery of services and a data storage system for patients' information. The main concern of the former is availability (e.g. being robust against DoS attacks), while the storage component should guarantee data integrity by protecting customer information and securing access to them. For some of the information, confidentiality is critical. In our scheme, the cloud provider will host each of these components in a different server group.

Each server group has its own IDS which have been customized according to the attacks that are determined in the CC policy for each of the confidentiality, integrity, and availability attacks, respectively. Although each IDS is customized for one set of attack, in order to be safe against the remaining attacks, their rules can be included selectively but with a lower priority. The rules used in each IDS can be customized based on the functionality of that IDS. The objective of this customization is to improve its performance and efficiency in resource utilization. For each customized IDS we shall improve the quality of its rules based on a functional knowledge of the IDS (and threats against it), and by tuning its rules accordingly. For example, rules that are not properly tuned can cause an IDS to waste time by redundantly checking them due to an improper sequence of rule checking. Using tuning approach, when designing IDS rules, leads to a significant improvement in performance when checking real-time traffic. The high level view of the proposed architecture has been illustrated in Fig. 1.

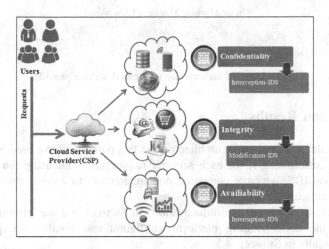

Fig. 1. An overview of the proposed IDS architecture

In the proposed architecture for each server in a server group, one instance of the customized IDS is activated on each virtual machine (VM) that corresponds to a customer cloud service. In addition, each server has an intrusion detection system manager (IDSM). The main duty of this component is to provide flexibility. For instance it can upgrade the rule set of all the IDSs on this server, it can coordinate the alerts among them to address distributed attacks to the server, it can also coordinate with the other IDSMs on other servers in the same group or servers in other groups. The detailed view of the proposed architecture is illustrated in Fig. 2.

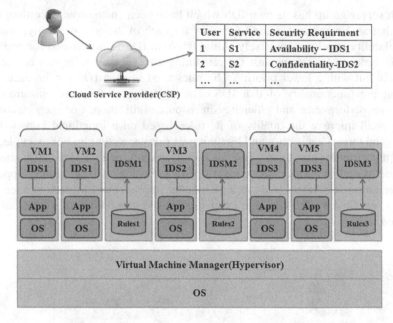

Fig. 2. Detailed architecture of a cloud service provider

4   Evaluation Results

In order to evaluate the proposed architecture, in this paper we have used Snort [14] as our IDS. By customizing it for each security requirement and using the customized version on each IDS, we have compared our architecture to a conventional non cus-tomized IDS structure.

In Subsect. 4.1 we briefly introduce Snort. In Subsect. 4.2 we introduce the used dataset and the corresponding platform configurations. Finally, we provide the simulations results in Subsect. 4.3.

4.1   Background

Snort. Snort is an open source signature based sniffer and network intrusion detections system (NIDS) utilizing a rule-driven language. It captures packets and checks their content with its predefined set of patterns and signatures. The detection engine of Snort allows registering, alerting and responding to any known attack. Snort utilizes descriptive rules to determine what traffic it should monitor and a modular detection engine to pinpoint real time attacks. When an attack is identified, Snort can take a variety of actions to alert the system administrator. Each rule has parameters that can be tuned. We use this capability to customize and configure it in order to fit our architecture.

Snort Rules. Each rule in Snort indicates intent, impact and target of an attack. A rule is what tells the engine where and what to look for in network traffic and what needs to be done if an attack has been detected. A rule in Snort consists of a header and a body (option). The header defines the traffic source. Rule headers consist of six elements: rule action, protocol type, source IP address, source port.

A rule body has over thirty optional parameters. For any Snort rule to trigger an event, all its optional rule parameters must match. It is basically a message to Snort to inspect the packets for the values that we specified in this section and determine whether it is malicious or not. This option allows rules to be classified by type of attack, and have a default priority value associated with that type. By using the two rule section values, Snort makes a rule tree from the loaded rule database, and processes each receiving packet in this tree based on packet parameter values. Figure 3 presents an example of a Snort rule.

Header [alert tcp $HOME_NET any -> $EXTERNAL_NET any

Option [(msg:"Attack-Detect "; ttl:5; flow: established;
content: "ABC"; classtype:XXXX; priority:1; rev:9;)

Fig. 3. A sample Snort rule

This rule means that if there is an established TCP stream from HOME_NET to EXTERNAL_NET that contains the string "ABC" in its payload with a ttl[1] value equal to "5", Snort should generate an alert and log a file entitled "Attack-Detect". Rules can be labeled with classifications and priority numbers to be used for grouping and distinguishing them. The rule classification, specified by the *"classtype"* keyword, determines the type of malicious traffic that the rule is designed to detect. The Priority field has two meanings: precedence of the rule in processing and analyzing traffics (rules with higher precedence or lower priority value are processed earlier) and specifies a threshold for IDS alarm generation. It should be noted that Snort has set the default priority value for each type of attack according to its destructive effect. These classifications and priorities can adjusted and we are going to use this feature in our approach for improving the quality of rules for each service type.

Snort Detection Engine. The detection engine is the most important part of Snort. Its responsibility is to detect if any intrusion activity exists in a packet using Snort rules. The computational load or speed of the detection engine depends on parameters such as number of rules, network load and the processing power of the machine that is executing Snort. One important property of Snort is its ability to search a data pattern inside a packet, with *"content"* keyword. For rules that have this property, *content* string pattern matching is one the most computationally expensive Snort processes. Hence, *content* keywords should be selectively and carefully used in IDS rules [20].

---

[1] Time to live.

The signature matching used in Snort IDS rule tree consists of two main parts: (i) packet classification, which involves examining the values of packet header fields, and (ii) deep packet inspection, in which the packet option is matched against a set of predefined patterns. The combination of header and payload search determines whether a packet is an intrusion attempt or not. According to [19], these two are the most computationally consuming parts of Snort.

Through improving IDS rules quality, by employing methods likes tuning classifications and priorities of rules, we can distinguish between high and low-risk alerts. These features are very useful when we want to differentiate high-risk alerts or want to pay attention to them first. In other words, a parameterized search will use a customized search order based on each parameter's relative ability to terminate a useless search quickly or limit the search space efficiently.

4.2 Implementation

In order to evaluate the DIDSCC architecture we used Snort (version 2.9.4.6) installed on CentOS Linux platform and used the DARPA99 dataset [15]. The DARPA dataset has five weeks of network traffic, with a list of when and where the attacks have occurred. Weeks 1–3 are for training, weeks 4–5 are for testing. The attacks in this dataset can be categorized into Probe, Denial of Service (DoS), Remote to Local (R2L) and User to Remote (U2R) attacks. In this simulation we consider R2L to exploit Confidentiality, U2R and Probe to exploit Integrity and DoS to exploit Availability.

We considered two scenarios for the evaluations and for each scenario we have three users that were assigned to three VMs and three IDSs that run in parallel. In the first scenario, based on the CIA security requirements the Snort rules have been categorized and then customized. The selected rules are presented in Table 1. In the second scenario, in all of the virtual machines the same Snort rules are deployed. In other words, rule sets and other Snort configurations are the same in all IDSs in this latter scenario.

The rule customization that is used to improve rule quality in the first scenario consists of the following two parts: (i) in each IDS group, their selected rules have the maximum priority and other rules have the normal priority. (ii) as mentioned before, Snort arranges rules using the header field and according to the *"content"*. For rules with *content* a pattern matching algorithm is used to select rules according to the *content* keyword. The optional *fast-pattern* property of the *content* keyword can be used to speed up the *content* string matching process by guiding Snort detection engine to avoid unnecessary matches. If a packet does not match the *content* keyword that has the *fast-pattern* property, we know that at least one of the rule options will not match, and an alert will never be generated. Hence, additional searches for the remaining parameters are no longer necessary and can be avoided, resulting in an improved performance [14].

Each VM has a 2.2 GHz CPU, 2 GB RAM and 50 GB Hard Disk. The virtual machines run on a Xen hypervisor. All evaluations for both scenarios are performed with the same settings and conditions.

Table 1. Selected Snort rules

IDS type	Snort rule files
Availability	dos.rules, ddos.rules, dns.rules, icmp.rules, icmp-info.rules, local.rules, netbios.rules, other-ids.rules, snmp.rules, web-cgi.rules, web-client.rules, web-iis.rules, web-misc.rules, bad-traffic.rules, attack-responses.rules, experimental.rules
Confidentiality	backdoor.rules, exploit.rules, finger.rules,ftp.rules, tftp.rules, icmp.rules, misc.rules,imap.rules, local.rules,netbios.rules, other-ids.rules, pop3.rules, rservices.rules, smtp.rules, snmp.rules, telnet.rules, web-iis.rules, web-misc.rules, web-php.rules, x11.rules,, attack-responses.rules, experimental.rules
Integrity	bad-traffic.rules, exploit.rules, misc.rules, info.rules, local.rules, mysql.rules, nntp.rules.oracle.rules, sql.rules, other-ids.rules,rpc.rules, scan,rules, shellcode.rules, web-attacks.rules, web-cgi.rules, web-coldfusion.rules, web-frontpage.rules, web-iis.rules, web-misc.rules, web-php.rules, attack-responses.rules, experimental.rules

4.3   Simulation Results

Our performance criteria consist of processing time and accuracy rate. Processing time is the required time for Snort to detect intrusions based on its preconfigured rules. This time is reported by Snort. Accuracy rate is the total percentage of detected intrusions per category. We have tested the two mentioned scenarios ten times and reported the average results in Tables 2 and 3.

Table 2. Processing time

Scenario/Time	t(s)
Scenario1- IDS 1 (Confidentiality)	228
Scenario1- IDS 2 (Integrity)	219
Scenario1- IDS 3 (Availability)	207
Scenario 2	264

Table 3. Detection rate

Scenario/Requirement	C	I	A
Scenario1- IDS 1 (Confidentiality)	84 %	56 %	82 %
Scenario1- IDS 2 (Integrity)	65 %	72 %	79 %
Scenario1- IDS 3 (Availability)	77 %	60 %	90 %
Scenario 2	88 %	76 %	94 %

As we can see above, in the first scenario with customized IDSs, the processing time has decreased by 17.5 % on average in comparison to the second scenario. This is an indication of a more efficient use of processing resources. Clearly, this customization enables our cloud provider to handle more traffic loads with the same resources.

Table 4 compares several general aspects of our proposed architecture and other approaches. In this table, "Optimized processing" property refers to performing intrusion detection processing efficiently and based on each service or security needs. "Adaptation to any customer requirement" refers to the ability to create an adjustable mapping between each service and its corresponding security requirement. "The Overall protection" implies that in addition to the ability to focus on high-priority security needs in each situation, other security requirements are also considered. "Parallelism" refers to the ability to perform the detection process in parallel. "The structure of IDS" represents how the system works in distributed or centralized mode (Fig. 2). In distributed mode, IDSs perform the intrusion detection operation individually while in other modes only one central IDS carries out the intrusion detection operation. "Scalability" means the IDS can scale as network traffic increases.

Table 4. Comparison of DIDSCC with few existing IDSs for CC

Property/System	DIDSCC	[7]	[8]	[9]
Optimized processing	✓			✓
Adaptation to any customer requirement	✓			✓
Overall Protection	✓	✓		✓
Parallelism	✓		✓	
Distributed(D)/Centralized(C) Intrusion detection	C + D	C	C + D	C
Scalability	✓		✓	

5   Conclusion and Future Work

Cloud computing has provided a framework for dynamic and saleable use of a wide range of services that can provide an infrastructure, a platform or software. Despite the advantages of cloud computing, security is a major challenge for cloud computing. In this paper, an efficient architecture for intrusion detection has been proposed for CC. The proposed distributed intrusion detection system for cloud computing (DIDSCC) has been evaluated using Snort and by optimally customizing it for each cloud service security requirement. Results from simulation, using Snort as our IDS, show that the proposed architecture is able to reduce processing time by 17.5 % on average. Also this customization enables our cloud provider to handle more traffic loads with the same resources.

In future work, we would try to configure IDSs dynamically according to the needs of services. Due to features of CC environment and diversity in service and security concerns, we can generate and configure rule and signatures based on user/service behavior or requirements dynamically. Also we can determine classes of services other than CIA model or classify security rules based on other criteria. Communication model between IDSMs of different groups and alert/message aggregation of these created models in each or between group can be extended. Also checking extra important factors such as scalability and other performance parameters like false alarm rate can be the next step for improving the proposed architecture.

References

1. TOP 10 PREDICTIONS, IDC Predictions 2013: Competing on the 3rd Platform. http://www.idc.com/research/Predictions13/downloadable/238044.pdf
2. Tanzim Khorshed, Md., Shawkat Ali, A.B.M., Wasimi, S.A.: A survey on gaps, threat remediation challenges and some thoughts for proactive attack detection in cloud computing. Future Gener. Comput. Syst. 28(6), 833–851 (2012)
3. Subashini, S., Kavitha, V.: A survey on security issues in service delivery models of cloud computing. J. Netw. Comput. Appl. 34(1), 1–11 (2011)
4. Zissis, D., Lekkas, D.: Addressing cloud computing security issues. Future Gener. Comput. Syst. 28(3), 583–592 (2012)
5. Lee, J.-H., Park, M.-W., Chung, T.-M.: Multi-level intrusion detection system and log management in cloud computing. In: 13th Interntional Conference on Advanced Communication Technology (ICACT), Seoul, pp. 552–555 (2011)
6. Modi, C., Patel, D., Borisaniya, B., Patel, H., Patel, A., Rajarajan, M.: A survey of intrusion detection techniques in Cloud. J. Netw. Comput. Appl. 36(1), 42–57 (2013)
7. Chebrolu, S., Abraham, A., Thomas, J.P.: Feature deduction and ensemble design of intrusion detection systems. Comput. Secur. 24(4), 295–300 (2005)
8. Lo, C.-C., Huang, C.-C., Ku, J.:A cooperative intrusion detection system framework for cloud computing networks. In: 39th International Conference on Parallel Processing Workshops (ICPPW), San Diego, vol. 39, pp. 280–284 (2010)
9. Roschke, S., Cheng, F., Meinel, C.: Intrusion detection in the cloud. In: 8th IEEE International Conference on Dependable, Autonomic and Secure Computing, Chengdu, pp. 729–735 (2009)
10. Tsamardinos, I., Aliferis, C.F., Statnikov, A.: Time and sample efficient discovery of Markov blankets and direct causal relations. In: 9th ACM SIGKDD International Conference on Knowledge Discovery and Data Mining, pp. 673–678 (2003)
11. Sander, V., Shenai, S.: Economic denial of sustainability (edos) in cloud services using http and xml based ddos attacks. Int. J. Comput. Appl. 41(20), 11–16 (2012)
12. Nguyen, H.H., Harbi, N., Darmont, J.: An efficient local region and clustering-based ensemble system for intrusion detection. In: 15th Symposium on International Database Engineering & Applications, pp. 185–191 (2011)
13. Armbrust, M., Fox, A., Griffith, R., Joseph, A.D., Katz, R., Konwinski, A., Lee, G., Patterson, D., Rabkin, A., Stoica, I., Zaharia, M.: A view of cloud computing. Commun. ACM 53, 50–58 (2010)
14. Snort-Homepage. https://www.snort.org/
15. Darpa 99 Intrusion detection data set. http://www.ll.mit.edu/mission/communications/cyber/CSTcorpora/ideval/data/1999data.html
16. National Institute of Standards and technology (NIST), Computer Security Devision, Special Publications Series (800 Series). http://csrc.nist.gov/publications/Pubs3Ps.html

17. Stoneburner, G.: Underlying Technical Models for Information Technology Security. Technical Report. NIST SP 800-33, United States (2001)
18. Greene, S.: Security Policies and Procedures: Principles and Practice. Prentice-Hall Inc., Upper Saddle River (2005)
19. Fisk, M., Varghese, G.: Fast Content-Based Packet Handling for Intrusion Detection. Technical report, University of California at San Diego (2001)
20. Yoshioka, A., Shaikot, S.H., Kim, M.S.: Rule hashing for efficient packet classification in network intrusion detection. In: 17th International Conference on Computer Communications and Networks (ICCCN), US Virgin Island, pp.1–6 (2008)
21. Meenakshi, R.M., Saravanan, E.: A data mining analysis and approach with intrusion detection/prevention with real traffic. In: IJCA Proceedings on EGovernance and Cloud Computing Services, EGOV(4), pp. 13–17 (2012)

Detection of Sybil Nodes in Mobile Sensor Networks Using the Context of Nodes Mobility

Rezvan Almas-Shehni[1](✉) and Karim Faez[2]

[1] Department of Electrical, Computer and Biomedical Engineering, Qazvin Branch,
Islamic Azad University, Qazvin, Iran
r.a.shehni@gmail.com
[2] Department of Electrical Engineering, Amirkabir University of Technology,
Tehran, Iran
kfaez@aut.ac.ir

Abstract. With the deployment of wireless sensor network applications in several fields such as military, the need to improve the security and detection attacks of these networks will also become more important. Sybil attack is one of the serious attacks in this network that a malicious node with the publication of his several fake IDs wants to corrupt several network operations such as routing protocols, data aggregation and voting. Due to the mobility of nodes and also variable network topology in the mobile sensor network, detection of this attack is more difficult. In this paper, a lightweight algorithm based on the context of node mobility is proposed to detect the Sybil in the mobile sensor networks. Simulation results using J-SIM indicates that the algorithm is able to detect the malicious nodes up to 99 % and also the false detection rate of nodes in the proposed method is lower than 2 % even the Sybil nodes are added to the network.

Keywords: Mobile sensor networks · Sybil attack · Watchdog node

1 Introduction

Wireless sensor network is a kind of Ad-Hoc networks that is employed in some applications such as military, environment, Medicine, explorations and so on. Each sensor network contains a large number of small sensor nodes which have small memory and low power. In addition, broadcast nature of data and operation without keeping also with increasing of applications of wireless sensor networks necessitate the implementation and improvement of security in this kind of networks which are considered by many researchers [2,16].

Sybil attack is one of the known attacks on wireless sensor networks. In this attack, the legitimate node captured or an illegitimate node is inserted to the network by the adversary are called malicious nodes. These nodes present multiple identities which are Fabricated or are Stolen from the other legitimate nodes in the other parts of network. After the development of malicious nodes

© Springer International Publishing Switzerland 2014
A. Movaghar et al. (Eds.): CNDS 2013, CCIS 428, pp. 117–128, 2014.
DOI: 10.1007/978-3-319-10903-9_10

in the network, the nodes are presented a large number of Sybil ID and neighboring nodes think have many neighbor so, the traffic of Sybil nodes is made traffic around themselves where it may be affected on routing protocol and some operations such as data aggregation, resource allocation, voting and detection of misuse [7,16].

On the fixed wireless sensor networks, some methods [4,5,9,13,14,17] are proposed for the detection of Sybil nodes while these methods are useless for the detection of Sybil nodes in the mobile sensor networks because most of these algorithms are based on the location of nodes or the Received Signal Strength Characteristics (RSSI) or neighborhood information. Therefore a new method should be proposed to identify the Sybil nodes in the mobile sensor networks.

In [10,15], some algorithms are introduced to countermeasure the Sybil attack in the mobile Ad-Hoc networks. Also in [12,13], some new solutions are employed to detect the Sybil nodes in the mobile sensor networks. In [12], the proposed method is high complexity and based on the base station. In [13], the main algorithm is based on the node ID and the detection process of Sybil attack is applied using the registration of nodes in the base station. Both of the methods in [12,13] are based on the base station and so suffer from the scalability.

This paper, we present a lightweight, accurate and practical algorithm to identify Sybil Nodes in mobile wireless sensor networks so that it can eliminate the disadvantages of previous algorithms. This paper is organized in the following way: Sect. 2 contains the previous works. In Sect. 3, system assumptions and attack model are described. The proposed method will be presented in Sect. 4 and the evaluation of proposed method is shown in Sect. 6. Finally, the paper is concluded in Sect. 7.

2 Related Works

The Sybil attack is introduced for the first time in [5] for the peer-to-peer networks. According to [7], this attack is serious threat in the sensor networks which can be harmful to many important functions of the sensor network such as voting, resource allocation, routing, data aggregation, misuse detection. In [9], the detailed analysis of the attack in wireless sensor networks is done and some mechanisms were proposed to defend against it. Also, the taxonomy of Sybil attack is shown in [9] which are referenced by the most researchers. In [9], several methods have been introduced to detect attacks Sybil: (1) radio source test; (2) random key pre-distribution; (3) Position Verification; (4) Code attestation.

In [20], a placement algorithm based on RSSI provided that uses the ratio of RSSIs from several receivers to estimate the location of nodes in the networks. In [4], the proposed method of [20] is applied on the detection of Sybil nodes. It uses four monitoring node to detection which is able listen to packets. In this method, the location of each packet sender is estimated by the association of all monitoring nodes where these estimated locations are sufficient for identification of Sybil nodes. It is important that the Sybil nodes are located in the same place.

In [14], a new method of Sybil node detection is introduced for fixed sensor networks that uses information of neighbors and is not required to hardware or signal strength. This distributed algorithm based on no base station and node trackers. A different method for the detection of attacks on multicast routing protocol based on geographical location of Sybil nodes is provided in [3].

In [8], another method based on the advance RSSI is proposed to identify the Sybil nodes when nodes adjust their transmission power. The proposed method in [6] is focused on the detection of Sybil nodes in the networks which employs Leach protocol for the classification task. This algorithm is based on the RSSI mechanism and the main result of paper is that the Sybil nodes increase the number of cluster headers and the result can be employed for the detection of Sybil nodes.

Another algorithm on Sybil attack detection is presented in [17] where Time Difference Arrival (TDOA) between source node and beacon nodes is used to identify the Sybil attack and the location of Sybil nodes. Due to the Sybil nodes can create multiple IDs and also are located in the same physical location, the main idea of [19] is that beacon nodes identifies the Sybil nodes where their signal phase difference is less than the threshold value (which is calculated by assessing the degree of accuracy of the neighboring sensor nodes). In [10,15], several algorithms to identify Sybil nodes in mobile Ad-Hoc networks have been proposed. An algorithm to defend against wormhole and Sybil attacks in multicast routing protocols based on location is proposed in [11].

Other methods of Sybil nodes detection are proposed in [12,13]. The algorithm [12] contains three phases. In the first phase, with participation base stations and according to the number of packets dropped, some of nodes are selected as valid nodes and head nodes. Then according to the received power of packet from other nodes in cluster, detection the Sybil nodes. In the second phase, the nodes close to Sybil node must simultaneously send messages to Sybil node. Because all Sybil nodes are related to a same physical node, collision occurred, so the Sybil nodes are identified due to collisions. In the third phase, routing scheme is checked to verify whether an intermediate node exists between the Sybil nodes or not; if it exists, the nodes are non-Sybil otherwise they are considered as the Sybil nodes. The proposed method in [13] is based on the registration of node in the base station. The algorithm consists of two phases and the node identifier assignment is done dynamically. These algorithms have a scalability problem.

3   System Assumption and Attack Model

Sensor network consists of two node sets, Sensor Node (SN) and Watchdog Node (WN). The task of SN nodes are gathering information, sending data to the base station and so on. The WN nodes are responsible for the task of identifying Sybil nodes. Each node has a unique identifier and is not aware of its location. Radio range of all nodes are set to r. Sensor nodes, SN and WN nodes, are mobile and moves according to mobility models such as Random Way point. The SN nodes are not robust against influence. When the adversary captures a node can access to confidential information and reprograms the captured nodes. It can be assumed that the WN nodes are robust against influence and cannot reprogram the captured nodes. Also, with the considering the mobility of sensor nodes in the environment, the nodes should sends a message such as "Hello", route request, data transferring and so on (in every t units of time or after a new location of nodes in the network) [10]. This is actually one of the requirements of mobile sensor network that each node is able to identify its neighbors at each time. If the node needs to communicate with its neighbors, it sets up the secure keys with them and creates its routing table. In this paper, it is assumed that the WN nodes are hidden because they are responsible to detect the Sybil nodes.

According to [9], in this paper, the attack model of Sybil nodes are direct, simultaneous and fabricated IDs. Suppose that a network is insecure and the adversary captures M sensor nodes of the network, then reprogram them and insert them as the malicious nodes to the network. After the development of malicious nodes in the network, number of S fake IDs (the Sybil nodes) is presented. Also, assume that the malicious nodes in networks as sensor nodes have mobility. The final assumption, if the malicious node in the network moves to a new place, it sends a message "Hello" or a route request message to other nodes for each Sybil identifiers (according to the Sybil attack model [9]). This last assumption is required to affect the attack by the adversary because the Sybil node can disorder the routing protocol or affect on the operation of network such as data aggregation, resource allocation and so on if the Sybil node releases all its IDs at the same time.

4   Proposed Method

As the mentioned before, a sensor network consists of two sets of WN and SN nodes where the task of SN nodes are gathering information, sending data to the base station and while the WN nodes are responsible for the task of identifying Sybil nodes. with the considering the mobility of sensor nodes in the environment, the nodes should sends a message such as "Hello", route request, to introduce to other nodes (in every t units of time or after a new location of nodes in the network). The WN node transmits with no SN nodes or other WN nodes and so, the Sybil node will be hidden from sensor and malicious nodes. Sybil detection procedure of nodes in the proposed algorithm consists of two phases:

4.1   Phase I (Registration of Context of Mobility Nodes)

In this phase, each WN node registers the information about mobility of other nodes independently in a matrix called M_{occur} (Fig. 1). This phase is composed of n iterations which the ith iteration is shown with R_i. In this figure, H refers to the total number of Sybil and SN nodes where it is set to where $|SN|$, M and S are the total number of SN nodes, malicious nodes and Sybil IDs therefore, the total number of Sybil nodes equals to $|SN| + M * S$.

Each WN node in cell $[ID_i ID_j]$ of its matrix M_{occure} shows the number of times that the both or just one of the ID_i and ID_j nodes are appeared in its

	ID_2	ID_3	ID_4	ID_5	...	ID_{H-1}	ID_H
ID_1							
ID_2							
ID_3							
ID_4							
ID_5							
				...			
ID_{H-1}							

Fig. 1. Structure of matrix M_{occur}.

neighborhood. It should be noted that the initial values of all cells of this matrix is set zero. Assume that the neighboring set of a WN node in R_k is $Set_n eighbor = ID_2, ID_5, \cdots$. At the first time, the value of cells $[ID_i, ID_j]$ (or $[ID_j, ID_i]$) of matrix M_{occure} will be incremented if $(ID_i, ID_j) \in Set_n eighbor$. Then, for every two nodes $(ID_i ID_l)$ that $ID_i \in Set_n eighbor$ and $ID_l \notin Set_n eighbor$, the value of cells $[ID_i ID_l]$ (or $[ID_l ID_i]$) of matrix M_{occure} will be decreased. Hence, after n rounds of registration, the value in each cell $[ID_i, ID_j]$ of M_{occur} matrix for a WN node is obtained using (1):

$$[ID_i, ID_j] = P_{ij} - p_{i \varepsilon j} - p_{j \varepsilon i} \tag{1}$$

where p_{ij} is the number of nodes in the neighborhood of the WN node. $p_{i \varepsilon j}$ is the number of times that the node ID_i without node ID_j is appeared in neighboring of the WN node and in this way, $p_{j \varepsilon i}$ is the number of times that the node ID_j without node ID_i is appeared in neighboring of the WN node.

4.2   Phase 2 (Detection of Sybil Nodes)

After the first phase, each WN node independently specifies the Sybil nodes according to its M_{occure} matrix. It means that each WN node checks its M_{occure} matrix and identify the nodes ID_i and ID_j as the Sybil nodes if the value of cell $[ID_i ID_j]$ is greater than a threshold $T_s > 0$ and finally, the IDs of ID_i and ID_j are added to the Sybil list (called $Sybil_l ist$). If the value of cell $[ID_i ID_j]$ is positive, it means that both of the nodes ID_i and ID_j are located as the neighboring of the WN node in the most cycles (or all cycles) because the Sybil nodes are simultaneously moved and located as the neighbors of the WN node.

However, in two cases, there may be occurred that some legitimate nodes (non-Sybil) are detected as the Sybil nodes mistakenly. In the first case, a legitimate node with the Sybil nodes are (randomly in one or more rounds) placed around a WN node and so, value of the cell related to this node and the other Sybil nodes, will be positive. The second case is that both of the legitimate nodes ID_i and ID_j of a network are presented simultaneously around a WN node or absent simultaneously and therefore the value of cell $[ID_i ID_j]$ will be positive.

To defend against such situations, it is possible to increase the value of n and so, the probability of occurring of this situation is greatly reduced. At the end of the second phase, the WN nodes give the $Sybil_list$ to the base station in order to inform the entire of network from Sybil nodes.

5   Computational, Communication and Memory Overhead

Memory overhead is amount of memory that is occupied in the implementation of the algorithm and is equal to $H \times H$ where the parameter H is computed as follows:

$$H = |SN| + M * S \tag{2}$$

It should be noted that the memory overhead is appeared in the WN nodes while the network nodes do not need to maintain additional data in their memories.

Communication overhead is the number of packets that the security algorithm is utilized to identify Sibel nodes in the network. The proposed algorithm is free of the overhead due to one-way communication between watchdog nodes and other nodes in the network and packets can only be sent to the sink node to identify the Sibel notes.

Computational overhead is the operations which is imposed due to the use of the proposed algorithm and is equal to the navigate and edit matrix with size of $H \times H$ in order to find the elements which are greater than a threshold and finally the time complexity is equal to $O(n^2)$.

6   Simulation Results

In this section, we conduct some tests to evaluate the performance of the proposed algorithm which is compared with other existing algorithms. The proposed method is simulated in $J - SIM$ Simulator [1] and compared with other algorithms presented in [3,6,8]. Our evaluation criteria to evaluate the performance are as the same in [20]:

True Detection Rate (TDR): Percentage of Sybil nodes identified by the algorithm.

False Detection Rate (FDR): Percent of the SN nodes identified as Sybil nodes mistakenly.

The parameters of simulation are, the total number of network nodes is shown by N, $|WN| = q$ is the number of WN nodes and M is malicious node. Nodes are randomly developed in an area of 100×100 m. Each malicious node generates S fabricated IDs. The radio range of all nodes is set as the same and equals to 10 meters. In all tests, $T_s = 1$ and. Also, we considered the movement model proposed in [18] to move all nodes in the network. In order to ensure the validity of the results, each simulation was reiterated 50 times and the final results is obtained from the average results of 50 repetitions.

Test 1. In this Test, the performance of the proposed algorithm in terms of TDR of Sybil nodes has been studied and the parameters are set as $S = 10$,

$q = 4$, $M = 5$, $N = 300$. Figure 2 shows the results of proposed algorithm for the iteration of 20 to 160 times. As is clear from Fig. 2, results of TDR are increased when the number of iteration is increased and after 100th iteration, the proposed algorithm obtains the TDR of 99 %. In 20th iteration, the measure of TDR is low because the context of mobility of nodes is required for true detection. After increasing of iteration, context of mobility of nodes is achieved, so the TDR will be increased.

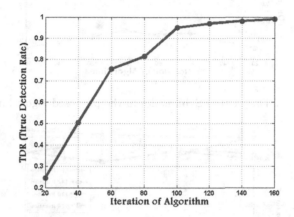

Fig. 2. The TDR of Sybil nodes in the proposed algorithm.

Test 2. The Test is applied to evaluate the FDR measure of algorithm for $S = 10$, $q = 4$, $M = 5$, $N = 300$. Figure 3 presents the testing results of proposed method for the iteration of 20 to 160 times. According to Fig. 3, the obtained FDR has a little fluctuation because we considered that the value of cell of matrix M_{occure} related to a legitimate node which is not appear around the WN node, will be decreased. As can be seen in Fig. 3, this mechanism forces the algorithm to achieve the FDR of 1 % even in high iteration.

Test 3. This Test is used to evaluate the effect of number of Sybil IDs on the performance of the proposed algorithm on the TDR and FDR. In this test, the parameters are set to as $q = 4$, $M = 5$, $N = 300$. The results of this test are shown in Figs. 4 and 5. Figure 4 illustrates the effect iteration of algorithm on the TDR. As can be observed in Fig. 4, better results have been achieved when the iteration of algorithm is increased. So that, with increasing of Sybil nodes, the TDR is linearly increased (in 160_{th} iteration). Due to the mobility of nodes, the higher correct detection rate obtained iteration of 160 is better than other iterations. Since the number of nodes in a network is fixed, increasing the number of Sybil nodes increases the density of Sybil nodes and detection of Sybil node is easier so the TDR will be improved. As can be shown in Fig. 5, increasing the number of Sybil nodes is affectless on the FDR measure and this value is lower than the 1 % and is not exceeded than 3 %. In this figure, the effect of

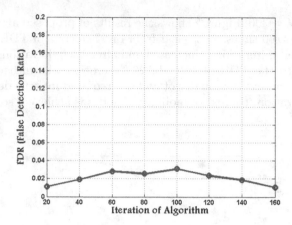

Fig. 3. The FDR of Sybil nodes in the proposed algorithm.

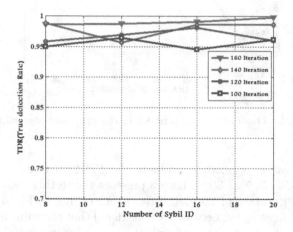

Fig. 4. Effect of number of Sybil IDs on the TDR measure in the proposed algorithm.

iteration of algorithm on the FDR measure is presented that increasing it, can keep the value around 1 % (minimum value).

Test 4. In this test, the effect of number of network nodes on the FDR measure has been studied. In this Test, the parameters are set as $S = 14, q = 4, M = 5$. The results of this test on the TDR measure are illustrated in Fig. 6. Since the number of Sybil nodes are fixing, increasing the number of nodes in a network decreases the density of Sybil nodes and so it can be hard to detect correctly and finally the TDR measure will be decreased to 90 %. This rate is increased to 99 % when the iteration of algorithm is increased.

In Fig. 7, the FDR measure will be shown. According to the Fig. 7, FDR is increased to 5 % because the density of Sybil nodes is decreased and if the iteration of algorithm increase, pplied on the detection of Sybil this rate will be decreased to 1.5 %.

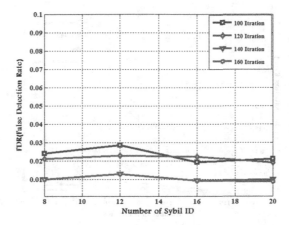

Fig. 5. Effect of number of Sybil IDs on the FDR measure in the proposed algorithm.

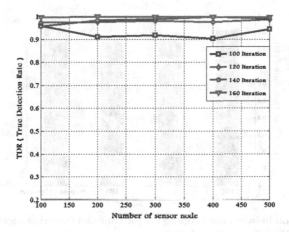

Fig. 6. Effect the number of nodes on the TDR measure in the proposed algorithm.

Test 5. The performance of the proposed algorithm and other algorithms are compared in terms of averaged TDR. As can be observed in Fig. 8, the rate of Sybil nodes (in average) in the methods proposed in [3,6,8] are 92%, 90% and 98%, respectively. According to Fig. 8, the values of aforementioned algorithms are lower than our proposed method that shows the superiority of the proposed method to the other methods. Other algorithms often used method of determining the location of nodes. And they are based on the energy level of nodes in the network or just based on the neighborhood information. While the proposed algorithm does not require determining the locations of nodes, or it does not need to check the node energy level and this algorithm is based on the nodes mobility.

Figure 9 shows the average false detection rate of the proposed algorithm and other algorithms. The results of this comparison show that the average false

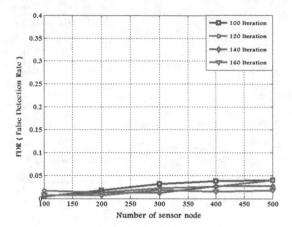

Fig. 7. Effect the number of nodes on the FDR measure in the proposed algorithm.

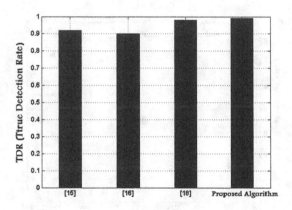

Fig. 8. Comparison between the proposed algorithm and the other algorithms in terms of average of TDR of the Sybil nodes.

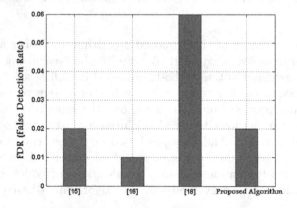

Fig. 9. Comparison between the proposed algorithm and the other algorithms in terms of average of FDR of the Sybil nodes.

detection rate in proposed algorithm is lower than the average false detection rate in other algorithm except the algorithms proposed in [6].

In [6], it is just considered the special case of Sybil attack where malicious node attempts to be selected as the cluster heads in LEACH and the Sybil nodes are detected by the base station. So the false detection rate in this algorithm is lower than the other algorithms.

7 Conclusion

This paper presented a new algorithm, using WN node and context of node mobility for the identification of Sybil nodes in mobile sensor networks. The algorithm is able to detect the Sybil node up to rate 99 %. This algorithm is successful in false detection rate of legitimate nodes, so that the value of the number of rounds in high run times is less than 1 %. The proposed algorithm is also compared with other algorithms. The results indicate good performance of the proposed algorithm in comparison to the other algorithms which is discussed previously. The results illustrate the appropriate performance of the proposed algorithm in terms of average TDR and the average FDR in comparison to the other algorithms.

References

1. J-sim simulator. http://www.j-sim.org
2. Akyildiz, I., Su, W., Sankarasubramaniam, Y., Cayirci, E.: A survey on sensor networks. IEEE Commun. Mag. 40(8), 102–114 (2002)
3. Chen, S., Yang, G., Chen, S.: A security routing mechanism against sybil attack for wireless sensor networks. In: 2010 International Conference on Communications and Mobile Computing (CMC), vol. 1, pp. 142–146 (2010)
4. Demirbas, M., Song, Y.: An RSSI-based scheme for sybil attack detection in wireless sensor networks. In: Proceedings of the 2006 International Symposium on World of Wireless, Mobile and Multimedia Networks, WOWMOM '06, Washington, DC, USA, pp. 564–570. IEEE Computer Society (2006). http://dx.doi.org/10.1109/WOWMOM.2006.27
5. Douceur, J.R.: The sybil attack. In: Druschel, P., Kaashoek, M.F., Rowstron, A. (eds.) IPTPS 2002. LNCS, vol. 2429, p. 251. Springer, Heidelberg (2002)
6. Jangra, A., Swati, P.: Securing LEACH Protocol from Sybil Attack using Jakes ChannelScheme (JCS). In: Proceeding of International Conference on Advances in ICT for EmergingRegions 2011 (2011)
7. Karlof, C., Wagner, D.: Secure routing in wireless sensor networks: attacks and countermeasures. In: Proceedings of the First IEEE International Workshop on Sensor Network Protocols and Applications, pp. 113–127 (2003)
8. Misra, S., Myneni, S.: On identifying power control performing sybil nodes in wireless sensor networks using RSSI. In: Global Telecommunications Conference (GLOBECOM 2010), pp. 1–5. IEEE (2010)
9. Newsome, J., Shi, E., Song, D., Perrig, A.: The sybil attack in sensor networks: analysis defenses. In: Third International Symposium on Information Processing in Sensor Networks, IPSN 2004, pp. 259–268 (2004)

10. Piro, C., Shields, C., Levine, B.: Detecting the sybil attack in mobile ad hoc networks. In: Securecomm and Workshops 2006, pp. 1–11 (2006)
11. Ramachandran, S., Shanmugan, V.: Impact of sybil and wormhole attacks in location based geographic multicast routing protocol for wireless sensor networks. J. of Comput. Sci. **7**(7), 1–973 (2011)
12. Sharmila, S., Umamaheswari, G.: Detection of sybil attack in mobile wireless sensor network. Int. J. Eng. Sci. Adv. Technol. [IJESAT] **2**(2), 256–262 (2012)
13. Sharmila, S., Umamaheswari, G.: Node ID based detection of sybil attack in mobile wireless sensor network. Int. J. Electron. **100**(10), 1441–1454 (2013). http://www.tandfonline.com/doi/abs/10.1080/00207217.2012.743093
14. Ssu, K.F., Wang, W.T., Chang, W.C.: Detecting sybil attacks in wireless sensor networks using neighboring information. Comput. Netw. **53**(18), 3042–3056 (2009). http://www.sciencedirect.com/science/article/pii/S1389128609002394
15. Vasudeva, A., Sood, M.: Sybil attack on lowest ID clustering algorithm in the mobile Ad hoc network. Int. J. Netw. Secur. Appl. **4**(5), 1–135 (2012)
16. Walters, J.P., Liang, Z., Shi, W., Chaudhary, V.: Wireless sensor network security: a survey. In: Xiao, Y. (ed.) Security in Distributed, Grid, Mobile, and Pervasive Computing, vol. 1, pp. 311–367. Auerbach Publications, CRC Press, Boca Raton (2007)
17. Wen, M., Li, H., Zheng, Y.F., Chen, K.F.: TDOA-based sybil attack detection scheme for wireless sensor networks. J. Shanghai Univ. (English Edition) **12**(1), 66–70 (2008). http://dx.doi.org/10.1007/s11741-008-0113-2
18. Yu, C.M., Lu, C.S., Kuo, S.Y.: Mobile sensor network resilient against node replication attacks. In: 5th Annual IEEE Communications Society Conference on Sensor, Mesh and Ad Hoc Communications and Networks, SECON'08, pp. 597–599. IEEE (2008)
19. Zhang, Y., Fan, K.F., Zhang, S.B., Mo, W.: AOA based trust evaluation scheme for sybil attack detection in WSN. Appl. Res. Comput. **27**(5), 1847–1849 (2010)
20. Zhong, S., Li, L., Liu, Y.G., Yang, Y.R.: Privacy-preserving location-based services for mobile users in wireless networks. Yale Computer Science, Technical report, YALEU/DCS/TR-1297 (2004)

Clouds and Grids

A Two-Level Energy-Aware ILP Formulation for Application Mapping on a Mobile Cloud Infrastructure

Hamid Tabani[✉] and Mahmoud Reza Hashemi

Multimedia Processing Laboratory, School of Electrical and Computer
Engineering, College of Engineering, University of Tehran, Tehran, Iran
{tabani, rhashemi}@ut.ac.ir

Abstract. Despite recent progresses in mobile technology, processing power and energy constraints are still the two main challenges of mobile devices. The processing constraint has been addressed in recent years with the introduction of the concept of mobile cloud computing where a computationally intensive task is distributed among several mobile devices each consisting of an MPSoC. Application mapping and scheduling in the mobile cloud environment is an important and also complex issue. The mapping result has a significant impact on both performance and energy consumption of the MPSoC platforms. The goal of this paper is to efficiently distribute application tasks among heterogeneous NoC-based MPSoCs. In this paper, we propose an ILP formulation that considers the two levels of intra-device and inter-device simultaneously to reach an optimal mapping. In this framework, an application is represented by its task graph. We assume that each application should meet its own deadline while the overall energy consumption that consists of both communication and computation energies should be minimized. Experimental results indicate that the proposed method consumes 8 % less energy on average, in comparison with an ILP method with the aim of minimizing just computation energy consumption. The energy reduction of the proposed scheme is more than 23 % on average in comparison to a Genetic based mapping method.

Keywords: Task mapping · Integer linear programming · Heterogeneous MPSoC · Mobile cloud computing

1 Introduction

In recent years, we have witnessed a rapid growth in mobile technologies. Mobile devices such as smartphones, tablets, and netbooks have not only gained popularity, but their processing power is increasing each day. Most such devices benefit from a multi-core processing element and a large amount of memory. This increased processing capability along with the global increase in access to mobile broadband networks has created the new paradigm of mobile cloud computing (MCC) [1]. Similar to conventional cloud computing, MCC helps overcome some of the inherent limitations of mobile environments such as processing power constraints, limited battery life, and

© Springer International Publishing Switzerland 2014
A. Movaghar et al. (Eds.): CNDS 2013, CCIS 428, pp. 131–144, 2014.
DOI: 10.1007/978-3-319-10903-9_11

bandwidth by exploiting the advantages of the cloud. The mentioned constraints, specially when a mobile device has to run multiple applications, may well justify offloading tasks to other available devices despite the extra costs and delays of an off-chip network.

Energy consumption is still a main concern in most mobile platforms. In recent years, power management and power reduction have become critical issues not only in conventional cloud environments where we are dealing with server farms, but also in mobile environments where the tasks of a complex application is distributed among several connected mobile devices. Hence, energy reduction is one of the main objectives of any mapping algorithm [2]. Generally, we can model the total energy consumption of a distributed system as a combination of computation and communication energy components. Communication energy is the energy that is consumed by network components when data is transmitted from one node to another, while computation energy represents the total energy that is consumed by the PEs. Most recent multi-core processing elements have a network on-chip (NoC) based interconnect. On-chip communication energy itself consists of link energy and router energy. The former is consumed by network links, while the latter is consumed by components within the router such as buffers, switches, arbiters, etc. The communication energy between devices depends on the network topology, communication technology, distance between nodes, and amount of transmitted data.

At inter-device level, a mapping algorithm defines the required policies and procedures for allocating each task within an application to a device in a distributed infrastructure. Within each device, and at the intra-device level, the mapping algorithm should determine the PE among several heterogeneous PEs that are generally connected using an NoC to which each task should be assigned. Although the concept is generally the same, but the corresponding parameters differ in inter-device and intra-device mapping. Although on-chip power consumption is generally much less than off-chip communication cost, but as the size of the NoC and the on-chip traffic increases, an optimized mapping becomes more important.

In this paper, we focus on the problem of energy efficient mapping on a cloud of heterogeneous MPSoC based mobile devices. For solving this problem, we propose an integer linear programming (ILP) formulation that provides a mapping and scheduling of an application task graph at both the cloud and device levels such that the overall energy consumption is minimized while performance constraints are satisfied. Although ILP solutions do not scale well and their execution time might increase with the complexity of the task graph and the dimensions of the NoC [3], nevertheless ILP solutions can help researchers and designers to not only apply them to schedulers but also to create new heuristic functions that approximate the optimal solutions well, and get a solution in a quicker way.

In this paper, we consider both computation and communication energy consumption to obtain the exact formulation for energy consumption in a system. We also consider task deadline which is a very important performance measure in multimedia applications.

It should be noted that considering the similarities between mobile cloud and conventional cloud computing, the proposed scheme can be easily extended to the latter environment.

The rest of the paper is organized as follows. Section 2 reviews the related works. The system model, objective functions, and constraints of the proposed ILP formulation are presented in Sect. 3. The proposed scheme is evaluated in Sect. 4. Finally, the paper concludes in Sect. 5.

2 Related Work

Many task mapping and scheduling algorithms for heterogeneous MPSoCs have been proposed in the literature, each with a different objective function [4–7].

Several ILP based mapping methods have been proposed as well. Chou et al. [8] have proposed an ILP based solution for contention-aware application mapping on NoCs. However, they have not considered the computation energy that is consumed by the PEs. Authors in [9] have proposed an ILP formulation to minimize the total energy consumption on a non NoC based architecture. In [10] authors have presented a framework that manages errors in a hardware-software system to obtain a good trade-off between energy, performance and reliability in a multicore system but in their formulation the details of interconnection network to obtain an exact formulation for communication energy have not been considered. Authors of [11] have presented an ILP formulation for energy minimization. However, the energy is not partitioned well and the exact formulation is not reported. In [12] authors have considered both computation and communication energies in its almost exact formulation to minimize energy consumption just in one MPSoC, but they do not consider network parameters and timing constraints in details. Also they have tried to reduce the overall energy consumption that usually results in an increase in processing energy consumption. Furthermore, since they only consider on chip communication cost, this work cannot be extended to multiple MPSoCs.

Authors in [13] proposed a Genetic Algorithm (GA) as an evolutionary algorithm to solve the problem of mapping on heterogeneous MPSoCs. The results of evolutionary approaches such as GA are not guaranteed to be optimal. Erbas et al. [14] proposed an evolutionary algorithm for a bus-based heterogeneous MPSoCs. In [15] authors do not consider the computation energy that is consumed by PEs and have proposed a run-time heuristic to minimize communication energy for task mapping on heterogeneous MPSoCs. Authors in [16] have also proposed a run-time method to minimize communication energy. They have used the communication between tasks to map the connected tasks in places with the shortest distance. This method does not consider the energy that is consumed by PEs. Furthermore, it assumes that the MPSoCs are homogeneous and they have not considered the heterogeneity of MPSoC.

Khajekarimi et al. [17] have proposed an energy-aware ILP formulation for task mapping on NoC-based MPSoC platforms. They consider both communication and computation energy consumption, heterogeneity of PEs and also application deadline, but their ILP formulation is just for one MPSoC based device.

To the best of our knowledge no existing method has considered entire available characteristics of the system to obtain an exact ILP formulation that satisfies the timing constraints. Application deadline is an important constraint in most of the applications.

Most existing methods do not consider both computation and communication energies together. In this paper, an ILP approach has been presented that addresses all these concerns.

3   Proposed ILP Formulation

In this section, we present the problem and the underlying models that have been considered for solving it. We start with describing the application and infrastructure models. Then, we define our constraints and formulation method.

3.1   Application Model

Each application is composed of a collection of tasks that represent indivisible units of computation. These tasks and their data dependencies create a task graph, in which vertices represent tasks and weighted edges represent the data volume communicated between two nodes of the graph. Task graphs may have more than one initial task. In this model, a parent-task should be completed before data is sent to its child. A child-task cannot start before it receives all its required data. In addition to the deadline constraint for the entire application, each task can have its own deadline. The computational requirement of each task is represented at run-time, which is presented in terms of clock cycles. To get the absolute time, the task run-time should be divided by the clock frequency of the PE that is running it.

3.2   Network Model

The network model consists of two levels; namely: inter-device and intra-device.

3.2.1   Inter-device Model

Each device can communicate through the mobile cloud, and share its resources and provide a distributed processing platform. To offload a task onto another PE or to another device we should consider the energy consumption among devices and this could be determined by the power consumption of the communication link and channel condition. In a mobile cloud, devices are usually connected through a wireless network. In this paper, we consider a set of mobile devices, as illustrated in Fig. 1(a) each consisting of an MPSoC, and propose an ILP formulation according to this model. For simplicity we do not consider other network parameters such as communication delay and software overhead. We assume that devices are connected wirelessly through a Wi-Fi access point. For simplicity and without lack of generality, we do not consider the power consumption of the access point in our calculations because it just adds a constant to our formulation. Neither do we consider the mobility of the devices. We consider that an extra device is responsible for running the mapping algorithm and managing the task distribution process.

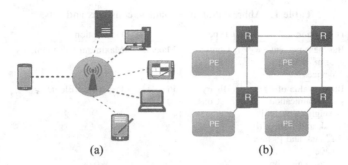

Fig. 1. (a) System model for a mobile cloud computing framework. (b) Architectural model of a mobile device

3.2.2   Intra-device Model

In our model, each device is generally an MPSoC that consists of heterogeneous PEs. Each PE in this paper is modeled with its clock frequency and static/dynamic power consumption. The PEs are connected through an NoC interconnect and we consider a 2D mesh topology. The architectural model of a simple device is shown in Fig. 1(b).

3.3   Computation Functions

In this subsection we present an ILP-based approach to obtain an optimal solution for mapping the application tasks. We provide the variables, sets and constants used in this formulation in Table 1. As described above, to satisfy the deadline of the entire application, we define some extra variables for each task. We define ready time, Rd_i, as the time that all the parents of the current task are finished and the selected PE is not busy with another task. If the selected PE on the selected device is busy with another task, the current task will start after the selected PE is free.

$$\forall i,j \in T : Rd_i \geq Fh_j * CB_{j,i} \tag{1}$$

Start time, St_i, represent the time at which the current task has started to run. The communications happen at the completion of the parent task and the parent task sends the dependent task a message size of CW bits. Each ready task starts when all its parents are finished and all the required data has arrived.

$$\forall i,j \in T : St_i \geq Rd_i + CW_{j,i}*$$
$$\sum_{n,k \in CH} \sum_{m,l \in PE} Z_{i,n,m,j,k,l} \left[\frac{Dp_{lo} * DCB_{n,k}}{TP_1} + \frac{(DC_{n,ac} + DC_{ac,k}) * DCB_{n,k}}{TP_{ac}} \right.$$
$$\left. + \frac{Dp_{om} * DCB_{n,k}}{TP_2} + \frac{Dp_{m,l} * Uc_{n,k}}{TP_1} \right] \tag{2}$$

Table 1. Abbreviation of variables, constants and sets.

Term	Description	Type	Term	Description	Type
$Bu_{n,m}$	Busyness percentage of mth PE on n^{th} device	Const	Maxval	Maximum value (Infinity)	Const
$CB_{j,i}$	Binary value of communication weight between i^{th} task and j^{th} task (if i^{th} task and j^{th} task have communication $CB_{j,i} = 1$	Binary Const	PE	Processing Elements	Set
CH	Devices	Set	$Pr_{i,j}$	Priority between i^{th} task and j^{th} task	Binary var
$CW_{i,j}$	Size of the message being transmitted between i^{th} task and j^{th} task in bits	Const	$PW_{i,n,m}$	Power consumption of ith task on m^{th} PE on n^{th} device	Const
$DCB_{n,k}$	Binary value of distance between n^{th} device and k^{th} device	Binary Const	Rd_i	Ready time	Var
$DC_{n,k}$	Distance between n^{th} device and k^{th} device	Const	St_i	Start time of the ith task	Var
Deadline	Deadline of entire application	Const	T	Tasks	Set
$Deadline_i$	Deadline of ith task	Const	TP_{ac}	Throughput of the access point	Const
$dif_{i,j}$	Auxiliary variable	Binary var	TP_i	Throughput of routers in the ith device $TP_i = f_i * channel\ width_i$ f_i is the frequency of the router in the ith device	Const
$DPB_{m,l}$	Binary value of distance between PEs in an MPSoC	Binary Const	$Uc_{n,k}$	Square matrix with binary variable and its main diameter is 0 and other elements are 1	Const
Dp_{lo}	Distance between a PE and output router in a link	Const	$U_{i,j}$	Diagonal matrix	Const
E_c	Communication energy consumption	Const	$Z_{i,n,m,j,k,l}$	Equal to $\beta_{i,n,m} * \beta_{j,k,l}$	Binary var
E_{hop}	Energy consumption of one hop for one bit in the NoC ($E_{router} + E_{link}$)	Const	$\beta_{i,n,m}$	PE assignment of ith task on n^{th} PE in m^{th} device	Const
$e_{i,n,m}$	Execution time of ith task on m^{th} PE in n^{th} device in terms of clock cycles	Const	$Fp_{n,m}$	Frequency of mth PE on n^{th} device	Const

(Continued)

Table 1. *(Continued)*

Term	Description	Type	Term	Description	Type
$E_{interface}$	Energy consumption of the interface between two devices	Const	Maxval	Maximum value (Infinity)	Const
E_p	Computation energy consumption	Const	PE	Processing Elements	Set
Fh_j	Finish time of the ith task	Var	$Pr_{i,j}$	Priority between i^{th} task and j^{th} task	Binary var
Fh_{total}	Finish time of entire application	Var	$PW_{i,n,m}$	Power consumption of ith task on m^{th} PE on n^{th} device	Const
$Fp_{n,m}$	Frequency of mth PE on n^{th} device	Const			

Finish time, Fh_i, that is the execution time of the task on the selected PE added to start time, is the time that the task is completed. When a task is assigned to a PE, it consumes a percentage of its processing power, referred to as percentage of busyness. The remaining processing power can still be used for the remaining tasks if assigned to it. Furthermore, our method tries to find the best solution such that all application tasks meet their deadline. It should be mentioned that $Bu_{n,m} < 1$.

$$\forall i \in T : Fh_i = St_i + \sum_{n \in CH} \sum_{m \in PE} \frac{e_{i,n,m} * \beta_{i,n,m}}{Fp_{n,m} * (1 - Bu_{n,m})} \tag{3}$$

3.4   Constraints Used in the ILP Formulation

In Eq. (4), we affirm that the finish time of the entire application is the maximum value of the finish times of all tasks. According to Eq. (5) the finish time of the application should be less than its deadline.

$$\forall i \in T : Fh_{total} \geq Fh_i \tag{4}$$

$$Fh_{total} \leq Deadline \tag{5}$$

According to Eq. (6) each task must be assigned to exactly one PE of the selected device.

$$\forall i \in T : \sum_{n \in CH} \sum_{m \in PE} \beta_{i,n,m} = 1 \tag{6}$$

As mentioned before each task may have its own deadline, in addition to the application deadline. For satisfying this constraint, the finish time of the task should be less than its deadline, as expressed in (7).

$$\forall i \in T : Fh_i \leq Deadline_i \tag{7}$$

We must also ensure that if two tasks are mapped on the same PE on a same device, they will be executed sequentially. In other words their execution time must not overlap.

$$\forall i,j \in T : dif_{i,j}$$
$$= \sum_{n,k \in CH} \sum_{m,l \in PE} \left[Z_{i,n,m,j,k,l} * \left[1 - \left(1 - DCB_{n,k} \right) \left(1 - DPB_{m,l} \right) \right] \right] + \left(1 - U_{i,j} \right) \quad (8)$$

In Eq. (8), $dif_{i,j}$ becomes 0 just when two distinct tasks are mapped on the same PE on the same device. In (9) when corresponding tasks are mapped on the same PE on a device, $Pr_{i,j}$ will be 1 and $Pr_{j,i}$ will be 0. In other words, this means that the priority of the ith task is higher than the jth task.

$$\forall i,j \in T : Pr_{i,j} * u_{i,j} + Pr_{j,i} * u_{j,i} + dif_{i,j} = 1 \quad (9)$$

In addition to Eq. (2), if the ith task and the jth task are mapped on the same PE on the same device and the jth task has a higher priority than the ith task, according to Eq. (10) the ready time of the ith task should be greater than the finish time of the jth task.

$$\forall i,j \in T : Rd_i \geq Fh_j + \left(pr_{j,i} - 1 \right) * Maxval \quad (10)$$

In order to change our formulation to a linear form, Eqs. (11) and (12) were added to the other equations. In (11) and (12) we consider β to be a binary variable. With this assumption the following equations are valid.

$$\forall i,j \in T, \forall m,l \in PE, \forall n,k \in CH : Z_{i,n,m,j,k,l} \geq \beta_{i,n,k} + \beta_{j,m,l} - 1 \quad (11)$$

$$\forall i,j \in T, \forall m,l \in PE, \forall n,k \in CH : 2 * Z_{i,n,m,j,k,l} \leq \beta_{i,n,k} + \beta_{j,m,l} \quad (12)$$

3.5 Objective Functions

As previously mentioned, our goal is to minimize the energy consumption. Hence, the objective function can be expressed as in (13).

$$E_{total} = E_p + E_c \quad (13)$$

Where E_p is the computation energy and it represents the energy consumed by all PEs that run tasks and is calculated according to Eq. (14). E_c is the communication energy and it represents the energy consumed by the interconnection network in each device and the energy consumed to communicate among devices and is calculated using Eq. (15). In this paper, we do not consider the effect of device mobility.

$$E_p = \sum_{i \in T} \sum_{n \in CH} \sum_{m \in PE} \left(\frac{\beta_{i,n,m} * e_{i,n,m} * PW_{i,n,m}}{fp_{n,m}} \right) \tag{14}$$

$$E_c = \sum_{i,j \in T} CW_{i,j} * \left[\sum_{n,k \in CH} \sum_{m,l \in PE} Z_{i,n,m,j,k,l} [(Dp_{lo} * DCB_{n,k} * E_{hop})\right.$$
$$\left. + 2 (DCB_{n,k} * E_{interface}) + (Dp_{om} * DCB_{n,k}) + (Dp_{m,l} * Uc_{n,k})] \right] \tag{15}$$

4 Experimental Results

To evaluate the validity of our proposed ILP formulation we have compared its optimal mapping results that were obtained using GAMS [18] with a mapping algorithm that uses GA to find the optimal solution, and the same ILP formulation that does only consider minimizing the computation energy consumption in its objective function. An ILP mapping algorithm is more complex than other heuristics such as GA, but there is always a tradeoff between algorithm complexity and reaching an optimum solution.

In this implementation, the GA process ends when no change is observed after 2000 iterations. The reported results for GA are average results of 20 separate GA executions.

In our evaluations, we have used 9 task graphs as benchmarks to evaluate the proposed ILP formulation. The characteristics of the benchmarks are described in Table 2. We use TGFF [19] to generate random task graphs (Task graph 1–6). Furthermore, we use MP3 decoder, GSM decoder and GSM encoder task graphs [20].

In our formulation we consider m devices each consisting of an $n*n$ heterogeneous MPSoC connected through an NoC interconnect with a mesh topology. In the first part of our simulations we consider two different heterogeneous devices. Similar to most current mobile devices that use a quad-core CPU, we consider that each device consists of a 2×2 heterogeneous MPSoC connected through an NoC interconnect with a mesh topology. For simplicity we consider that PEs are architecturally identical but might

Table 2. Characteristics of the benchmarks.

No	Benchmark	# Node	# Edge
1	Task graph 1	11	15
2	Task graph 2	14	12
3	Task graph 3	15	18
4	Task graph 4	23	27
5	Task graph 5	28	50
6	Task graph 6	38	37
7	GSM decoder	34	55
8	GSM encoder	53	80
9	MP3 decoder	17	18

Table 3. NoC Parameters [21].

Parameter	Value (pJ)
Energy link bit	0.6
Energy switch bit	0.3325

running at different frequencies. Our mapping algorithm can assign only one task to each PE, but a PE might have other tasks prior to this mapping (represented by percentage of busyness).

We use the NoC router and link energy consumption reported in Table 3. The execution time and power consumption of PEs are borrowed from [22]. Devices are connected through a wireless network based on IEEE 802.11n standard [23]. The link capacity is considered to be 54 Mbps.

We have conducted our simulations in two different scenarios. In the first scenario we do not consider the busyness of the PEs. In the second scenario we consider a situation in which some PEs are partially busy from their prior tasks. Figure 2 illustrates the characteristics of target PEs borrowed from [24, 25]. The conditions of experiments are shown in Fig. 3. In Fig. 4, our proposed ILP method has been compared with two other cases in terms of energy consumption in the first scenario. In this figure, ILP1 is the ILP formulation with the aim of minimizing only the processing energy and ILP2 is our proposed approach.

Clearly, since our proposed method has considered both communication and computation energies, the total energy consumption of its mapping result is less than the other two evaluated methods. The presented results illustrate that the proposed method has been able to improve overall energy consumption (consisting of processing and communication energies) by 8 % on average in comparison to the ILP1 method, and to reduce energy more than 23 % on average in comparison with the GA based

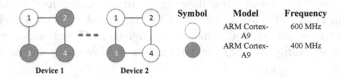

Fig. 2. Characteristics of target PEs

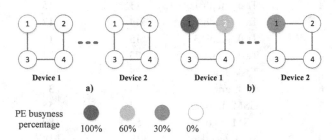

Fig. 3. CPU busyness in (a) scenario 1, (b) scenario 2

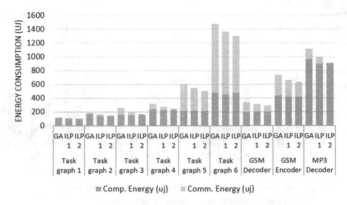

Fig. 4. Experimental results of three different methods in terms of energy consumption in the first scenario

mapping algorithm. As Fig. 5 shows, for larger task graphs the communication energy consumption is more significant. Because of the busyness of some PEs in the second scenario the data transmission among devices increases. The simulation results confirm the validity of our proposed method for the second scenario similar to the results of the first scenario. We present the comparison between our proposed method and the ILP1 and GA based mapping algorithms in Fig. 5. As this figure indicates, in the second scenario the communication energy consumption becomes more significant.

Whether a task runs on a device or is offloaded to the mobile cloud strongly depends on the application deadline, priority of the tasks, busyness of the PEs and also the battery status or power saving mode of the device. Furthermore, parallelism in the application and dependencies between the tasks is an important factor in distribution of the tasks. In Fig. 5, the deadline of the task graph 6 is much less than the MP3 decoder application. Hence, to meet the application deadline, most of the tasks of this application are inevitably offloaded to the mobile cloud. We also extended the previous

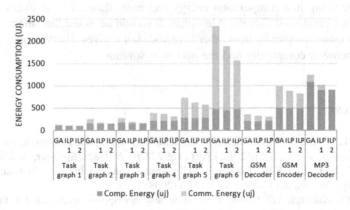

Fig. 5. Experimental results of three different methods in terms of energy consumption in the second scenario

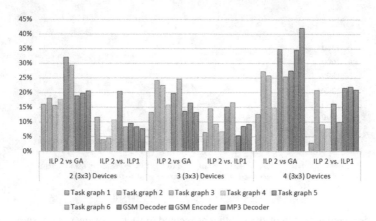

Fig. 6. Energy consumption savings for three different cases

scenarios for devices with 9 PEs (3 × 3) and 16 PEs (4 × 4). In addition, we increased the number of devices to up to 4 devices. As illustrated in Fig. 6, the results show that our proposed method can reduce the energy consumption by up to 42 %. It should be noted that as the size of the NoC and number of devices increase, the effectiveness of our proposed method becomes more significant.

5   Conclusion

In this paper, we have presented a two-level ILP formulation to minimize energy consumption in task allocation among devices and on each device among PEs. Our proposed ILP formulation can compute the global optimal mapping and yields better energy consumption in comparison with existing methods. Our proposed formulation considers two level task mapping in a mobile cloud, intra-device and inter-devices. Simulation results in two different scenarios indicate that the proposed approach has been able to save energy by 8 % in average in comparison to the ILP method with the aim of minimizing just computation energy and more than 23 % in average in comparison with a conducted Genetic Algorithm. It should be noted that although the ILP method has more complexity than other heuristics but it gives a better solution and it is a tradeoff between complexity and the optimum solution.

References

1. Durga, S., Mohan, S.: Mobile cloud media computing applications: a survey. In: Mohan, S., Suresh Kumar, S. (eds.) ICSIP 2012. LNEE, vol. 222, pp. 619–628. Springer, Heidelberg (2013)
2. Chen, G., Li, F., Son, S.W., Kandemir, M.T.: Application mapping for chip multiprocessors. In: Design Automation Conference (DAC) (2008)
3. Derin, O., Kabakci, D., Fiorin, L.: Online task remapping strategies for fault-tolerant network-on-chip multiprocessors. In: IEEE/ACM International Symposium on Network on Chip (NOCS) (2011)

4. Beltrame, G., Fossati, L., Sciuto, D.: Decision- theoretic design space exploration of multiprocessor platforms. IEEE Trans. Comput. Aided Des. Integr. Circ. Syst. **29**(7), 1083–1095 (2010)
5. Carvalho, E.L.D.S., Calazans, N.L.V., Moraes, F.G.: Dynamic task mapping for MPSoCs. IEEE Des. Test Comput. **27**(5), 26–35 (2010)
6. Antunes, E., Soares, M., Aguiar, A., Johann, F.S., Sartori, M., Hessel, F., Marcon, C.: Partitioning and dynamic mapping evaluation for energy consumption minimization on NoC-based MPSoC. In: Thirteenth International Symposium on Quality Electronic Design (ISQED), pp. 451–457 (2012)
7. Mandelli, M., Ost, L., Carara, E., Guindani, G., Gouvea, T., Medeiros, G., Moraes, F.G.: Energy-aware dynamic task mapping for NoC-based MPSoCs. In: IEEE International Symposium on Circuits and Systems (ISCAS), pp. 1676–1679 (2011)
8. Chou, C.L., Marculescu, R.: Contention-aware application mapping for network-on-chip communication architectures. In: IEEE International Conference on Computer Design, pp. 164–169 (2008)
9. Yi, Y., Han, W., Zhao, X., Erdogan, A.T., Arslan, T.: An ILP formulation for task mapping and scheduling on multi-core architectures. In: Proceedings of Design Automation and Test Europe Conference (DATE), pp. 33–38 (2009)
10. Yetim, Y., Malik, S., Martonosi, M.: EPROF: An Energy/Performance/Reliability optimization framework for streaming applications. In: Asia and South Pacific Design Automation Conference (ASP_DAC) (2012)
11. Tosun, S.: Energy- and reliability-aware task scheduling onto heterogeneous MPSoC architectures. J. Supercomput. **62**, 265–289 (2012)
12. Huang, J., Buckl, C., Raabe, A., Knoll, A.: Energy-aware task allocation for network-on-chip based heterogeneous multiprocessor systems. In: Euro-micro International Conference on Parallel, Distributed and Network-Based Processing (PDP) (2011)
13. Weng, N., Kumar, N., Dechu, S., Soewito, B.: Mapping task graphs onto network processors using genetic algorithm. In: Proceedings of AICCSA 2008: the IEEE/ACS International Conference on Computer Systems and Applications, pp. 481–488 (2008)
14. Erbas, C., Cerav-Erbas, S., Pimentel, A.: Multi-objective optimization and evolutionary algorithms for the application mapping problem in multiprocessor system-on-chip design. IEEE Trans. Evol. Comput. **10**, 358–374 (2006)
15. Khajekarimi, E., Hashemi, M.R.: Communication and congestion aware run-time task mapping on heterogeneous MPSoCs. In: Computer Architecture and Digital Systems (CADS) (2012)
16. Hu, W., Tang, X., Xie, B., Chen, T., Wang, D.: An efficient power-aware optimization for task scheduling on NoC-based many-core systems. In: Proc Computer and Information Technology (CIT), pp. 172–179 (2010)
17. Khajekarimi, E., Hashemi, M.R.: Energy-aware ILP formulation for application mapping on NoC-Based MPSoCs. In: 21st Iranian Conference on Electrical Engineering (ICEE2013) (2013)
18. Rosenthal, R.E.: GAMS-a User Guide. GAMS Development Corporation, Washington, DC (2010)
19. Dick, R.P., Rhodes, D.L., Wolf, W.: TGFF: task graphs for free. Hardware/Software Co-design. In: Proceedings of the Sixth International Workshop on CODES/CASHE 1998, pp. 97–101, 15–18 (1998)
20. Schmitz, M.T.: Energy minimization techniques for distributed embedded Systems. Ph.D. Dissertation, Dept. Electronics and Computer Science., Univ. Southampton, UK (2003)
21. Yan, S., Lin, B.: Joint multicast routing and network design optimization for networks-on-chip. IET Comput. Digital Tech. **3**(5), 443–459 (2009)

22. Svanfeldt-Winter, O.: Evaluation of the energy efficiency of ARM based processors for cloud infrastructure. TUSS Technical Report, No. 991 (2010)
23. Luo, F.: Digital Front-End in Wireless Communications and Broadcasting: Circuits and Signal Processing. Cambridge University Press, Cambridge (2011)
24. Svanfeldt-Winter, O.: Energy efficiency of ARM architectures for cloud computing applications. M.S. Thesis, Department of Information Technologies, Abo Akademi University Turku (2011)
25. CoreTile Express A9x4 Cortex-A9 MPCore (V2P-CA9) Technical Reference Manual

A Multi-criteria Resource Allocation
Mechanism for Mobile Clouds

Simin Ghasemi Falavarjani[1](✉), Mohammad Ali Nematbakhsh[1],
and Behrouz Shahgholi Ghahfarokhi[2]

[1] Department of Computer Engineering, University of Isfahan, Isfahan, Iran
`simin.ghasemi@gmail.com, nematbakhsh@eng.ui.ac.ir`
[2] Department of Information Technology Engineering,
University of Isfahan, Isfahan, Iran
`shahgholi@eng.ui.ac.ir`

Abstract. Due to resource scarcity of mobile devices in Mobile Cloud Computing (MCC), intensive computing applications are offloaded into the cloud. There is a three-tier architecture for MCC consisting of distant cloud servers, nearby cloudlets and adjacent mobile devices. In this paper, we consider third tier. We propose an Optimal Fair Multi-criteria Resource Allocation (OFMRA) algorithm that minimizes the completion time of offloading applications along maximizing lifetime of mobile devices. Furthermore to stimulate selfish devices to participate in offloading, a virtual price based incentive mechanism is presented. The paper also designs an Offloading Mobile Cloud Framework (OMCF) which collects profile information and handles the offloading process. A prototype of the proposed method has been implemented and evaluated using a high computational load application. The results show that the proposed algorithm manages the tradeoff between optimizing completion time and energy well and improves the performance of offloading using the incentive mechanism.

Keywords: Mobile cloud computing · Offloading · Resource allocation · Multi-criteria optimization · Cooperation incentive · Fairness

1 Introduction

Recent years have witnessed an increasing popularity of mobile applications. The latest study by Juniper Research forecasts that market for cloud-based mobile applications will rise to $9.5 billion by 2014 [1]. However, some mobile devices cannot execute intensive computing applications such as image processing, speech recognition and data mining due to their resource (processing power, memory, battery life) restrictions [2]. To address this problem, it has been suggested to offload computation from mobile device to the cloud [2, 3].

A three-tier architecture is defined for MCC which consists of remote cloud servers, nearby computing servers known as cloudlets and neighboring mobile devices [2]. However, offloading to remote cloud servers causes long delay and offloading to local cloudlets limits mobility of devices [2, 4]. Therefore in this paper third tier is

© Springer International Publishing Switzerland 2014
A. Movaghar et al. (Eds.): CNDS 2013, CCIS 428, pp. 145–154, 2014.
DOI: 10.1007/978-3-319-10903-9_12

considered which consists of vicinal mobile devices where both service requester and service providers are mobile devices. It is also assumed that mobile devices are always connected (single hop). It is a usual case in scenarios such that all mobile devices belong to the same user or devices that are carried by a group of people on a trip or a mission e.g. in military or disaster relief scenarios [2, 5].

One of the most challenging issues in MCC is allocating appropriate resources for a given offloading service request towards satisfy QoS requirements.

Most of the previous works on resource allocation in mobile clouds have tried to decide which parts of application should be offloaded to the cloud towards optimizing time or energy. They delegate the resource allocation problem to the cloud [6, 7].

On the other hand, some researchers try to select appropriate devices among available mobile devices to allocate tasks to them optimizing specific metrics [4, 5, 8, 9]. Scavenger [8] provides a dual-profiling scheduler to assign tasks to available surrogates in order to minimize response time. In Serendipity [9], initiator mobile device allocates tasks to resource providers among mobile devices which intermittently encounter to it. In time-optimizing Serendipity, the objective is minimizing completion time while in energy-optimizing Serendipity; minimizing local energy consumption is regarded. Wei et al. [4] define a Hybrid Local Mobile Cloud Model (HLMCM) which consists of mobile devices and local cloud infrastructures and present an application scheduling algorithm which aims to maximize the profit of HLMCM while minimizing energy consumption of mobile devices. In [5] the authors consider environments which offloading is occurred among a set of mobile devices forming a Mobile Device Cloud (MDC) where nodes are highly collaborative and propose an offloading schema objects to maximize lifetime of the MDC.

However, none of the previous literatures in MCC provides a fair resource allocation method that optimizes both response time and consumed energy with respect to QoS constraints.

In this paper, an Optimal Fair Multi-criteria Resource Allocation (OFMRA) algorithm is proposed which minimizes both response time of offloading service and consumed energy of mobile devices (provides fairness via maximizing lifetime of all mobile devices) and considers deadline and budget constraints. In addition, an approach is needed to stimulate selfish mobile devices in order to participate in other's offloading process. To overcome this problem, a virtual price based incentive mechanism is presented and is considered in OFMRA. Moreover, an Offloading Mobile Cloud Framework (OMCF) is designed which gathers profile information and manages offloading process.

In summary, the main contributions of this paper are as follows: (1) proposal of OFMRA, a QoS constrained and fair resource allocation algorithm that optimizes completion time and energy consumption of offloading; (2) considering a virtual price based incentive mechanism in OFMRA to stimulate selfish mobile devices; and (3) design and implementation of OMCF to handle offloading process.

The rest of the paper is organized as follows. Section 2 explains how to stimulate mobile devices to cooperate and describes the OFMRA algorithm. In Sect. 3, Architecture of OMCF and profile estimation is stated. Implementation and evaluation of the framework is explained in Sect. 4 and the paper is concluded in Sect. 5.

2 Optimal Fair Multi-criteria Resource Allocation

In mobile cloud, when a mobile client wants to execute an intensive computing application, it requests offloading service from neighboring mobile devices. It first collects information about the application and available mobile devices (as will be described in Sect. 3) and then selects appropriate service providers among neighboring mobile devices. In this paper, it is assumed that only one mobile client can request offloading service at any time and other clients should wait until termination of current offloading process.

In the following, the price based incentive mechanism is explained which is used in OFMRA. Then QoS constrained resource allocation problem is formulated and the proposed Optimal Fair Multi-criteria Resource Allocation algorithm is discussed.

2.1 Price Based Incentive Mechanism

In offloading process, some mobile devices may be selfish and refuse to cooperate in others' offloading process in order to save themselves battery and computing resources. Therefore encouraging such selfish mobile devices is a challenging issue in mobile cloud computing. Fernando et al. [2] explain that it is essential to persuade users to collaborate and share their resources.

In order to motivate mobile devices to participate in offloading processes, we use a virtual price based incentive mechanism inspired from [10] where imaginary credits are paid to mobile devices for executing tasks. The more tasks a mobile device executes the more credits it will obtain. The mobile device can then use these credits to pay for its future offloading requests. For each device, the price of computation service is proportional to its computing power i.e. more powerful devices are more expensive.

In this paper, we assume that all mobile devices are honest and trustworthy. So the incentive mechanism is as follow: at initiation time, credits of mobile devices are initialized to a specific fee. When mobile device A requests a computing service from service provider B, the mobile device B executes the requested service and returns the results and charging information to A (e.g. time it takes for B to run the service). After that, depending on the amount of computation, remaining credit of mobile device A decreases and credit of mobile device B increases.

Next, the QoS constrained resource allocation problem considering above incentive mechanism is modeled as a multi-criteria optimization problem which minimizes completion time and energy consumption together. Then, an algorithm is proposed to solve this problem.

2.2 Problem Modeling

Suppose we have a task consisting of n parallel and independent subtasks. We assume all subtasks are the same with equal amount of computation, and m mobile devices have been discovered around the initiating mobile device. Let R_1 shows initiating mobile device and R_j represents j^{th} resource provider. t_j is the time it takes to execute a subtask on resource provider R_j, p_j denotes price per time unit running a subtask on j^{th} mobile device, e_j is amount of energy consumed by R_j to run a subtask per second, and $E0_j$ indicates the initial energy level of device R_j. Also assume that et_j denotes the energy expenditure on device R_j to transmit a unit of data and V_{in} and V_{out} represent size of input/output of each subtask. A solution of resource allocation problem is an array b of m + 1 entries where b_j is the amount of subtasks allocated to R_j.

As mentioned in [11], due to running subtasks in parallel, execution time of the task is the maximum entry of tl_j where tl_j is the turnaround time it takes for resource provider R_j to complete b_j subtasks.

$$completeTime = \max_{j \in \{1...m+1\}} tl_j, \quad tlj = bj * \left[t_j + \left(\frac{Vin + Vout}{BandWidth} \right) \right] \quad (1)$$

In virtual price based incentive modeling, a mobile device should pay off to Rj based on the amount of resources it consumes to run the subtasks on that surrogate. We use the formula proposed in [11] where the price p_j is a virtual price as described in Sect. 2.1. Thus the overall expense of task is sum of payments as below:

$$expense = \sum_{j=1}^{m} b_j * t_j * p_j \quad (2)$$

Reducing time and expense as the goal of resource allocation problem, it may leads to assigning more subtasks to devices with more computing power and lower price. Thus the energy of those devices is consumed drastically and they will drain-out of batteries while other slower devices remain intact. However in a fair resource allocation, subtasks should be assigned in a manner that the minimum residual energy between all devices be maximized. In order to provide fairness, we consider energy consumption as another criterion regarding the method of [12] which assigns subtasks in proportion to residual energy of mobile devices. That mechanism consumes lesser energy while avoids devices with low residual energy to be contributed in offloading. Consumed energy involves the amount of energy consumed to execute the subtasks and the amount of energy consumed to transfer related data. Therefore, the system energy consumption is sum of all devices' consumed energy:

$$energy = \sum_{j=1}^{m+1} \frac{consumedE_j}{E0_j - consumedE_j}, \quad (3)$$

$$consumedE_j = b_j * \left[t_j * e_j + et_j * (Vin + Vout) \right]$$

Thus the multi-criteria optimization problem of resource allocation is formulated as:

Minimize   *CompleteTime*
Minimize   *expense*
Minimize   *energy*

Subject to

$$completeTime \leq T_0, \tag{4}$$

$$expense \leq M_0, \tag{5}$$

$$EO_j - b_j * \left[t_j * e_j + et_j * (Vin + Vout) \right] \geq 20/100 * EO_j \\ for\ all\ j = 1 \ldots m + 1, \tag{6}$$

$$\sum_{j=1}^{m+1} b_j = n. \tag{7}$$

Above constraints satisfy some QoS requirements and check the feasibility conditions. Equation (4) is a QoS feature to ensure that completion time does not exceed to deadline T0. Equation (5) expresses budget constraint i.e. maximal expense that initiating mobile can pay for (M0). Equation (6) avoids allocating subtask to device Rj with energy level less than 20 % of E0j, preventing mobile devices from draining out of battery. Finally Eq. (7) guarantees all subtasks to be offloaded to remote devices or be executed locally.

A Pareto solution set is achieved solving above multi-criteria optimization problem. To obtain the best solution, following weighted sum method is used to calculate total "cost" and to determine the minimum cost as the best solution:

$$Cost = w_t * completeTime + w_m * expense + w_e * 1000 * energy \tag{8}$$

Let w_t, w_m and w_e represent the weights of completion time, expense and remaining energy, respectively. These weights determine the importance of each criterion with respect to user preferences. For example, a user may consider one unit of time as valuable as one unit of price and both are as valuable as energy, then weights are set to $w_m : w_t : w_e = 1 : 1 : 1$. Weights are normalized i.e. $w_t + w_m + w_e = 1$. So in above example, $w_m = 0.33$, $w_t = 0.33$ and $w_e = 0.33$. We multiply the energy criterion by 1000, to unify the scale of energy to other criteria.

2.3 Solving Optimization Problem

It is NP-complete to find optimal solution for the above resource allocation problem. We exploit a branch and bound algorithm to solve the optimization problem (see Algorithm 1).

In lines 8–11, time, expense, energy and cost are calculated according to Eqs. (1), (2), (3) and (8), respectively. In line 13, QoS constraints in Eqs. (4), (5), (6), and (7) are checked by promising function and bound function determines bound of time and energy. To estimate bound of completion time, a greedy approach is used that iteratively chooses the surrogates with minimum completion time for each remaining subtask. In energy bound, for each remaining subtask, the destination device with maximum residual energy is selected. If the current solution is dominated none of solutions in Pareto solution set, it is added to Pareto solution set in line 15. At the end of algorithm, the best solution with minimum cost is selected. The complexity of above algorithm is $O(n^m)$ where n is number of subtasks and m is number of neighboring mobile devices. But the number of neighboring mobile devices is limited.

Algorithm 1. OFMRA

```
1: OFMRA(n, m, profiles) // n and m are number of subtasks
   and mobile devices, respectively. Profiles represent
   task, devices and network information
2:   queue = initPriorityQueue();
3:   While !queue.empty()
4:     parentState = queue.poll();
5:     remTsk = parentState.remaingSubtasks();
6:     for t=1 to remTsk do
7:       curState = initState(parentState, t);
8:       time = comleteTime(curState, profiles);
9:       expense = serviceExpense(curState, profiles);
10:      energy = residual_Energy(curState, profiles);
11:      cost = totalCost(curState, profiles);
12:      curState.setCriter(time, energy, expense, cost);
13:      if promising(curState) & bound(curState)
14:        if remTsk+t=n & paretoSet.NonDominate(curState)
15:          paretoSet.addPareto(curState);
16:        else
17:          queue.put(curState);
18:  bestSolution = paretoSet.selectMinimumCost();
```

3 OMCF System Architecture

Offloading Mobile Cloud Framework comprises two parts: client side which requests offloading service and server side which provides services. A mobile device contains both parts. When an application starts in a mobile device, OMCF client gathers profile information to solve the task allocation problem, assigning subtasks to appropriate devices. After execution of all subtasks, OMCF client gathers partial results from OMCF servers and merges them.

Figure 1 shows high-level overview of OMCF's architecture. The client consists of three components: profiler, solver and client proxy. Profiler gathers task, device and network information.

Task profile includes execution time and input/output size of the subtasks. It is assumed that developers of an application have annotated remoteable parts (methods) and provided task partitioning information via task profile. In this paper techniques explored in [8] is used to estimate runtime and output size of each subtask based on benchmarking.

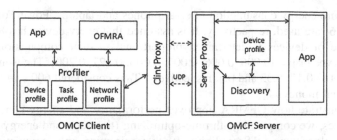

Fig. 1. High-level view of OMCF's architecture

Device profile contains execution speed and energy consumption model of each device. We use PassMark benchmark [13] and PowerBooter [14] to obtain processing power and energy consumption model of devices. Using task and device profiles, we can estimate time and consumed energy it takes to execute a subtask on every device, which is required for resource allocation.

Network profiler measures network bandwidth and latency, and monitors network connectivity. In this paper, we use the method explored in MAUI [6] i.e. 1 KB of data is sent periodically and transmission duration is measured to calculate network throughput. If network disconnection occurs, OMCF resumes offloaded subtasks and runs them locally. Collected profiles are passed to the OFMRA to find optimum solution for resource allocation problem.

On the server side, there are three components: device profiler, discovery component and server proxy. Every device intends to cooperate in offloading, introduces itself through proactive discovery protocol [15]. It broadcasts advertisement messages containing device's profile periodically. Client/Server proxies manage communication between client/server sides in local/remote mobile devices.

When offloading process ends, OMCF collects profiling information and makes a history-based profile. It uses the history-based profiles to learn and improve profile estimation for future offloading.

4   Evaluation

A prototype of OMCF (single-thread) has been implemented on Android and Windows OS. To evaluate performance and energy consumption of OMCF, a face detection application has been used which takes 1 MB picture as a subtask and identifies all faces in the picture.

The proposed framework has been tested on six devices: four HTC Wildfire S smartphones powered by 600 MHz ARMv6 processor and 512 MB of memory running Android 4.0.4 OS, a DELL Vostro with 2.2 GHz core 2 duo CPU and 4 GB of RAM and a Sony VAIO CB laptop with 2.4 GHz core i5 CPU and 6 GB of RAM. One of the smartphones requests for offloading service while others play the role of resource providers. The devices are connected to each other via an ad hoc network using Wi-Fi with 4 Mbps measured bandwidth.

To measure energy consumption of smartphones and laptops, PowerTour [14] and Joulmeter [16] are used, respectively. It is assumed that every device has 80 % initial energy. Price of devices is determined proportional to their computation power as presented by vector p = [0.006, 0.006, 0.006, 0.006, 0.127, 0.200]. The weights w_t, w_m and w_e are set to 0.17, 0.33 and 0.5, respectively. T_0 is considered 600 s while M_0 is 10 units of virtual money.

To demonstrate how OFMRA improves performance and energy conservation of mobile devices, we compare it with time-optimizing (time-opt) and energy-optimizing (energy-opt) algorithms in Serendipity [9] that minimize only completion time or consumed energy greedily in contrast to OFMRA that tries to minimize time and energy together.

The experimental results are as followed. Figure 2 shows the comparison of completion time, energy consumption, cost and fairness between OFMRA, time-opt and energy-opt algorithms, running face detection application on 7–80 pictures. Energy consumption is calculated using Eq. (3) while the total cost is determined from Eq. (8). As shown in Fig. 2, OFMRA stands in second place considering time or energy independently while it gives the minimum cost comparing to mentioned algorithms.

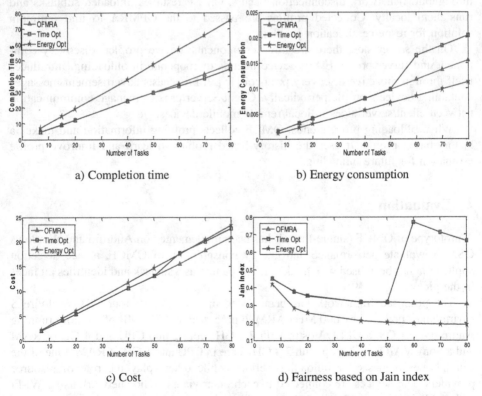

a) Completion time

b) Energy consumption

c) Cost

d) Fairness based on Jain index

Fig. 2. A comparison of (a) completion time, (b) energy consumption, (c) cost and (d) fairness (based on Jain index), between OFMRA, time-opt and energy-opt algorithms.

Energy-opt algorithm always gives subtasks to VAIO laptop which has the most battery capacity. Considering up to 50 pictures as input, both of time-opt and OFMRA algorithms give subtasks to Dell and VAIO laptops. When the number of input subtasks reaches over 50 pictures, time-opt uses other smartphones to reduce the completion time but it yields to higher energy consumption and cost. The results illustrates that OFMRA manages the tradeoff between time and energy and tries to allocate subtasks in a way that minimize both of them. In addition, Fig. 2(d) shows Jain index based on ratio of consumed energy to initial energy of each device and demonstrates that OFMRA allocates subtasks among devices more fairly than energy-opt, however time-opt provides the best fairness.

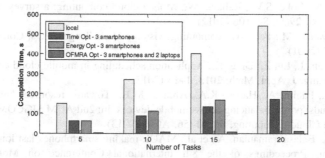

Fig. 3. The impact of virtual price based incentive on completion time.

Another experiment is also performed to show the impact of virtual price based incentive mechanism which is used in OFMRA. Figure 3 indicates completion time of 5, 10, 15 and 20 subtasks running locally or offloading to cooperative resource providers. It is assumed that two laptops are selfish and refuse to cooperate in offloading process. So time-opt and energy-opt algorithms without any incentives, offload subtasks to three smartphones which causes to take longer time. It is shown that using virtual price based incentive mechanism in OFMRA, stimulates mobile devices to participate which causes a great decrease in completion time. In addition Fig. 3 shows that offloading subtasks to remote devices improve performance comparing to local execution.

5   Conclusion

In this paper, an Optimal Fair Multi-criteria Resource Allocation algorithm is proposed which minimizes the completion time and energy consumption of offloading service, considering QoS constraints and provides fairness among mobile devices. Furthermore a virtual price based incentive mechanism is presented to stimulate selfish mobile devices to cooperate in offloading process. An Offloading Mobile Cloud Framework is also designed that enables mobile devices to offload intensive parts of their applications to the mobile cloud.

The experimental results show that in comparing to time-optimizing and energy-optimizing algorithms which lead to optimize time and energy respectively, the proposed algorithm achieves better results considering both criteria together and manages the tradeoff between them well. In addition, using virtual price based incentive mechanism stimulates all mobile devices to participate in offloading process and improves the response time.

References

1. Perez, S.: Mobile cloud computing: $9.5 billion by 2014. http://www.readwriteweb.com/archives/mobile_cloud_computing_95_billion_by_2014.php
2. Fernando, N., Loke, S.W., Rahayu, W.: Mobile cloud computing: a survey. Future Gener. Comput. Syst. **29**(1), 84–106 (2012)
3. Satyanarayanan, M.: Pervasive computing: vision and challenges. Pers. Commun., IEEE **8** (4), 10–17 (2001)
4. Wei, X., Fan, J., Lu, Z., Ding, K.: Application scheduling in mobile cloud computing with load balancing. J. Appl. Math. **2013**, 1–13 (2013)
5. Mtibaa, A., Fahim, A., Harras, K.A., Ammar, M.H.: Towards resource sharing in mobile device clouds: power balancing across mobile devices. In: 2nd ACM SIGCOMM Workshop on Mobile Cloud Computing, pp. 51–56. ACM (2013)
6. Cuervo, E., Balasubramanian, A., et al.: MAUI: making smartphones last longer with code offload. In: Proceedings of the 8th International Conference on Mobile Systems, Applications, and Services (MobiSys), San Francisco, CA, USA, pp. 49–62. ACM (2010)
7. Chun, B.G., et al.: Clonecloud: elastic execution between mobile device and cloud. In: 6th Conference on Computer Systems, EuroSys 2011, pp. 301–314. ACM (2011)
8. Kristensen, M.: Scavenger: transparent development of efficient cyber foraging applications. In: IEEE International Conference on Pervasive Computing and Communications (PerCom), pp. 217–226 (2010)
9. Shi, C., Lakafosis, V., Ammar, M.H., Zegura, E.W.: Serendipity: enabling remote computing among intermittently connected mobile devices. In: 13th ACM International Symposium on Mobile Ad Hoc Networking and Computing, pp. 145–154 (2012)
10. Lu, R., Xiaodong L., Haojin Z., Xuemin S., Bruno P.: Pi: a practical incentive protocol for delay tolerant networks. IEEE Trans. Wirel. Commun. **9**(4), 1483–1493 (2010)
11. Wei, G., Vasilakos, A.V., Zheng, Y., Xiong, N.: A game-theoretic method of fair resource allocation for cloud computing services. J. Supercomput. **54**(2), 252–269 (2010)
12. Chang, J.H., Tassiulas, L.: Energy conserving routing in wireless ad-hoc networks. In: 19th Annual Joint Conference of the IEEE Computer and Communications Societies (INFOCOM), vol. 1, pp. 22–31. IEEE (2000)
13. PassMark Benchmark. http://www.cpubenchmark.net
14. Zhang, L., et al.: Accurate online power estimation and automatic battery behavior based power model generation for smartphones. In: 8th IEEE/ACM/IFIP International Conference on Hardware/Software Codesign and System Synthesis, pp. 105–114. ACM (2010)
15. Kristensen, M.D.: Scavenger-mobile remote execution. DAIMI Report Series 37(587) (2008)
16. Joulmeter. http://research.microsoft.com

An Efficient Scheduling of HPC Applications on Geographically Distributed Cloud Data Centers

Aboozar Rajabi[1]($\boxtimes$), Hamid Reza Faragardi[2], and Thomas Nolte[2]

[1] School of Electrical and Computer Engineering,
University of Tehran, Tehran, Iran
ab.rajabi@ut.ac.ir
[2] Mälardalen Real-Time Research Centre,
Mälardalen University, Västeras, Sweden
{hamid.faragardi,thomas.nolte}@mdh.se

Abstract. Cloud computing provides a flexible infrastructure for IT industries to run their High Performance Computing (HPC) applications. Cloud providers deliver such computing infrastructures through a set of data centers called a cloud federation. The data centers of a cloud federation are usually distributed over the world. The profit of cloud providers strongly depends on the cost of energy consumption. As the data centers are located in various corners of the world, the cost of energy consumption and the amount of CO_2 emission in different data centers varies significantly. Therefore, a proper allocation of HPC applications in such systems can result in a decrease of CO_2 emission and a substantial increase of the providers' profit. Reduction of CO_2 emission also mitigates the destructive environmental impacts. In this paper, the problem of scheduling HPC applications on a geographically distributed cloud federation is scrutinized. To address the problem, we propose a two-level scheduler which is able to reach a good compromise between CO_2 emission and the profit of cloud provider. The scheduler should also satisfy all HPC applications' deadline and memory constraints. Simulation results based on a real intensive workload indicate that the proposed scheduler reduces the CO_2 emission by 17 % while at the same time it improves the provider's profit by 9 % on average.

Keywords: Cloud computing · Data center · Energy-aware scheduling · CO_2 emission · Multi-objective optimization

1 Introduction

Cloud computing has emerged as a new paradigm to support the utility computing idea [1]. The advantages of this computing model motivate the IT industries, which require a High Performance Computing (HPC) infrastructure to run IT applications, to utilize this model and have access to a flexible HPC infrastructure. Cloud providers promise to prepare such infrastructure on demand with a minimum investment for customers through the cloud data centers. The data centers are geographically distributed over the world to support users in any corner of the world. In such a large-scale system, energy-efficient computing is a tremendous challenge [2].

© Springer International Publishing Switzerland 2014
A. Movaghar et al. (Eds.): CNDS 2013, CCIS 428, pp. 155–167, 2014.
DOI: 10.1007/978-3-319-10903-9_13

Cloud data centers consume a large amount of energy which directly affects the cost of services. Based on a set of recent estimations, energy consumption strongly contributes to the total operational cost of data centers [3]. Higher energy consumption would make the services more expensive. In addition, an increase of the energy consumption will result in destructive impacts on the environment along with more greenhouse gas emissions [4]. In 2007, Gartner estimated that the Information and Communication Technologies (ICT) industry generates about 2 % of the total global CO_2 emissions, which is equal to the aviation industry [5].

In this paper, the problem of scheduling HPC applications in the geographically distributed data centers (i.e., a cloud federation) is investigated. The goal is to schedule a set of HPC applications in such a way that CO_2 emission is minimized and the profit of the cloud provider is maximized. As the locations of data centers are spread over the world, some energy efficiency factors such as electricity cost, CO_2 emission rate and Coefficient of Performance (COP) usually vary across various data centers. In addition, in order to provide a suitable solution for real-time applications, the proposed scheduler attempts to meet application deadlines. Moreover, memory constraint is considered to present a realistic solution that can run on cloud federation infrastructure. The problem is formulated and then in order to cope with the scheduling problem, a two-level scheduling algorithm is introduced. The scheduler is an online scheduling approach in which the federation-level is the first level scheduler and the Highest Execution time-Lowest Power consumption (HELP) scheduler is the second one. The former scheduler is based on a powerful meta-heuristic approach known as the Imperialist Competitive Algorithm (ICA) [6]. The latter scheduler is a greedy heuristic algorithm employed as a local scheduler at each data center. These two schedulers cooperate with each other in such a way that the memory and deadline constraints are satisfied while achieves a right compromise between the profit and the amount of CO_2 emission.

The main contributions of this paper are: (1) Proposing an online scheduling approach which works based on a two-level scheduling architecture, (2) Considering heterogeneous resources, (3) Contemplating real-time HPC applications and various system constraints.

The remainder of this paper is organized as follows. A short brief of the related works are reviewed in Sect. 2. The problem definition is stated in Sect. 3. After describing the problem and underlying models, Sect. 4 discusses the proposed solution. Section 5 evaluates the solution approach and presents the obtained results. Finally, concluding remarks and future works are presented in Sect. 6.

2   Related Work

The energy consumption of data centers has been recently considered in several works rather than performance and dependability metrics. However, most of these approaches focus on scheduling of applications within one data center (e.g. [9, 16–18]). Also, CO_2 emission has been ignored in a wide range of previous works. There are some studies in Grids which investigate energy efficiency of resources in multiple locations, similar to our work. Orgerie et al. [7] proposed a prediction algorithm that consolidate workloads on a portion of CPUs and turn off unused CPUs. Patel et al. investigated allocating Grid workload at different data centers considering temperature [8]. The main goal of their work is reducing the temperature based on the energy efficiency at different data centers however, they ignored the CO_2 emission.

In the scope of cloud computing, a similar problem has discussed recently. Garg et al. [10] proposed some heuristics for scheduling of HPC workloads in several data centers. They considered the provider's profit and CO_2 emission as the scheduling objectives. Although the proposed heuristics strive to find a good tradeoff between objectives, this approach can only optimize one goal at time. Kessaci et al. [11] have solved the same problem by using a meta-heuristic approach. They have proposed a meta-scheduler using a multi-objective genetic algorithm to optimize the objectives. Both mentioned studies, consider a homogeneous data center in which the servers are the same despite the difference with other data centers' servers.

This work is different from the mentioned works, because it addresses the problem of scheduling HPC workloads in heterogeneous cloud data centers. The proposed method uses a two level scheduler to make the scheduling decisions. The scheduler considers both the CO_2 emission of each data center and the profit of cloud provider.

3 Problem Definition

3.1 System Model

The system is a set C of c data centers which compose a cloud federation. Execution price, CO_2 emission rate, electricity price and COP are considered as energy efficiency factors. These factors vary across different data centers depending on their locations, architectural designs and management systems. In addition, the number and hetero-geneity of servers within the data centers directly impact on the complexity of the problem. Each data center is a set P of p heterogeneous servers. Each server also has a specific amount of memory.

The presumed service delivery model in this work is the Infrastructure-as-a-Service (IaaS). The service presented by the cloud provider is the offering of an infrastructure to run the clients' HPC applications. A set A consists of N elements represents the applications. Each application has a deadline that must be met. A user submits his requirement for an application a_i in the form of a tuple $(d_{a_i}, n_{a_i}, e_{a_i p_j}, m_{a_i})$, where d_{a_i} is the deadline to complete a_i, n_{a_i} is the number of CPUs needed to execute a_i, $e_{a_i p_j}$ is a vector that represents the execution time of a_i on server p_j when that server is operating at the maximum frequency, m_{a_i} is the memory required by a_i.

3.2 Energy Model

The energy consumption of a data center is related to IT equipment such as servers and network, or other auxiliary equipment like cooling equipment and lightning. The lightning portion could be neglected because of its little impact on the total energy consumption of a data center [11]. As the energy consumption of the servers and cooling system are accountable for the significant portion of a datacenter's energy consumption, we ignore the network energy in this work, and it can be considered as part of our future work.

Due to the heterogeneity of servers within the data centers, the energy consumption of each application depends on both the data center to which the application is assigned and the server within the data center to which the application is allocated. Therefore, the server which is in charge of running the application should be known in order to calculate the total energy consumption by a set of applications. It should be mentioned that in this work, only energy usage of the CUP is considered as the energy consumption of a server. In other words, the energy consumption by other components (e.g., memory and disk) is ignored because CPU is the dominant part in terms of energy consumption when running CPU-intensive workloads. Hence, the power consumption in each server is derived from the power model in Complementary Metal-Oxide Semiconductor (CMOS) logic circuits which is defined by

$$P = A'C'V^2f + I_{leak}V + P_{short} \tag{1}$$

where A' is the number of switches per clock cycle, C' is the total capacitance load, V is the supply voltage, f is the frequency, I_{leak} is the leakage current and P_{short} is the power dissipation resulting from switching between a voltage to another. As A' and C' are constant, we replace their product by α. Moreover, the second part of the equation represents the static consumption, let it be β. In CMOS processors the voltage can be expressed as a linear function of the frequency and thus, V^2f can be replaced by f^3. Therefore, the energy consumption of the Computing Equipment (CE) for execution of a_i is computed by

$$E_{a_ic_k}^{CE}(X) = \sum_{j=0}^{P}(\alpha_{p_j}f_{p_j}^3 + \beta_{p_j}) \times e_{a_ip_j} x_{ij} \tag{2}$$

where x_{ij} is equal to one if a_i is assigned to the jth server and otherwise, it is zero. The energy consumed by the cooling equipment is directly related to the location of the data center due to variance of temperature. The COP parameter could be used to compare the energy consumption of the cooling system [12, 13]. The COP indicates the ratio of energy consumed for execution of the service to the amount of energy which is required for cooling the system. Indeed, COP represents the efficiency of the cooling system. Although the COP varies over time, we suppose that it is constant during our scheduling period. The energy consumption of the Cooling System (CS) of the data center c_k, $E_{c_k}^{CS}$, is defined by

$$E_{c_k}^{CS} = E_{a_ic_k}^{CE}/COP_{c_k} \tag{3}$$

According to Eqs. 2 and 3, total energy consumed by application a_i executing on data center c_k is computed by

$$E_{a_ic_k}^{total} = E_{a_ic_k}^{CS} + E_{a_ic_k}^{CE} = (1 + 1/COP_{c_k}) \times E_{a_ic_k}^{CE} \tag{4}$$

3.3 CO$_2$ Emission Model

The amount of CO$_2$ emissions of the data center c_k is related to a coefficient. This coefficient, $r_{c_k}^{CO_2}$, is determined based on the method that the required electricity of c_k is generated. As we know, there are different ways for generating electricity such as using fossil fuels like oil and natural gas or using renewable resources like water, solar and wind power. The renewable resources are green and will make less destructive impacts on the environment. Due to the diverse methods of generating electricity in various places, the value of $r_{c_k}^{CO_2}$ is different for each cloud data center. The CO$_2$ emission due to the execution of application a_i on the data center c_k is computed by

$$CO_2 E_{a_i c_k} = r_{c_k}^{CO_2} \times E_{a_i c_k}^{total} \tag{5}$$

where $r_{c_k}^{CO_2}$ is the CO$_2$ emission rate of c_k. As a result, the total CO$_2$ emission incurred by the execution of all HPC applications is defined by

$$TCO_2 E(X) = \sum_{i=0}^{N} \sum_{k=0}^{c} CO_2 E_{a_i c_k}(X) \tag{6}$$

3.4 Profit Model

Profit is equal to income minus cost. In this paper, we define the income as the price that should be paid by the user. Also, the cost is the price which is incurred by electricity usage. The achieved profit due to the execution of application a_i in the data center c_k is computed by

$$Prof_{a_i c_k} = n_{a_i} \times e_{a_i c_k} \times p_{a_i}^c - p_{c_k}^e \times E_{a_i c_k}^{total} \tag{7}$$

where $e_{a_i c_k}$ is the average execution time of a_i on c_k, $p_{a_i}^c$ is the static price of a_i, $P_{c_k}^e$ is electricity price of the area in which the c_k is located and $E_{a_i c_k}^{total}$ is the total energy consumption of a_i on c_k. Therefore, the total profit can be computed as $TProf(X)$ by

$$TProf(X) = \sum_{i=0}^{a} \sum_{k=0}^{c} Prof_{a_i c_k}(X) \tag{8}$$

4 Proposed Solution

In this section, an online scheduling algorithm is suggested to cope with the mentioned problem. The architecture of the proposed solution consists of a two-level scheduling algorithm. In the following, the architecture is explained in details and it is demonstrated how this scheduling architecture can be applied.

4.1 Architecture

Federation-level Scheduler: This scheduler is located at the high level to distribute a set of applications among the available data centers in a cloud federation. In this level, the applications are mapped to the data centers in such a way that a right compromise between the profits and CO_2 emission can be achieved. Although this decision is made at the federation level, the high-level scheduler should be aware of servers which are executing the applications. However, in most of the previous studies only homogenous data centers are taken into account in which the high-level scheduler does not need to be aware of data center-level scheduling. Because, if the servers of a data center are the same, calculating the energy consumed by the application is not dependent to which server of this data center is executing the application. Nevertheless, we introduce an intelligent architecture which is able to separate these two scheduling levels even for heterogeneous data centers and provides a two-level scheduler. The federation-level scheduler is inspired by the ICA algorithm intensified by a fast local search. As we mentioned above, ICA is responsible to find an appropriate mapping of services among the data centers. Each mapping is represented by a vector of N elements, and each element is an integer value between one and c. Figure 1 shows an illustrative example for a mapping of applications. The third element of this example is two, which means that the third application is mapped to the second data center. Furthermore, this representation causes satisfaction of the no redundancy constraint in the sense that each application should be mapped to no more than one data center. Section 4.2 describes the ICA in more details.

a_1	a_2	a_3		a_N
1	1	2	...	1

Fig. 1. Representation for mapping of services to the data centers

Data Center-level Scheduler: Each data center has a local scheduler. The submitted applications to this data center are scheduled by the corresponding scheduler. The scheduler at this level aims to find an allocation which can meet the memory and deadline constraints while at the same time it attempts to minimize the energy consumption. Decreasing the energy consumption potentially leads to mitigation of CO_2 emission and increasing the cloud provider profit. It should be noted that the data center-level scheduler may not be able to find a feasible allocation. In other words, if all the applications mapped to this data center are allocated to its servers, then some applications may miss their deadlines or the sum of memory demands by the applications exceeds the available memory on the servers. It can happen because the mapping of applications onto the data centers is done at the federation-level irrespective of schedulability consideration within the data centers. Accordingly, the second-level scheduler attempts to allocate all applications in a feasible manner and if it fails, then it tries to allocate the most possible number of applications without violation of the constraints. Finally, it returns the number of applications that could not be scheduled in this data center. Based on the value achieved from all data centers, Eq. 9 defines a penalty function to calculate the total percentage of unscheduled applications.

$$P(X) = \frac{\sum_{i=1}^{c} \emptyset_i(X)}{N} \qquad (9)$$

where X is an assignment of services to the servers, and $\phi_i(X)$ represents the number of unscheduled services by the assignment X in the ith data center. The second-level scheduler receives a mapping of services onto the data centers from the ICA as an input and it generates both X and $\phi_i(X)$. The HELP algorithm is suggested in this paper as the data center scheduler and it will be explained in Sect. 4.3.

4.2 Imperialist Competitive Algorithm (ICA)

ICA is used to find a right compromise between profit and CO_2 emission. ICA, a socio-politically inspired optimization strategy, was originally proposed from the work of Atashpaz-Gargari and Lucas [6]. It begins by an initial population similar to many other evolutionary algorithms. Population individuals called country are divided into two groups: colonies and imperialists. Imperialists are selected from the best countries (i.e. the lowest cost countries) and the remaining countries form the colonies. All the colonies of the initial population are divided among the imperialists based on their power. The power of an imperialist is inversely proportional to its cost. The imperialists with lower costs (i.e. higher powers) will achieve more colonies. The next step in the algorithm is moving colonies to their relevant imperialists. The movement is a simple assimilation policy which is modeled by a directed vector from a colony to the corresponding imperialist. If the assimilation causes any colony to have a lower cost compared to its imperialist then, they will change their positions. Subsequently, the revolution process begins between the empires. Each imperialist along with its colonies form an empire. The total cost of an empire is determined by the cost of its imperialist along with the cost of its colonies. This fact is modeled by the following equation.

$$TC_n = Cost(imperialist_n) + \varepsilon.mean\{Cost(colonies\ of\ empire_n)\} \qquad (10)$$

where TC_n is the total cost of the nth empire and ε is the colonies impact rate which is a positive number between zero and one. Increasing ε will increase the role of the colonies in determining the total power of an empire. It should be mentioned that each country (either empire or colony) is corresponding to a mapping like Fig. 1. Furthermore, $C(i)$ represents the cost of the ith mapping. To compute $C(i)$, the ith mapping is given as an input to the HELP algorithm and then it returns an assignment of services to the servers namely, X_i. Subsequently, $C(i)$ can be achieved by Eq. 11.

$$C(i) = \theta TCO_2E(X_i) - \rho TProf(X_i) + \omega P(X_i) \qquad (11)$$

where ω is the penalty coefficient and it is applied to scale the penalty value to the proper range. For evaluations, its value is set to 10. θ and ρ are the coefficients which can tune the importance of the CO_2 emission and profit respectively. All the coefficients should be selected in such a way that solving the above-mentioned problem to be equal to find a right compromise between the objectives (profit and carbon emission) while all the constraints are met.

The competition among imperialists forms the basis of the algorithm. During the competition, weak empires collapse and the most powerful ones remain. This process continues until the stopping condition is met. In the imperialistic competition, the weakest colony of the weakest empire will be exchanged from its current empire to another empire with the most likelihood to possess it. The imperialist competition will gradually result in an increase in the power of the powerful empires and a decrease in the power of the weak ones. Any empire that cannot succeed in the competition to increase its power will ultimately collapse.

The final step in the algorithm is global war. If the best imperialist in the imperialistic competition did not get any better after a certain iteration time, the global condition is satisfied. This way a new empire will be formed with the same random amount of the initial population as in the initialization step. Then the best empires from the new existing empires will be selected and the algorithm repeats again. Global war can efficiently lead to escape from local optima. The algorithm stops when the stopping condition is satisfied. It can be simply defined as the time when only one empire is left. The pseudo code of the ICA is provided in Algorithm I.

In this scheduling architecture, the second-level scheduler plays a supplementary role for the high-level scheduler. As the information must be prepared quickly, a simple heuristic is proposed to solve the optimization problem at each data center.

ALGORITHM I. ICA

```
1. Initialize the empires randomly;
2. Move the colonies towards their empires (Assimilation);
3. Randomly change characteristics of some countries (Revolu-
tion);
4. if there is a colony which TC_col < TC_imp then
5.      Exchange the positions of that imperialist and colony;
6. end if
7. Compute the total cost of all empires (TCemp);
8. Pick the weakest colony from the weakest empire and give to
the empire that has the most likelihood to possess it;
9. if there is an empire with no colonies then
10.     Eliminate this empire;
11. end if
12. if there is only one empire then
13.     Stop condition satisfied;
14. else
15.     go to 2;
16. end if
```

4.3 Highest Execution Time-Lowest Power Consumption (HELP) Heuristic

The execution time of HELP should be short enough to make it practically beneficial. Indeed, its run time must be admissible because the federation-level scheduler would run it several times. Hence, HELP is implemented based on a simple and quick idea. It schedules longer applications on the servers which have lower power consumption. As a result, the system will save energy consumption. It is worth noting that the mentioned application and system constraints are also taken into account by HELP.

First of all, HELP sorts the applications according to their deadlines in ascending manner. Then, an application is picked up from the sorted list and is scheduled on a server which has the minimum value of "HELP Score". This metric is calculated for each application and has a different value for each server. The various values are because of different execution times of each application on each server's type. The "HELP Score" is computed by

$$HELP\_Score_{a_i p_j} = (\alpha_{p_j} f_{p_j}^3 + \beta_{p_j}) \times e_{a_i p_j} \tag{12}$$

where $e_{a_i p_j}$ is the execution time of application a_i on p_j and $\alpha_{p_j} f_{p_j}^3 + \beta_{p_j}$ is the power consumption of the p_j. HELP attempts to schedule an application on a server with the minimum value of the $HELP\_Score$ which is able to satisfy all the constraints. If no one of the servers can meet the constraints, then HELP leaves the application and tries to allocate the next application. In addition, if the application requires more than one server, it will cover its needs from other servers. Therefore, it is common for an application to be scheduled on more than one server. In this case, in order to satisfy the application's deadline, the longest completion time of the application on the assigned servers should be less than the corresponding deadline.

5   Performance Evaluation

As the proposed solution is designed for cloud federations, it is essential to perform evaluations on large-scale cloud data centers. However, it is difficult to conduct similar and repeatable experiments on a real cloud federation. To cope with problem, simulation has used as a common solution to evaluate energy-aware scheduling. Thus, the addressed system is simulated precisely considering all entities and constraints.

To model the HPC applications, we use workload traces from Feitelson's Parallel Workload Archive (PWA) [14]. The PWA provides workload traces that reflect the characteristics of real parallel applications. We obtain the submit time, requested number of CPUs and actual runtime of applications from the PWA. Also, the methodology proposed by [15] is used to synthetically assign deadlines through two classes namely Low Urgency (LU) and High Urgency (HU). We suppose that 20 % of all applications belong to the HU class and the other 80 % belong to the LU class. In addition, three classes of application arrival rates are considered in our experiments, Low, Medium and High. We vary the original workload by changing the submit time of the applications. Each move from an arrival rate class to another means ten times more applications are arriving during the same period of time. In the other words, each time we divide the submission time by 10. Furthermore, the initial values of ICA are presented in Table 1. Finally, the scheduling period in our algorithm is set to 50 s.

A cloud federation which is composed of 8 geographically distributed data centers with different configurations is modeled as listed in Table 2 similar to [10, 11]. Carbon emission rates and electricity prices are derived from the data provided by US Department of Energy [19] and Energy Information Administration [20]. These values are average over the entire region that the cloud data center is located. Each data center consists of several heterogeneous servers. We consider three different types of servers which are tabulated in Table 3. The power related parameters are derived from a recent work presented by [10]. For the lowest frequency f_i^{min}, we use the same value as used by Garg et al. [10], i.e. the minimum frequency is 37.5 % of f_i^{max}.

Table 1. Initial values of ICA

Parameter	Description	Value	Parameter	Description	Value
$N_{country}$	Number of initial countries	80	R	Revolution Rate	0.1
N_{imp}	Number of initial imperialists	8	Af	Assimilation Coefficient	2
N_{col}	Number of initial colonies	72	ε	Colonies impact rate	0.02

To evaluate the proposed algorithm, scheduling of 4026 HPC applications is simulated. The proposed solution is compared with the Genetic Algorithm proposed earlier by Y. Kessaci [11]. The two algorithms are compared in three different situations. Each situation is defined by values of θ and ρ which are used to weight the objectives. Also, experiments conducted for each situation are in three different classes of service arrival rates. In the first situation ($\theta = 1, \rho = 0$), the CO_2 emission is only considered and the algorithm has attempted to minimize its value. The second situation establishes equilibrium of both objectives. Finally, the last situation considers provider's profit. The CO_2 emission is neglected in this situation and the profit is maximized.

Table 2. Characteristics of the cloud data centers

Location	CO_2 Emission rate (kg/kWh)	Electricity Price ($/kWh)	COP	Number of Servers
New York, USA	0.389	0.15	3.052	2050
Pennsylvania, USA	0.574	0.09	1.691	2600
California, USA	0.275	0.13	2.196	650
Ohio, USA	0.817	0.09	1.270	540
North Carolina, USA	0.563	0.07	1.843	600
Texas, USA	0.664	0.1	1.608	350
France	0.083	0.17	0.915	200
Australia	0.924	0.11	3.099	250

As the Table 4 indicates, the proposed algorithm produces better solutions in comparison with the traditional GA approach. The proposed scheduling architecture outperforms about 9 % on average in terms of the profit. CO_2 emission is improved in the meanwhile about 17 % on average. Additionally, our average execution time is shorter than GA for all experiments. Our proposed scheduler improves the execution time 11.13 % on average. It should be noted that the increase in execution time of each situation is related to the increase in the number of arrival services which makes the problem space larger.

In addition, the generated results are in form of Pareto solutions. Consequently, the system designers can choose appropriate θ and ρ values to reach an acceptable level of CO_2 emission and profit. In the other words, cloud providers will be able to present flexible infrastructures with the lowest cost and destructive environmental impacts.

Table 3. Characteristics of the servers

Type	CPU power factors		CPU frequency level		Disk (GB)	Memory (GB)
	β	α	f_i^{max}	f_i^{opt}		
1	65	7.5	1.8	1.630324	500	4
2	90	4.5	3.0	2.154435	600	8
3	105	6.5	3.0	2.00639	900	16

Table 4. Simulation results

	Service arrival rate	Proposed algorithm			Genetic Algorithm		
		Avg. Profit ($)	Avg. CO_2 (kg)	Avg. Exe. Time (ms)	Avg. Profit ($)	Avg. CO_2 (kg)	Avg. Exe. Time (ms)
$\theta = 1$ $= 0$	Low	2647086	10528	46	2382376	11581	51
	Medium	9352924	39984	64	7482338	47979	72
	High	25895514	162864	221	24601738	195435	255
$\theta = 0.5$ $= 0.5$	Low	3879236	13292	47	3675274	14621	53
	Medium	11691461	63929	68	9937741	76716	76
	High	31549144	311575	219	28394229	405048	244
$\theta = 0$ $= 1$	Low	5187142	19896	45	4149713	21885	53
	Medium	14212546	84926	71	12791283	93419	78
	High	35776097	429752	233	33987292	504902	259

6 Conclusions and Future Work

In this paper, the problem of scheduling HPC applications on a set of heterogeneous data centers which are located all over the world is investigated. The problem has two objectives, minimizing CO_2 emissions and maximizing cloud provider's profit. As the solution, a two-level scheduling algorithm is proposed which combines two meta-heuristic and heuristic algorithms. The first level scheduler, federation-level, utilizes ICA to solve its bi-objective optimization problem. Due to heterogeneity of the cloud data centers, the scheduling decision making is directly related to the servers which the applications are scheduled on. Therefore, the second level scheduler, data center-level, schedules its assigned applications and provides required information for the federation-level scheduler. Based on the simulation results, the proposed scheduling approach outperforms the other mentioned related work which is based on GA in terms of CO_2 emission, profit and execution time. For future works, we plan to integrate Dynamic Voltage Frequency Scaling (DVFS) techniques to save more energy.

References

1. Buyya, R., Yeo, C.S., Venugopal, S., Broberg, J., Brandic, I.: Cloud computing and emerging IT platforms: vision, hype, and reality for delivering computing as the 5th utility. Future Gener. Comput. Syst. **25**(6), 599–616 (2009)
2. Voorsluys, W., Broberg, J., Buyya, R.: Introduction to cloud computing. In: Buyya, R., Broberg, J., Goscinski, A. (eds.) Cloud Computing: Principles and Paradigms, pp. 1–41. Wiley Press, New York (2011). ISBN-13: 978-0470887998
3. Belady, C.: In the data center, power and cooling costs more than the IT equipment it supports, http://www.electronics-cooling.com/articles/2007/feb/a3/
4. Buyya, R., Beloglazov, A., Abawajy, J.: Energy-efficient management of data center resources for cloud computing: a vision, architectural elements, and open challenges. In: Proceedings of the 2010 International Conference on Parallel and Distributed Processing Techniques and Applications (PDPTA 2010), Las Vegas, USA, 12–15 July 2010
5. Gartner, Gartner estimates ICT industry accounts for 2 percent of global CO2 emissions, April 2007. http://www.gartner.com/it/page.jsp?id=503867
6. Atashpaz-Gargari, C., Lucas, E.: Imperialist Competitive Algorithm: An algorithm for optimization inspired by imperialistic competition. IEEE Congress on Evolutionary Computation (2007)
7. Orgerie, A., Lefèvre, L., Gelas, J.: Save watts in your grid: green strategies for energy-aware framework in large scale distributed systems. In: Proceedings of the 2008 14th IEEE International Conference on Parallel and Distributed Systems, Melbourne, Australia (2008)
8. Patel, C., Sharma, R., Bash, C., Graupner, S.: Energy aware grid: global workload placement based on energy efficiency. Technical Report HPL-2002-329, HP Labs, Palo Alto, November 2002
9. Rajabi, A., Faragardi, H.R., Yazdani, N.: Communication-aware and energy-efficient resource provisioning for real-time cloud services. In: The 17th CSI International Symposium on Computer Architecture & Digital Systems (CADS 2013), Tehran (2013)
10. Garg, S., Yeo, C., Anandasivam, A., Buyya, R.: Environment-conscious scheduling of HPC applications on distributed cloud-oriented data centers. J. Parallel Distrib. Comput. **71**(6), 732–749 (2011)
11. Kessaci, Y., Melab, N., Talbi, E.: A Pareto-based metaheuristic for scheduling HPC applications on a geographically distributed cloud federation. Cluster Computing, 1–21 (2012)
12. Moore, J., Chase, J., Ranganathan, P., Sharma, R.: Making scheduling "cool": temperature-aware workload placement in data centers. In: Proceedings of the 2005 Annual Conference on USENIX Annual Technical Conference, Anaheim, CA (2005)
13. Tang, Q., Gupta, S.K.S., Stanzione, D., Cayton, P.: Thermal-aware task scheduling to minimize energy usage of blade server based datacenters. In: Proceedings of the 2nd IEEE International Symposium on Dependable, Autonomic and Secure Computing, DASC 2006. IEEE Computer Society, Los Alamitos (2006)
14. Feitelson, D.: Parallel workloads archive. http://www.cs.huji.ac.il/labs/parallel/workload

15. Irwin, D., Grit, L., Chase, J.: Balancing risk and reward in a market-based task service. In: Proceedings of the 13th IEEE International Symposium on High Performance Distributed Computing, Honolulu, USA (2004)
16. Faragardi, H.R., Rajabi, A., Shojaee, R., Nolte, T.: Towards energy-aware resource scheduling to maximize reliability in cloud computing systems. In: 15th IEEE International Conference on High Performance Computing and Communications (HPCC 2013), China (2013)
17. Ebrahimirad, V., Rajabi, A., Goudarzi, M.: Energy-aware scheduling algorithm for precedence-constrained parallel tasks of network-intensive applications in a distributed homogeneous environment. In: 3rd International Conference on Computer and Knowledge Engineering (ICCKE 2013), Mashhad (2013)
18. Faragardi, H.R., Shojaee, R., Tabani, H., Rajabi, A.: An analytical model to evaluate reliability of cloud computing systems in the presence of QoS requirements. In: 12th IEEE/ACIS International Conference on Computer and Information Science, Japan (2013)
19. US Department of Energy, Voluntary reporting of greenhouse gases: Appendix F. Electricity emission factors (2007). http://www.eia.doe.gov/oiaf/1605/pdf/Appendix20F_r071023.pdf
20. US Department of Energy, US Energy Information Administration (EIA) report (2007). http://www.eia.doe.gov/cneaf/electricity/epm/table5_6_a.html

Author Index